THE ASSESSMENT
OF OBJECT RELATIONS PHENOMENA
IN ADOLESCENTS
TAT AND RORSCHACH MEASURES

The LEA Series in
Personality and Clinical Psychology
Irving B. Weiner, Editor

THE ASSESSMENT OF OBJECT RELATIONS PHENOMENA IN ADOLESCENTS TAT AND RORSCHACH MEASURES

Francis D. Kelly
Franklin Medical Center
Greenfield, Massachusetts

LEA LAWRENCE ERLBAUM ASSOCIATES, PUBLISHERS
1997 Mahwah, New Jersey

Lawrence Erlbaum Associates, Inc., Publishers
10 Industrial Avenue
Mahwah, New Jersey 07430

Cover design by Gail Silverman

Library of Congress Cataloging-in-Publication Data

Kelly Francis D., Ed.D.
  The assessment of object relations phenomena in the adolescent : TAT
and Rorschach measures / by Francis D. Kelly.
    p.   cm.
  Includes bibliographical references and index.
  ISBN 0-8058-2235-6 (alk. paper).
  1. Projective techniques for teenagers. 2. Object relations
(Psychoanalysis). 3. Personality assessment of teenagers.
4. Projective techniques for teenagers—Case studies. 5. Object
relations (Psychoanalysis)—Case studies. 6. Personality assessment
of teenagers—Case studies. I. Title.
RJ503.7.P76K45 1997
616.89'17'0835—dc20   96-38321
                                                                  CIP

Printed in the United States of America
10 9 8 7 6 5 4 3 2 1

*To those I love most—Susan, Kristen, and Kathryn.
And for Karen, whose memory
still burns brightly in my heart.*

Contents

Preface

This book discusses object representation assessment of the adolescent. It is designed to introduce the reader to essential theoretical tenets of object relations theory, especially as they apply to the adolescent, and to illustrate how this theoretical model lends itself to the clinical situation regarding the psychological assessment of object representation parameters in normal and disturbed adolescents. Several key assumptions guide this work.

The first assumption is that object representations are psychological constructs that capture the multidimensional aspects of the individual's inner template. More specifically, they order, categorize, and detail the vicissitudes of affective and cognitive experiences related to past and present experiences that relate to the self and others.

The second assumption is that these representations or multi-faceted schemata serve as a type of lighthouse or beacon that helps to orient, direct, and guide the nature of a person's relatedness with others. The bulk of the emphasis stresses the examination and exploration of how object representation information, vividly depicted by empirically derived measures, can provide a rich, clinically relevant and multidimensional perspective capturing the nuance and uniqueness of a given adolescent's inner representational world. An attempt is made to illustrate how this information may in turn be translated into hypotheses and prognostications regarding the adolescent's preferred transactions with his or her interpersonal world. This also extends to musings and informed hunches regarding patterns of relatedness in relation to the clinical situation.

This volume offers an assessment paradigm complementary to the more widely used approaches to the interpretation of the Rorschach and the Thematic Apperception Test (TAT), one that emphasizes a more nomothetic and atheoretical direction. The volume provides an opportunity for clinicians to consider an alternative lens to view their data from TAT and Rorschach measures in their work with adolescents. It affords the opportunity to adopt and implement a more idiographic approach to test interpretation and analysis, one that is yoked to, and directly derived from, object relations theory.

This work should be useful to a diversified audience, whose common interests and concerns resonate around the clinical assessment of the object representational world of the adolescent. It should be of assistance in making treatment recommendations that are informed and derived from material that articulates, captures, and portrays the multidimensional aspects of a given adolescent's object representational inner map. Graduate students in clinical, counseling, and school psychology should find this a useful introductory experience that provides an orientation to essential theoretical aspects of object relations theory, and should come to appreciate how theory and clinical material converge in the assessment process.

More seasoned professionals, psychologists, psychiatrists, and clinical social workers as well, will resonate to the clinical material presented, and will consider the adoption of assessment approaches that allow for a more concerted evaluation of object representation dimensions in adolescent patients. I am optimistic that this volume will excite, stimulate, and generate curiosity, which will increase appreciation of how the adoption of an additional diagnostic lens (e.g., object representation material derived from the TAT and Rorschach) enhances and strengthens both the diagnostic and treatment processes with adolescent patients.

This effort would not have been possible without the assistance, encouragement, and thoughts of others. My sincere thanks go to Dr. Donn Brechenser and Dr. Rob Simpson for their patience with my quirky ways and their thoughtful support of my clinical work with children and adolescents. To my immediate colleagues on the Developmental Evaluation Team, I can hardly express my gratitude for all that you have taught me, and for the clinical work that inspired many of the thoughts contained in this volume. I am grateful for the able assistance and support given by Judy McNamara, Beverly Blatt, John Kolodin, Kathy Coutu, Sharon Thuillard-Rohrs, and Karin Newcomb, and to Dr. Norton Garber, Dr. Sheri Katz, Dr. Terese Weinstein, and Dr. Carey Dimmitt.

To the responsive and vocal cadre of post-doctoral fellows and colleagues who contributed their clinical material, sometimes in heated disagreement, I am thankful for your presence and acknowledge your helpful assistance, stimulating critical comments, and supportive manner. I hope that in the course of our interaction, we all learned much about projective assessment. My gratitude also goes to Dr. Marcia Black, Dr. Kent Higgins, Dr. Peter Jackson, Dr. Denise Greene, Dr. Joyce Mahaffey, Dr. Joe Mangine, Dr. Brooks McCutchen, Dr. Margaret Miller, Dr. Scott Rice, Dr. Debra Ross, Dr. Rick Schuetz, Dr. Pat Schumm, and Dr. Jim Shortell.

Amy Olener deserves a special thanks for her guidance, patience, and editorial assistance. From the outset, she has been a special presence, offering critique, support, and thoughtful observations that have helped to transform this volume into its final form. For this, I am most appreciative.

Lastly, and most deservedly, I reserve a special thank you for my wife and best friend, Susan. She read, edited, critiqued, and shaped this material, and provided a supportive and patient ambience and nest, which has allowed this effort to reach completion. A simple thank you hardly seems sufficient to acknowledge and compensate for the generous amount of her expended time with this project; and for her enduring patience with a sometimes impatient and irrascible husband who seemed, in the recent past, all too often wed to a word processor. Nonetheless, I express my sincere gratitude and love for your able and indomitable presence.

Introduction

Since the mid-1980s, child psychologists who are involved in conducting psychological assessments have been increasingly influenced by three major factors that have emerged and converged, resulting in a significant alteration in the way they conduct their work. In two instances, the results only served to improve and enhance the evaluative process, and ultimately enhanced pronouncements and observations in relation to diagnostic and therapeutic procedures. In the third case, there is measured judgment as to what the final results will be with respect to either adding something of benefit, or greatly detracting from optimal services to child and adolescent patients.

The aforementioned factors relate in the first case to the impressive efforts of Exner, Weiner, and their colleagues (Exner & Weiner, 1992; Exner & Weiner, 1995) who developed an encyclopedic empirical and nomothetic normative database utilized in the Rorschach assessment of children and adolescents. The second factor involves the gradual application of object relations theory and tenets to the idiographic interpretation of child and adolescent projective test material, particularly the Rorschach and TAT. The final factor represents the growing presence and impact of managed health care as it dictates and increasingly governs when, and when not, psychological assessments will be considered as an appropriate and necessary component of the evaluation process. Expanded discussion of how these three factors significantly influenced and impacted the arena of child and adolescent personality assessment follows.

Although the Comprehensive System (Exner, 1978; Exner & Weiner, 1992, 1995) continues to be the subject of criticism in select quarters

1

because of its lack of clear theoretical underpinnings (Kleiger, 1992; Ziskin & Faust, 1988) and the contention that it does not provide the clinical predictive power of a more content-based, idiographic interpretive paradigm (Aronow, Reznikoff, & Moreland, 1995) it represents the predominant Rorschach scoring and classification system in use today. As Acklin (1995) thoughtfully noted, this is important for at least two reasons. In the first case, the Comprehensive System brought the various previously scattered scoring systems under one roof into a unified framework that can only allow for continued rich clinical and heuristic application and investigation. Second, the derivation of reliable and valid scores serves to ground inferences and disciplines inappropriate or arbitrary interpretations (Schafer, 1954).

For child psychologists who espouse a psychoanalytic theoretical orientation in their approach to Rorschach interpretation, the Comprehensive System should hardly be eschewed as it obviously has much to offer, providing a rich and detailed vista of a child's or adolescent's ego resources and functioning. Salient and important material is readily available and easily extracted from the empirical material (e.g., scores, ratios), allowing for a composite profile of ego functioning in relation to parameters such as reality testing; thought organization; defensive operations; regulation and control of drives, affects, and impulses; object relations; and so on. The Rorschach provides a broad measure of cognitive structuring and organization (Weiner, 1994). Many experienced clinicians utilize the Comprehensive System in this way as they gradually piece together the nomothetic material and weave it into a tapestry, eventually reflecting a product bound together by idiographic and nomothetic thread.

The diagnostic tools of the clinical child psychologist were greatly improved by the application of the Comprehensive System, especially the most recent revision of volume III (Exner & Weiner, 1995), as the updated material provides more extensive normative data that can be readily utilized in a nomothetic and idiographic interpretive frame. Expansion of clinical material serves to more accurately differentiate between children and adolescents with varying degrees of developmental disturbance, especially those in the moderate to severe range of psychopathology. This revised normative material will ultimately be of considerable assistance to clinicians as they will be able to evaluate data in a more accurate manner.

Juxtaposed against the impressive growth of the Comprehensive System was an equally impressive, albeit somewhat smaller, development of idiographic approaches to child and adolescent projective data relying on contemporary object relations theory (Blatt & Lerner, 1983). Rorschach data (Kelly, 1986; Leifer, Shapiro, Martone, & Kassem, 1991) with younger adolescents was translated into a phenomenological matrix informing clinicians about inner cognitive representative schema and templates serving to define the nuances of inner and external dimensions of relatedness, with this extending to the treatment situation. With respect to older adolescents, several clinicians cogently articulated how object relations dimensions are vividly portrayed on the Rorschach, and how this material has relevant diagnostic and treatment implications (Blatt & Ford, 1994; Blatt & Lerner, 1983; Gacano & Meloy, 1994; Kwawer, Lerner, Lerner, & Sugarman, 1980; Lerner, 1992; Lerner & Lerner, 1988; Lerner & St. Peter, 1984).

The TAT also benefited from the application of object relations theory to interpretive material. Most notably, Westen and colleagues (Westen, Barends, Leigh, Mendel, & Silbert, 1988; Westen et al., 1991; Westen, Ludolph, Block, Wixom, & Wiss, 1990; Westen, Ludolph, Silk, et al., 1990) developed an elaborate scoring and interpretive paradigm assessing four dimensions of object relations functioning and allowing for clear and cogent diagnostic conceptualizations in addition to offering the clinician clear therapeutic direction. Additional research reflects the adoption of the SCORS (Westen et al., 1988) applied to adolescent populations with histories of sexual abuse (Ornduff, Freedenfeld, Kelsey, & Critelli, 1994; Pistole & Ornduff, 1994).

With children and adolescents, the continued application of an interpretive lens emphasizing object relations theory can only continue to reap rewards in the way of improved, relevant, and pragmatic diagnostic and treatment formulations and direction as theory nicely melds with practice. Just as child clinicians will continue to improve and hone diagnostic and assessment skills as a result of the continued utilization of the Comprehensive System, informed child psychologists will probably want to sample the best of two worlds in adding an idiographic interpretive framework to their repertoire of diagnostic and treatment options. The integration of object relations psychoanalytic theory with test material is reminiscent of the earlier integration of ego psychology (Hartmann, 1958) and psychoanalytic test theory (Rapaport, Gill, & Schafer, 1968). The implications are manifold, providing cogent diagnostic information and dictating indicated treatment directions, briefly outlined by Blatt and Lerner (1983a) in the section to follow.

They delineate discrete impressions in relation to diagnostic and treatment concerns. First, object representations obtained from Rorschach material afford the clinician important information about the developmental level of personality organization and the quality of interpersonal relationships to which an individual is predisposed. Second, they provide material in relation to an individual's construction of reality and the nature of the cognitive structures that mediate between needs, drives, present, and past experiences. Third, they help to inform clinicians as to the existing multidimensional cognitive–affective template, which serves to guide internal and external relatedness. Lastly, object representations serve to inform clinicians as to what the likely response to treatment will be as this relates to probable transference issues and phenomena.

To briefly highlight some of the important diagnostic advantages of utilizing an idiographic approach to the viewing of Rorschach and TAT material, I underscore the following points. First, test material is organized and interpreted within the context of a well-conceptualized theoretical matrix, contemporary psychoanalytic object relations theory, which provides for clear, cogent, reliable and valid structural developmental information by way of the interpersonal world of a child or an adolescent. Second, such material provides the clinician with important and clear diagnostic material in relation to how adolescents manifesting varying degrees of psychopathology present clinically, even when their manifest symptomatology may ostensibly suggest a similar diagnostic syndrome or disorder (e.g., anorexia nervosa). Third, an object relations interpretive perspective permits thorough and informed commentary in relation to treatment directions and the likely pitfalls and problems that may be encountered, based on careful analysis of object representations.

The 1980s and early 1990s witnessed major growth and development in the area of child and adolescent personality assessment with respect to nomothetic and idiographic approaches. This was an exciting and stimulating period and was positive in that it gave child psychologists powerful evaluative devices to implement in the psychological assessment of children and adolescents. But it is ironic that these exciting advances in personality assessment came at a time in which managed health care already managed to impose significant constraints on the allocation of funds provided for psychological assessment. Although it is premature to speculate on where this will eventually go, it is already obvious that the lumping of treatment and assessment dollars will result in the denying of requests for psychological assessment. This is unfortunate because most requests for psychological assessment are legitimate, indicated, and necessary for diagnostic closure and thoroughness. It is also ironic that the tendency of managed health to shrink assessment funds may ultimately be cost ineffective and result in inappropriate treatment recommendations and programs (Appelbaum, 1990). It is obvious to psychologists who work with children and adolescents that reliance on more traditional and actuarial approaches to assessment (e.g., interviews, behavior checklists, manifest behavior) often fall short of the mark in ensuring diagnostic closure. Subsequent treatment plans are hastily or inappropriately contrived only to result in a treatment path that subsequently reveals an uneven course, or in the worst scenario, a regressive odyssey.

Not every adolescent should be routinely subjected to a comprehensive psychological assessment, but the current situation suggests that we now have at our disposal impressively reliable and valid nomothetic and idiographic measures with which to assess adolescents. We can do so in a manner that ensures, in the majority of cases, precise diagnostic profiles and informs clinicians as to treatment directions and options tailored to the individual. In order to meet the challenge of justifying personality assessment, several factors must be kept in mind.

First, in commenting on the importance of considering psychological assessment for enhancing the conceptual basis and power of treatment decisions, Hayes (1993), although not referring to projective or personality assessment, made several observations, easily applying to situations where psychological tests are employed in the assessment process.

He noted that the complexity of clinical treatment decisions, especially in this climate of short-term, focused treatment, can highlight the potential utility of psychological assessment prior to and during therapy. The theoretical and conceptual advances mentioned in the previous sections provided psychologists the opportunity to shorten the gulf between assessment and treatment and to enhance the power of treatment decisions. And as Hayes further observed, continued conceptual and methodological advances in psychological assessment and treatment increasingly made for more fusion between the assessment and treatment process. As Appelbaum (1990) observed, assessment can be quite compatible in this climate calling for brief, focused work. Psychological material provides additional quick, cogent, diagnostic information and serves to buffer those superficial and overly simplistic diagnostic formulations that lack conceptual grounding.

Personality testing will only retain its credibility in this capricious climate if specificity and clarity are realized in the articulation of treatment objectives and goals. What specific type of intervention or treatment is required for a given patient along with predictions about the likely course of treatment should be the end result of a comprehensive personality assessment. Appelbaum (1990) candidly and succinctly observed that clinicians who believe in assessment will have to demonstrate the usefulness of the enterprise in a cost-efficient manner designed to answer practical clinical questions in ways that significantly contribute to a patient's welfare.

Thus, child psychologists who spend at least some of their time involved in psychological assessment find themselves in a culture urgently calling for more correspondence and connectedness between assessment and treatment, dictated by the realities of managed care and requiring well-honed clinical and fiscal accountability and restraint.

It is my intent with this volume to expand and advance the development of an idiographic approach to the assessment of adolescent projective material, specifically by emphasizing the utilization of TAT and Rorschach data. It is the intent of this volume to demonstrate how an application of the basic tenets and theoretical principles of object relations theory may be applied and utilized in the interpretation of Rorschach and TAT responses. My guiding assumption is that phenomenological evaluation of this material eventuates in a more comprehensive, theory-based, experience-near portrait of an adolescent's object relations representations and functioning. Ultimately, this results in the creation of a template allowing for understanding and predictions in relation to future interpersonal transactions, including those involving the psychotherapeutic process.

The remaining sections of this volume are divided into 10 chapters designed to introduce and familiarize the reader with an idiographic, object relations approach to the interpretation of adolescent TAT and Rorschach material.

Chapter 1 is concerned with the presentation of the pitfalls and limitations one encounters when sole adherence to the *DSM–IV* classification is employed in the diagnosis and assessment of adolescent patients. The contribution of projective material is presented in an attempt to explicate how this data can significantly improve the diagnostic picture, and will more accurately inform treatment decisions and direction.

Chapter 2 provides a brief overview of the recent trends evident in the projective assessment of adolescents, with the emphasis on detailing how two predominant interpretive approaches, the nomothetic and the idiographic, were utilized in the interpretation of both younger and older adolescents' TAT and Rorschach material, with a variety of clinical syndromes and psychological disorders.

Chapter 3 provides an overview of the major tenets of object relations theory as it relates to adolescent development, again with respect to younger and older adolescents. The chapter also discusses the construct of object representation, outlining how this phenomenon is portrayed in TAT and Rorschach material with discussion as to how this data is organized into a cohesive composite informing clinicians about the multidimensional nature and nuances of an adolescent's object relations capacity and functioning.

Chapter 4 provides the reader with a thorough introduction to the Mutuality of Autonomy Scale (MOA), an object relations scale first developed by Urist (1977), and later modified and applied to the evaluation of child and adolescent protocols by Tuber (1992). The second part of the chapter introduces another object relations scale, the Social Cognition and Object Relations Scale (SCORS) developed by Westen and associates (Westen, Lohr, Silk, Kerber, & Goodrich, 1985). The specific application of this assessment paradigm to younger and older adolescent patients is considered in depth via examination of scoring examples and interpretive guidelines.

Chapter 5 presents a representative sampling of six normal, well-adjusted younger and older adolescents' object relations functioning as captured by Rorschach and TAT measures. MOA and SCORS material is introduced to provide readers with a sense of how younger adolescents differ from older ones in order to illustrate the developmental changes reflected in object relations shifts and maturation.

Chapter 6 is subdivided into three sections and indroduces nine clinical cases. The overriding intent is to illustrate how adolescents of different ages and with an array of psychological problems and disorders depict disorders of self and object representations on structured measures—MOA and SCORS. The first section focuses on younger adolescents and includes cases representing diverse forms of psychopathology and clinical presentations. The second deals with adolescents in midadolescence and represents varied clinical presentations and a range of psychopathology. The last section considers the older adolescent with the focus being on illustrating how varying types of psychopathology influence object relatedness and representations. An effort is also made to illustrate how this material serves to guide, inform, and direct clinicians in subsequent treatment planning and psychotherapeutic endeavors.

Chapter 7 presents three cases of younger and older adolescents with histories of varying types of abuse and trauma in order to examine the impact of trauma experiences on object representations and object relations functioning.

Chapter 8 outlines how the material obtained from Rorschach and TAT measures is organized and integrated into a diagnostic perspective that allows for the creation of the treatment plan formulation. Younger and older adolescents are presented via examination of three clinical cases. Here, the primary emphasis is on the development of treatment formulations and recommendations tied to the diagnostic material and attuned to referral questions and concerns.

Chapter 9 is concerned with showing how a variety of therapeutic interventions and programs result in organizational changes as depicted by object representation measures. Illustration of two cases serves to demonstrate how manifest reported changes and alterations in overt behavior and object relations functioning are mirrored and captured by concomitant shifts and changes in object representation measures.

Chapter 10 provides an overview of this volume. Thoughts and recommendations in relation to future research and clinical endeavors involving the continued and expanded use of an idiographic model of interpretation for object representational material are discussed.

1

Diagnostic Difficulties in Adolescent Psychiatry: Limitations of DSM–IV and the Role of Projective Tests in Developmental Assessment

A large part of the clinician's work with adolescents continues to involve assessment and diagnosis. Differential diagnosis reveals a multifaceted procedure in which data is collected from an array of external and internal sources, and is then ordered into a conceptual schema designed to generate a profile or comprehensive composite representative of a syndrome or disorder. The clinician has to rely on direct and indirect sources of material with which to facilitate an ongoing, oscillating, inductive–deductive process that should suggest what the problem is and what can be done about it in order to facilitate optimal developmental functioning.

Increasingly, psychiatrists, psychologists, and clinical social workers tend to rely on devices that generate actuarial data in order to arrive at quick and accurate diagnostic impressions with adolescents. Data may be gathered from a variety of sources, some of the more frequently utilized being briefly referenced here.

The interview is the most commonly relied on procedure used to obtain an initial diagnostic picture. Structuring and standardizing interview procedures resulted in significant effort directed at developing more objective approaches to the interview process with adolescents. Attempts to provide standardization, reliability, and validity in the diagnostic process resulted in the development of a variety of structured interview procedures including: the Diagnostic Interview for Children and Adolescents (DICA), developed by Herjanic and Reich (1982); the Kiddie–SADS (K–SADS) written by Puig-Antich and Tabrizi (1983); and the Child Assessment Schedule (CAS) developed by Hodges and colleagues (Hodges, McKnew, Cytryn, Stern, & Kline, 1982).

Clinicians also frequently rely on standardized rating scales to provide actuarial information about an adolescent's behavior problems and symptoms, with the most common example being the well-researched Child Behavior Checklist (Achenbach & Edelbrock, 1983). Examples of additional rating scales used to classify and order problematic adolescent behavior include the Conners' Parent Rating Scale (Conners, 1982) and the Missouri Children's Behavior Checklist (Curry & Thompson, 1979).

The most widely used and researched instrument utilized by psychologists and their colleagues to gather and order diagnostic information into a taxonomy of mental disorders is the *Diagnostic and Statistical Manual of Mental Disorders* of the American Psychiatric Association (*DSM–IV;* American Psychiatric Association, 1994). This device serves the clinician by providing a relatively reliable taxonomy of psychiatric syndromes and disorders and can be used to provide impressions regarding differential diagnosis. But as experienced clinicians readily attest, this classification system has significant shortcomings when applied with adolescents.

Thus, it is possible to traverse multiple paths in arriving at diagnostic impressions and formulations regarding adolescent psychopathology. Adolescents are interviewed directly, with the clinician often relying on his or her own internal model for conducting the process; in other instances, a more structured format is followed. In other situations, scales and behavior reports of parents and teachers are added to the diagnostic material. In some cases, psychological test material is used to augment and strengthen information gleaned from other sources. In all instances, information is then ordered into some type of classification matrix, most frequently the *DSM–IV,* in order to organize symptoms, behavior, stressors, and adaptational levels of functioning. These methods often represent one superficial level of diagnosis, more appropriately termed *screening,* in that the results may offer little more than an ordering or taxonomy of manifest behavior and symptoms.

Clinicians who work with adolescents will in more humble and rational moments admit to the difficulties in arriving at an accurate diagnostic picture after spending time with an adolescent, particularly a younger or more disturbed one. Yet, the clinical interview most often remains the main method by which psychologists, psychiatrists, and clinical social workers obtain information and data in order to arrive at diagnostic and assessment impressions and subsequent treatment recommendations. Diagnostic closure is obtainable, however, and accurate formulations are not impossible if one looks to the interview as the primary vehicle for obtaining information.

There are many skilled clinicians who adroitly develop multidimensional portraits about adolescents' inner psychological landscapes after interviewing them. But this is often not what transpires, as interview material is difficult to obtain or provides scant and incomplete diagnostic material. Again, this is most likely to occur with younger, less verbal adolescents and those with more severe acute or chronic disturbance. In older adolescents, this may also be the case, although they are more inclined to verbally represent their concerns, problems, and conflicts. This leads to more easily conceived diagnostic impressions and treatment formulations.

Criticisms of the more descriptive–actuarial–behavioral approach to nosology with children and adolescents, embodied in the work of *DSM–IV*, reference at least two major areas of appropriate concern about the reliance on this device when it is employed as the primary diagnostic criterion utilized in the classification of childhood and adolescent psychopathology.

There are serious inherent diagnostic constraints due to the lack of a conceptual approach that takes into account a developmental perspective (Korenblum, 1993; Noam & Houlihan, 1990; Schwab-Stone, Towbin, & Tarnoff, 1991; Shapiro, 1989). There is also, as Shapiro (1989) observed, an incomplete diagnostic process, given the lack of opportunity for a dynamic formulation. This should be an integral part of the total assessment process, providing conceptual clarity and serving as the template for subsequent treatment planning.

The fact that *DSM–IV* does not allow for developmental considerations represents an overriding and glaring limitation. With respect to a variety of physiological, emotional, interpersonal, and cognitive variables, there are significant differences between younger and older adolescents, and between both of these groups and the group compromising middle adolescence. The developmental task of separation–individuation (Blos, 1967) epitomizes a variable that reveals cogent and significant differences in how early, middle, and late adolescents confront, cope, and master this developmental task.

The younger adolescent may present an array of behavioral, interpersonal, and emotional symptoms that ostensibly represent a variety of diagnostic possibilities, such as dysthymia, separation anxiety disorder, and conduct disorder. These are all widely used *DSM–IV* diagnoses and are useful in providing ordering and typology of symptoms, but not an inkling that the manifest presentation belies a motivational substrate fueled by phase-specific developmental tasks, neurotic disorders, characterological damage, environmental stressors, or psychobiological disorder.

The sensitive and experienced clinician would raise this as a possibility. It is equally possible that time constraints and lack of a theoretical position would mean this critical developmental motivational factor was overlooked, especially in an era where taking a developmental history is often viewed as inessential to the rendering of solution-focused approaches to treatment.

Consider the case of two 15-year-old adolescents, one male (Patrick), one female (Gina), seen for consultation on a short-term, generic inpatient psychiatric unit. Both had admitting diagnoses of conduct disorder, group type, along with polysubstance abuse involving alcohol and cannabis. More specific discussion of each patient follows in order to provide clinical material in relation to some of the issues touched on.

In Gina's case, there would hardly be any argument with the *DSM–IV* diagnosis. She was "running amok" for the past 2 years. Her mother and stepfather had little control over her and had relinquished temporary custody to the Department of Social Services in an attempt to provide some external control and leverage in her life. She was involved in shop-lifting, several incidents of assaults with peers, and was recently arrested, along with several of her peers, for two breaking-and-entering episodes. She was currently suspended from school. She drank and used marijuana since she was 12, reporting that she frequently found herself in homes of friends with no recollection of how she had gotten there.

The interview, conducted on her third day of hospitalization, produced material that embellished the clinical picture but did not allow for either a sense of complete developmental functioning or specifics of aftercare involving the scope and degree of psychological interventions. She proved to be a cooperative adolescent, but her ability to verbalize and represent her inner world suggested an impoverished and underdeveloped quality reflecting affective intrusion (i.e., depressed and apathetic attitudes and symptoms) as she recounted her tumbling and turbulent course over the past 3 years.

She noted she was an only child and that her parents had divorced when she was 10. She saw her father on an irregular basis, as he was alcoholic and unpredictable in his availability. Soon after the divorce, her mother became involved with a man who was alcoholic and physically and verbally abusive to her mother and Gina. It was also suspected that Gina was sexually abused by this man, but this had not been substantiated. Gina felt betrayed and cast adrift by her mother who, despite promises to leave this man, continued to tolerate and minimize his serious problems and abusive ways. As a result, Gina began to act out at age 12, gravitating to a peer group who provided her with a sense of belonging and helped to buffer the anger and hurt she experienced in relation to the sense of being abandoned by her mother. As the interview continued, she noted, in a bland and matter-of-fact manner, the escalating problems in all domains of her life. This suggested to the interviewer that the convergence of cognitive, biological, psychologi-cal phase-specific stressors of early adolescence now superimposed on a developmental structure (possibly reflecting ego as well as object relations limitations), would not bode well as Gina was faring poorly in her attempts to cope with internal and external developmental demands. The interviewer was particularly concerned about the mother–daughter connection for diagnostic reasons as well as for concerns relating to disposition. Gina tended to idealize her mother, glossing over her probable anger and hurt at her mother's inability to provide Gina with a crucible, which would have given her the requisite sustenance to better cope with the inherent psychological and reality-based stresses and demands of early adolescence.

The young man, Patrick, also 15 years of age, presented a troubling history and the *DSM–IV* diagnosis of conduct disorder, group type, along with mixed substance abuse and dependence (i.e., alcohol and cannabis along with periodic cocaine and LSD). He, too, had extensive clashes with authority. Currently suspended from school for assaulting a teacher, he recounted breaking-and-entering, disorderly conduct, larceny, and assaults as examples of additional infractions that had led to his involvement in the juvenile justice system (he was currently on probation).

The interview also provided an additional perspective, but left questions regarding diagnostic and disposition concerns. Like Gina, it was difficult for him to extensively elaborate his story because of what appeared to be attentional lapses, impoverished verbal skills, and increasing anger and rage as the interview progressed. His problems and developmental course suggested more pronounced and severe characterological damage and disruption. His parents were both polysubstance abusers and his father, with whom he most recently resided, had a violent temper, particularly when he was drinking. His parents were divorced when he was 5, and he subsequently lived with his mother for 7 years, with this being terminated after Patrick struck his mother while intoxicated. He had no recall of this incident. He admitted that he started drinking at age 12 and that this quickly developed into a major problem along with concomitant cannabis abuse. He said that he had been out of school more than he had been in, was a major behavior problem, and was getting into many fights with peers and teachers. At the time of his hospitalization, he was indefinitely suspended from his most recent school.

As the interview with Patrick progressed, the interviewer's concerns about major ego impairment and severely compromised object relations functioning came repeatedly to the fore as this adolescent became more disorganized and agitated when pressed for details about his life. Patrick said he could not recall much about his early childhood. He spoke mostly about his drinking, his fighting, his many and frequent encounters with the police. He talked in an angry and animated fashion about slashing "some guy's face" because he was giving Patrick and his friends "grief." He did not seem upset by his actions and said he slept with a butterfly knife because he was afraid of the dark and needed protection against unknown assailants. He could not recall events leading to his hospitalization because he was quite intoxicated at the time of his admission. In actuality, he was admitted following an altercation in a park where he threatened to kill a woman and her children because he felt they were making fun of him. The ensuing confrontation with police saw him out of control and voicing that he would harm himself or others if people did not stop "fucking with my mind."

The interviewer obtained material that supported the impression that this was a quite disturbed adolescent. His judgment was shallow, concrete, and eccentric. He evidenced tenuous impulse control even when not under the influence of alcohol, and was obviously a frightening young man when under the influence. He had poor capacity to learn from experience, and saw little connection between his actions and the consequences he incurred. His ability to contain and modulate emotions and feelings was tenuous at best and it was clear that diffuse rage and aggression easily came to the fore along with a sense of mistrust and paranoia, again exacerbated by the use of alcohol. His capacity for relatedness appeared superficial and undifferentiated.

The results of the interview certainly provided additional important information, only serving to heighten diagnostic and disposition concerns. Again, certain questions and issues were unaddressed based on the limitations of relying on material provided by a young man with questionable ability to accurately and objectively report on himself and his world, with this also being related to language and verbal problems. Important diagnostic and treatment questions remained, including: Is there indication of an underlying or incipient thought disorder hinted at in the interview? How deficient and depleted are his ego resources? What is his capacity for relatedness beyond what is suggested by historical and interview material? Aside from the obvious need for a more extensive posthospitalization treatment program, which continues to address his severe substance abuse, what other therapies would be appropriate?

Here is where the clinician reaches an impasse in the road to realizing further diagnostic clarity in order to make more precise and informed statements regarding the inner worlds and psychological structures of these two adolescents. Their respective behaviors within the context of a therapeutic milieu can provide additional diagnostic material, but this is less frequently the case where time-limited stays hardly allow for an unfolding and examination of troubling behavior and problems preceding and prompting hospitalization. In addition to providing no additional material for a more differentiated and individual diagnostic composite, the DSM–IV diagnoses provide no guidelines with respect to treatment, save for obvious immediate direction—in both cases, the initial order of business should address posthospitalization programming for the substance abuse aspect of their presentations. Beyond this, many critical questions remain. Is either one of these adolescents suitable for individual psychotherapy? If so, what type of therapy would be indicated: cognitive–behavioral; focused, short-term; supportive–expressive; different types of family treatment? Would group therapy be more appropriate or indicated? What would be the likely response to therapy? What is the level of structural– developmental functioning in both cases? What is the capacity for relatedness and what transference behaviors should be anticipated in the treatment situation?

These vignettes serve to highlight some of the aforementioned inherent limitations when there is exclusive reliance on a diagnostic–assessment paradigm providing categorization based on symptoms and manifest indices of behavior. The *DSM–IV* classification system is not intended to provide hard and necessary information and data in regard to the multidimensional matrix of psychological factors that coalesce and interact (e.g. cognitive, affective, interpersonal) to motivate and define these two adolescents' problematic developmental course. Nor does this type of typology provide critical information as to how well, or how derailed, are these adolescents mastering critical phase-specific developmental demands, such as separation–individuation (Blos, 1967).

Here is where alternative diagnostic methods and options are needed. Reliable and valid psychological tests provide a lens allowing the possibility for transformation of the static and unidimensional material provided by *DSM–IV*, into a multidimensional, dynamic diagnostic composite. Testing captures nuance and intricacy in relation to ego functions, focal conflicts, and parameters of self–object relatedness embodied in object representation measures as defined by TAT and Rorschach responses.

Ordering psychological test data into a conceptual schema (Sugarman, 1986) affords the clinician cogent impressions regarding differential diagnostic possibilities and impressions embedded within a powerful theoretical base. There is also the opportunity for theory-based treatment formulations and planning.

Utilizing information derived from the Comprehensive System (Exner & Weiner, 1995) provides the clinician ample and relevant information about the vicissitudes of ego functioning in the adolescent. As Meloy and Singer (1991) observed, conceptual linkages are possible between the Comprehensive System and more traditional methodological approaches embodied in the work of Rapaport, Gill, and Schafer (1968). This is especially the case when indices of thought disorder are the variable under consideration. A clear sense of the adolescent's reality testing, impulse control capacity, affect modulation, and cognitive functioning are critical areas potentially tapped by the Comprehensive System. Formal test scores and ratios translate into a diagnostic vista that is not available if one relies solely on the aforementioned interview or behavioral indices. The manifest presentation of the adolescent may belie a different inner panorama, one more comprehensively and vividly defined when viewed through the lens of projective test data, and one serving to more comprehensively and articulately define the structural–developmental landscape and motivational substrate directing a pathological and errant developmental course.

Additional developmental diagnostic clarity is further realized if the clinician looks to Rorschach and TAT object representation measures, which are derived from theoretical tenets relating to contemporary object relations theory, as this provides another lens to view the adolescent's world of relatedness. As Lerner (1986) observed in his discussion of a quite troubled, hospitalized, 16-year-old female adolescent's Rorschach protocol:

> Paradigmatic patterns of object relating and experience can be understood through a close examination of Rorschach responses and that these patterns may be particulary evident in the analysis of the human response. Rorschach human percepts may be conceptualized as powerful projections of drive-infused, either conflict-determined or developmentally arrested, imprints of earlier, formative interpersonal relationships and transactions carried forward by the patient's continually assimilating, shaping and coloring new situations, experiences, and relationships. (p. 140)

In order to illustrate how psychological test information provides the clinician with diagnostic and treatment formulation material that goes far beyond the typology of *DSM–IV*, it is necessary to return to Gina and Patrick. Rorschach responses to Card 3 and TAT responses to Card 4 are referenced in order to illustrate how the same *DSM–IV* diagnosis provides little more than perfunctory actuarial classification when juxtaposed against the results of psychological test data.

Patrick's response to Card 3 suggests several interpretive possibilities regarding his ego resources and aspects and dimensions of his object relations functioning:[1] "Looks like . . . I don't know. Yeah, two dudes there ripping . . . tearing, pulling apart some animal that they stomped . . . see the ribs there. (Q) Don't know . . . shaped like that . . . pulling . . . tearing it to bits. Don't know, just looks like that."

Borrowing from the Comprehensive System, his reality awareness is adequate, but beyond this, we see indication of ego frailty represented by the special score emphasizing aggressivity. Further analysis, relying on an object representation perspective, suggests that his expectations of relatedness are colored and imbued with dire and catastrophic expectations, reminiscent of his accounts (real or imagined) relating to slashing of adversaries with minimal provocation.

Gina's response to this card reveals a different percept, as represented by the following: "Not sure . . . maybe two ladies doing some kind of . . .

---

[1](Q) = query; (Future) = "What will happen next?"; (Feel) = "How does he or she feel?"

making some kind of . . . cooking something. That's a pot there at the bottom. Cooking some kind of meal or feast with the fire (red) there on top of it, sort of like in the background."

Using limited parts of the Comprehensive System as a starting point in order to comment on ego resources and functioning, her response is well-organized and integrated, suggesting a good capacity to synthesize and integrate her impulses and emotions. Reality awareness is obviously sound. Beyond this, one can make initial inferences about her object relations capacity, as the percept suggests differentiated, reciprocal, and cooperative involvement, suggestive of a high degree of mutuality and lack of conflict.

Turning to additional TAT material in order to provide additional diagnostic information, these two adolescents' responses to Card 4 are presented.

Patrick's response to this card continues to be troubling, as it converges with historical and interview material to again support the impression of a disturbed adolescent with probable significant characterological arrest and severe impairments in ego functioning. His response is as follows:

> Don't get this . . . Oh yeah . . . this guy here is getting ready to beat the shit of some guys who are giving him a bad time . . . look at his eyes, he's pissed. (Q) Don't know . . . really gonna stomp on them. (Q) She's not gonna be able to do much . . . just pulls away from her. (Future) He does a job on them . . . won't mess with him again. (Feel) He's pissed . . . like I said . . . don't care.

The story converges with Rorschach material to suggest that this is an angry, easily stimulated, probably paranoid young man who appears to have a compromised ability to organize, integrate, and regulate his emotions and impulses. Under stress or the influence of substances he appears capable of being dangerous and out of control. His object relations functioning suggests a markedly primitive, undifferentiated, and eccentric quality with significant concerns being raised about his ability to get along with others. He appears to see encounters as potentially destructive and harmful with little suggestion that they can be comforting or rewarding.

Gina's response to Card 4 of the TAT also serves to provide additional diagnostic information consistent with her Rorschach material, and like Patrick's, allows for a more defined and crystallized diagnostic and treatment picture:

> Like they're in love I guess . . . don't know . . . had a fight I guess. He's mad and wants to leave, upset about his job . . . got fired, just wants to be by self. (Q) She's worried about him . . . thinks he might do something stupid . . . get drunk . . . get in a fight. (Future) He cools off . . . goes away

for a while . . . comes back . . . finds another job. (Feel). He feels hurt, mad . . . she's concerned and worried, wants to help . . . don't know.

The material provided by this brief response again suggests that her ego resources and object relations functioning are more intact and developed than is the case with Patrick. We see the capacity for delay, planning, restraint, and good organization of her emotions and impulses. Her ability to reflect on and integrate conflict material seems apparent and is consistent with the brief Rorschach material and some of the interview data. Her object relations functioning suggests a more developmentally advanced and adaptive picture than does Patrick's, in that it is possible to see more in the way of self–object differentiation, a sense of relatively positive and cooperative relatedness, and the understanding that relationships are multifaceted and emotionally complex. In Gina's case, she should be able to utilize and benefit from therapeutic involvements as her capacity for relatedness is essentially positive. She should be expected to participate in psychotherapy, which, in part, will help her to understand the reasons why she has used alcohol to bind and buffer her underlying hurt and rage in relation to the past several years of her life.

Returning again to the issue of diagnosis and assessment with adolescent patients, several observations are warranted. We cannot expect that a nomenclature or taxonomy will provide all we need to comprehend about a given adolescent. Multidimensional perspectives in relation to diagnosis or treatment are not possible when clinicians look only to *DSM–IV* for additional help regarding inferences and hypotheses around what motivates behavior, what are a given adolescent's ego resources and limitations, what is the capacity for relatedness in given situations, how this youngster will respond to treatment. Interviews, both structured and unstructured, also have their limitations in relation to what type of treatment is suggested, with whom, and what the likely response will be.

The inclusion of psychological test information can only strengthen, in an efficient and cost-effective manner, tentative diagnostic impressions and global treatment formulation plans—especially with adolescents (in particular younger and more disturbed patients), who often lack the capacity to accurately represent their stories and situation because of a variety of cognitive and psychological constraints. This makes it exceedingly difficult to articulate appropriate and individual treatment formulations. The situation may be significantly improved and enhanced by the implementation of projective assessment as one component of the diagnostic procedure. The introduction of psychological test information, obtained from Rorschach and TAT data, may often significantly contribute to the diagnostic and treatment process, providing information that may not otherwise be available from other sources (i.e., interviews, historical material, *DSM–IV*).

2

Object Relations Assessment and Functioning in Adolescence: Theoretical and Clinical Considerations

The intent of this chapter is to provide some commentary and observations about object relations functioning in adolescence in order to acquaint the reader with contemporary and historical thinking. Most of this, until recently, paid little accord to the fact that the adolescent period is a developmental stage wherein considerable object relations change and potential growth may still occur. There was, as Lamia (1982) observed, insufficient attention to the revision and modification of self and object representations in adolescence, and to the attendant relationship between the adolescent's self and object representations. In order to illustrate some of the more essential theoretical and clinical points it is helpful to begin with a metaphorical example followed by a clinical exposition.

The trustees of a private school wish to commission a painting to be presented at the June commencement in order to honor a well-respected headmaster who is retiring after many years of long service. He had started there as a young science teacher fresh out of college. The painting is to be of the science building where he first taught as a young man. Three artists are contacted and advised that their efforts will be judged in the latter part of May, with one of the offerings to be selected by the trustees. The two remaining paintings will be offered to charity with the artists being generously reimbursed for their efforts and talent.

The first artist, a well-organized, conscientious, and fastidious person makes initial sketches, takes photographs, and begins the work in an orderly, efficient, and prompt manner. The painting is actually completed some time before the deadline, long before the days lengthen, and certainly long before the annual cornucopia of color explodes on the barren

New England landscape. The painting, although impressively detailed, lacks something.

The second artist, also accomplished, makes initial sketches, takes photographs, and creates some initial washes with which she is somewhat displeased. She ceases work on the project, turns to other tasks, and then returns to her painting at a later date. At this point, the artist again visits the site and encounters a different vista, a result of the blossoming of spring with all of its magnitude and splendor, which rendered an entirely different panorama than she encountered a few short weeks before. The light is different, shadows apparent that were absent in the recent past. By chance, she encounters her colleague who proudly reveals his completed effort. Similarities are apparent between the works, but this second artist feels her colleague's final work, although admirable, lacks something. Undaunted, she now returns to her own painting, embellishing and altering as she finds nuances of the new light and color vital to her increasingly defined and more integrated creation.

The third painter also begins her work in a similar manner to her colleagues. Initial sketches, photographs, and drafts are made in late winter as the days begin to lengthen. Then, unexpectedly, the artist falls ill and comes to the unfortunate realization that her initial efforts, defined and bearing her unique style, will not reach completion because of the unfortunate setback and time constraints. Her student, someone acquainted with her style and technique, offers to complete the work. Not wishing to alter the basic integrity and definition of the creator, the student nonetheless brings a fresh and unique style, ultimately broadening yet still retaining the essence of the initial effort. As was the case with the second painter, there is the opportunity for expanded time, given the unfortunate illness of the original artist. And in a fortuitous turn, the opportunity for additional time provides the chance to incorporate the nuances of an everchanging, rejuvenated spring environment. The ultimate effort suggests considerable breadth, richness, and uniqueness, despite the obvious precarious beginning.

This metaphor might suggest the theoretical musings of three clinicians who are asked to comment and reflect on their experiences and thoughts in relation to how object relations development proceeds during the adolescent years. In a similar vein, it could refer to the multiple paths that object relations development might take as a function of internal and external influences. An adolescent's object relations functioning is defined by ongoing transactions with others that serve to create a changing, multidimensional inner schema or template, *object representations*, that are altered, redefined, and assume complete articulation and cohesion at some point in the individual's life cycle.

For the majority of well-adjusted individuals, this completed product is probably displayed in late adolescence or young adulthood. But this is not necessarily the case with many other young adults—those with character disturbance, histories of early trauma, psychoses, and neuro-psychological impairment—as these individuals frequently continue to manifest incomplete, partially integrated and, in some instances, unfinished portraits of self and object representation landscapes.

In returning to the previous metaphor in order to illustrate some theoretical tenets regarding object relations development, specifically with an eye to addressing developmental issues and concerns unique to adolescents, we should note that the majority of theoretical and clinical interest is focused on the initial "wash" and early definition regarding the predominant theme and direction of the painting. This is akin to the voluminous clinical and theoretical material that highlights infancy, the toddler period, early childhood, and prelatency as the critical period for the entire painting. The first clinician would vigorously argue that object relations development transpires during infancy and subsequent earliest childhood with completion being realized by the time the oedipal conflict is addressed.

There is more than ample historical material to support the argument that major object relations development transpires over the course of the first 5 years (Bowlby, 1969; Kernberg, 1967, 1975; Klein, 1948; Kohut, 1984; Mahler, Pine, & Bergman, 1975; Sutherland, 1983; Winnicott, 1960). But as was pointed out by several authors (Pine, 1990; Rutter, 1989; Vaillant, 1987; Westen, 1990), personality changes continue to take place much later in the developmental cycle. This includes object relations development, with the possibility of demonstrating significant growth far beyond the preoedipal–oedipal years, continuing to expand and flourish during latency and throughout all the phases of adolescence (Blatt & Ford, 1994; Westen et al., 1991).

The second clinician would not argue with her colleague regarding the fact that the critical, and perhaps majority of, development and growth of an individual's object relations functioning takes place early in the developmental cycle. But here marks a point of departure, as the second clinician adopts a different perspective, one informed by the work of Blos (1967) and others who designated early and middle adolescence as a period of psychological rebirth in which the young adolescent revisits familiar terrain, and once again confronts developmental issues requiring the negotiation and mastery of phase-specific tasks involving separation and individuation. Regardless of the accomplishments of the young adolescent's passage up to this point, he or she is again required to organize, synthesize, and integrate not only old material in the way of psychological developmental tasks, but must now increasingly come to grips with emerging and different challenges generated by intrinsic psychobiological, cognitive, societal, and familial factors. The second clinician appropriately argues that her "composition" or developmental perspective cannot be completed until the opportunity arises to observe how the child traverses a new landscape, one offering new challenges and unique obstacles, and differing from the surveyed terrain of the past.

The third clinician in considering the positions and views of her colleagues finds much to concur with, although there are some points of disagreement. Her assessment of the patient also respects and underscores the importance of earliest developmental experiences as pivotal and basic in defining an organizational template of self and object representations. But she balks when the issue of relative closure is raised in relation to the oedipal period, siding with the second clinician. She raises the question of how major external events and stressors, many of them occurring beyond the oedipal period, impact and alter object representations and attendant relatedness. She cites clinical and research material (e.g., loss of a parent through divorce, death, or emotional unavailability; varied traumatic experiences like sexual and physical abuse, neglect, and homelessness), and offers evidence to suggest that these noxious events sometimes did not result in permanent adverse alteration of object relations functioning. Her observations suggest that temporary derailments were ameliorated or offset by the introduction of therapeutic environmental alterations and interventions, such as residential care, psychotherapeutic experiences, changes of environment, or introduction of a new, empathic caretaker.

Three major considerations are proposed with respect to the issue of object relations functioning in the adolescent period. First, although the preoedipal years provide a solid and defined bedrock that shapes and directs much of a child's later object relations development, it is important to suspend diagnostic judgment around the finality or completeness of a child's object relations functioning. The opportunity exists for critical modifications and growth well beyond the early years. As Westen (1990) observed, most object relations theories neglected to study functioning in the postoedipal years, somewhat of a surprise in view of the considerable opportunities for maturation.

Second, object relations capacity continues to develop well into and throughout the adolescent period, owing to the cognitive (Elkind, 1985; Harter, 1977; Piaget, 1954), psychological (Blos, 1967), societal, and psychobiological factors that emerge and coalesce to either further derail or provide the catalyst for heightened growth, organization, and increasing synthesis in this critical area of personality functioning.

Third, the unfortunate experiencing of trauma or extreme stress, although in some cases debilitating, does not necessarily permanently damage and adversely alter the course of object relations development. The experience of mutative environmental events can offset, ameliorate, and in some cases, curtail the derailments engendered by negative pathological experiences (Rutter, 1989; Westen, 1990).

At this point, it is helpful to provide clinical material to illustrate these three points. The case to be presented involves a 12-year-old adolescent who was subsequently seen for a 6-year period of ongoing intermittent psychotherapy.

CASE ILLUSTRATION:
TEDDY, A NARCISSISTIC ADOLESCENT

Teddy was 12 when first seen at the request of his pediatrician. He was manifesting gastrointestinal distress, anxiety, and possible depression, as well as episodic behavior problems at school. He was in the seventh grade at a boarding school with this being his first year. The middle child, with an older 14-year-old sister and a younger 10-year-old sister, he was the only one of the children not at home. Both siblings attended a private day school near their home and resided with their mother and father. Teddy was sent to boarding school because of his father's insistence that his son follow in his own footsteps, although there was clear indication that Teddy did not agree.

Teddy's earliest development was problematic according to his parents. He was described as an active, willful, and difficult infant and toddler who did not like to be cuddled or contained, with this suggesting a basic temperamental predisposition termed *the difficult child* (Chess & Thomas, 1984). As a preschooler, he attended a nursery school where he was frequently described as aggressive with peers, had difficulty with the give and take of games, and with peer encounters that elicited frustration (i.e., when he was unable to get his way). At home, he was difficult to discipline and his father's stern, punitive, and sometimes heavy-handed discipline was in distinct contrast to his mother, who either reacted out of frustration, usually screaming at her son, or left the situation for her husband to intercede.

As he headed off to a private elementary school, Teddy continued to behave in a manner reminiscent of his preschool experience. In addition, he began to experience more frustration because of increased learning demands. He was diagnosed as having a mild learning disorder, making it difficult for him to organize and express his thoughts and opinions when task demands required written output. Despite this area of concern, he also had obvious strengths and competence, as he was a solid reader and eagerly participated in oral class discussions. His father dismissed his learning problems, citing that Teddy was simply "lazy," and in more angry moments, that he was "stupid."

In the social arena, Teddy exhibited a variable course. He could usually maintain some connectedness with one or two other children, but in the long run these relationships usually waned and eventually ceased as he related in a coercive, controlling, and devaluing manner. Similarly, his relations with teachers was problematic. He derisively referred to most of them as "nerds" or "stupid" when they gave him constructive criticism or failed to heap praise on him. He experienced particular difficulty with female staff and teachers whom he chastised as "wimps" and weak in character. Staff saw him as unhappy, a bully, and a child who was increasingly "digging himself into a hole." Initial recommendations for psychiatric consultation fell on deaf ears, as his father offered that Teddy had no problems and that discipline and regimentation would bring him around. This, of course, did not happen and Teddy drifted through the elementary grades proving himself to be an average student, a mixed blessing to his peers, and a continual source of concern to his teachers, who consistently remarked that his manifest presentation was of an unhappy and insecure little boy.

When Teddy was first seen for consultation, he presented as a pubescent 12-year-old. Dressed in fashionable attire, he looked much like a model in an advertisement for Ralph Lauren. He was not sure why he was being seen, dismissed the concerns of his pediatrician, and complained bitterly about how much he disliked his new school and everything associated with it. He put down his new mates as "geeks" and "assholes" and related how many friends he had at his previous school, which, of course, was much better than this "dump." He angrily said he did not miss his parents much as they were glad to get rid of him anyway. Besides, they favored his sisters who, in his estimation, were also "wimps" because they did not possess his innate athletic talents. In discussing various aspects of his life, he made ample and boastful note of his material possessions, his father's wealth and business success—"he could buy this place if he wanted." He had little to say about his mother, who, interestingly enough, was a talented and well-acclaimed artist. When I inquired as to why he might be seeing me he feigned ignorance, making curt reference as to how his parents and doctor wanted this, but how he could see little reason for it, given the fact that he really did not have problems.

Over the course of the first several months of treatment, it became clear that Teddy lived up to his reputation as being a difficult child, a description that had been rendered long ago. Early on in therapy he announced that talking was for "wimps," and instead wanted to spend time playing chess, a game he sometimes played with his father. He proved to be both competent and sadistic in his play, gloated over his victories, and was insensitive and impatient with my mistakes or ineptness. He was not above cheating or attempting to bend the rules when threatened with momentary setbacks or defeat, behavior that was reminiscent of how he dealt with adversity in the classroom and on the athletic field. He derived little gratification from the intimacy or challenge of the game and often seemed distinctly self-absorbed.

Kernberg (1989) commented on the narcissistic child's inability to engage in relatedness unless there is the assurance of immediate need gratification. This was sadly the case with Teddy as he initially seemed oblivious to the fact that the therapist had any other purpose than to meet his immediate needs. In the course of our chess matches, which served to allow him some sense of distance and protection, he offered diagnostic material that served to reinforce my perception that he was a young adolescent with well-defined character organization and developmental arrest, suggestive of a preoedipal disorder emphasizing a narcissistic level of functioning (Bleiberg, 1984; Eagen & Kernberg, 1984; Kernberg, 1989; Ornstein, 1981; Rinsley, 1980).

In evaluating Teddy's object relations functioning, several conclusions are justifiable when we consider current and historical material with the additional consideration of family dynamics, which further serve to solidify the differential diagnostic formulation. His self representations were grandiose, unrealistic, transparent, lacking substance, and suggesting compensation for underlying anxieties in relation to fears of being seen as weak, not good enough and a "wimp." His pronounced tendency to devalue, criticize, and gloat, along with his inability to demonstrate the rudiments of empathic relatedness, suggested a clinical picture defined by prominent narcissistic features, as did his other traits (e.g., exploitativeness, insatiable need for admiration and acclaim).

What emerged over time was the fact that Teddy was the product of a family crucible that could be designated as narcissistic (Shapiro, 1982; Zinner & Shapiro, 1972) and that served to nurture and sustain his personality derailment. In Teddy's case, the father's projected and poorly integrated aspects of his own internal world were continuously played out on the stage of his son's psyche. So, too, was the case with his mother, although perhaps less dramatically so than with the father, whose presence was indelibly presented in Teddy's self and object relations. Teddy's self representations were dominated by the aggressive, competitive, grandiose, and pseudo self-reliant portrait he presented to the world—the dominant or *viable self* (Sutherland, 1983). Other self representations were split off, disavowed, and repressed, but ultimately gained expression as witnessed by his reliance on devaluation, grandiosity, and projective maneuvers. His object representations suggested a world view of others as inferior, "sponges," inadequate, envious, manipulative, and weak. Consequently, he found little enjoyment or satisfaction in his dealings with peers or adults, with most of his transactions being superficial and specious.

As Teddy commenced treatment, the goals were much in accord with those defined by Kernberg (1989) and others (Masterson, Baiardi, Fischer, & Orcutt, 1992) most familiar with the treatment of narcissistic adolescents. In a general sense, attempts were directed toward helping him develop a more integrated and realistic sense of himself, with this being intertwined with a second therapeutic goal. This consisted of helping him to better understand his own modus operandi of employing pathological defensive operations in his object relations dealings, assisting him in understanding the rationale for this, and gradually pointing out the ultimate negative ramifications as he readied himself for his adolescent journey—a course that would either witness continued entrenchment or gradual growth and a more positive turn.

Treatment with Teddy proved to be marked by expected initial difficulties as he mobilized his defenses and presented his narcissistic self on the therapeutic stage. His distant and at times contentious, deprecating relatedness with me repeatedly brought to the fore his grandiosity and negativity, serving as clear manifestation of resistance, and also offering a vivid portrayal of his identity. Over time, I became a participant in his story, with this probably first occurring after a prolonged, unpleasant Christmas holiday during which his father had slapped him and then pinned him to the floor following an altercation between Teddy and one of his sisters. Teddy tearfully and angrily went on to recount many similar episodes of physical maltreatment, exclaiming that, "he only cares for me when I do good in sports, then he is proud of me."

This incident proved to herald a significant transitional point in his treatment, marking the beginning of the introjective or definitive stage of therapy (Rinsley, 1980), wherein the narcissistic adolescent gradually begins to use psychotherapy in order to begin to appreciate and understand self and others. This stage suggests a shift away from using others as objects of derision, manipulation, devaluation, and as repositories for projections of unacceptable and negative self representations. During this phase of treatment, it was possible to witness subtle, yet perceptible and significant alterations in his self- and object relatedness as he became less critical and devaluing of me, his peers, and his teachers. A competent athlete, he no longer gloated over his singular accomplishments, gave hints and encouragement to less talented teammates, and seemed more interested in the efforts of the entire team. In class, he was less likely to be shunned by peers. His bravado and arrogance gave way to a more quiet and reserved presentation. He developed solid ties to a few of his teachers who worked with his learning problems and gradually helped him to realize a more realistic and differentiated sense of his strengths and limitations. The final stages of treatment coincided with the important separation from his high school experience and his imminent entrance into a college in the Midwest.

In commenting on his adolescent developmental odyssey, several observations are indicated. He initially presented as a troubled young adolescent with clear indication of compromised, arrested, and developmentally impaired object relations functioning. The overall clinical picture suggested a narcissistic disorder. His major derailment had its origin in the preoedipal period, but there was also indication that his turbulent latency years continued to ferment and fuel his problems. The family crucible hardly provided the emotional containment he needed, as his parents' own narcissistic disorders rendered them erratic, unavailable, and largely ineffectual in their dealings with Teddy. It was apparent that a change of environment offered the opportunity for a critical mutative experience, one that may well not have transpired had he remained in the home. His teachers and staff rode the waves of his obnoxious, devaluing, and self-centered tirades; and in the process provided a type of containment and therapeutic milieu that eventually allowed him to trust and begin to mend his ways with classmates and adults. His individual psychotherapy was a critical intervention, as were the consultations with teachers and school staff. These meetings proved indispensable, as they comprised the "family work," focused on transference and countertransference issues. Actual family psychotherapy was precluded because of the significant distance that the biological parents lived from their son's school.

In summary, this clinical presentation serves to illustrate several propositions and concerns referenced earlier. First, it was possible to witness significant signs of object relations impairment related to derailment and arrest in the preoedipal years. But it was also possible, as recent findings suggest, to see that object relations functioning continues to develop throughout childhood and adolescence (Palombo, 1990; Westen, 1990). For clinicians to cast their diagnostic lot exclusively on the preoedipal period, seeing this as the time in which one's object relations capacity is completely defined, is to lose the opportunity to witness the unfolding presentation of a broader panorama. Adolescence affords a continued viewing of significant structural–developmental growth and change in the object relations domain, extending far beyond the preoedipal years in normal and disturbed adolescents.

Second, one can witness substantive and enduring positive changes in both self and object relatedness as a function of mutative experiences that occur later in development, in this case the adolescent period. Clinicians who work with adolescents should hardly find this surprising or novel, but in actuality there is little support for this position aside from anecdotal and clinical material.

Third, the effects of noxious and pathogenic environmental events, in this case the protracted and intermittent physical and emotional abuse by the father, undoubtedly contributed to Teddy's object relations impairment, but did not prevent him from realizing and demonstrating considerably improved relatedness with self and others. In this regard, the observations of Westen (1990) are particularly relevant, as he noted that although trauma, that is, various types of abuse, may affect enduring object relational structures and is instrumental in producing pathology, this is not necessarily a given for several reasons. Consideration has to be paid to a variety of factors before more definitive clinical pronouncements are possible, including variables such as: the nature and interpretation of the abusive experiences, the cognitive–developmental level and capabilities of the adolescent, the nature of the adolescent's object relations capacities, and the potential mutative influence of the environment. Later abuse—for example, episodes occurring in latency—may be less debilitating than abuse experiences transpiring in the early formative years, because of the extent of maturation, resiliency, and robustness of object relations and ego systems.

The clinical and introductory metaphorical material provide some illustrative perspective with regard to contemporary issues and concerns involving object relations development in the adolescent period. There has been a lack of clinical investigation into how adolescents' object relations develop and change, how various experiences impact and influence maturation, and how mutative environmental events serve to create new opportunities for growth and differentiation. The next chapter begins to address some of these concerns, as extensive research pertaining to diagnostic and therapeutic issues is presented. An exposition follows regarding how cognitive structures (object representations) provide vital and relevant clinical information that accurately depicts personality functioning.

3

Object Representation Assessment in Adolescence: TAT and Rorschach Research in Relation to Different Clinical Populations

Greenberg and Mitchell's (1983) widely accepted definition of object re-lations functioning postulates internal and external transactions with self and others: "The term refers to individual's interactions with external and internal (real and imagined) other people and to the relationship between their internal and external object worlds" (pp. 13–14). Another term some-times used to define the domain of an individual's real or imagined definition to self and others is *object representation*. Although the term is sometimes used interchangeably with object relations, its more useful and appropriate place is the inner domain, as it is a psychological construct referring to a complex, multidimensional inner mental map, schemata, or template, providing graphic psychological definitions of self and others.

Blatt and Lerner (1983), expanding on earlier writings (Beres & Joseph, 1970; Sandler & Rosenblatt, 1962), offered a succinct definition: "Broadly defined, object representation refers to the conscious and unconscious mental schemata—including cognitive, affective, and experiential compo-nents—of objects encountered in reality" (p. 194).

These mental schemata are transmitted to the child within the context of a dyadic interpersonal relationship involving the child and the person or persons primarily entrusted with his or her care. Thus, object repre-sentations are mental constructs or models that develop first from the initial relationship via the process of internalization (Schafer, 1968). They subsequently serve to organize and integrate perceptions and experiences of self-systems, as well as the complex matrix of information involving significant others. This eventually ensures that the individual, at any given point in time, has at his or her disposal an array of ideas and feelings about self and others that subsequently inform, direct, and guide real or imagined interactions and relatedness—providing clarity, consistency, and organization in the arena of personality functioning.

In considering the constructs of self and object representations, it is helpful to consider additional definitions that provide a relevant theoretical and clinical perspective. Regarding *self representations*, Schafer's (1968) writings provided a comprehensive and useful definition.

> As used here, self representations refers to certain contents of subjective experience. It may be defined as an idea that the subject has about his own person. Terming it as an idea is not meant to discount the primarily somatic, affective, and diffuse experiential origins and referents of many self representations. (p. 25)

Kissen (1986), drawing on earlier work (Horner, 1979; Jacobson, 1964; Mayman, 1976), provided a helpful definition, as he observed that self representations refer to:

> The various physiognomic modes by which the individual symbolizes an experiential image of the self and its associated affects. The individual may utilize verbal or nonverbal means for expressing these internalized units of self-perception. Although these self-perceptions may be experienced at relatively conscious, preconscious, or even unconscious level, they are most likely to be consciously available. (p. 11)

Just as the child gradually develops and builds a self representational system, he or she is also developing an equally important parallel intrapsychic model involving the conceptualization and articulation of others. Object representations refer to mental structures involving memories, perceptions, feelings, and ideas about others: those in the present, those from the past, those loved, and those loathed. The vast array of conscious, unconscious, and preconscious information is organized into schemata, which serve to guide and inform the direction of current and future transactions and relatedness. More precisely, as Schafer (1968) observed:

> The so-called object is an aggregate of more or less organized representations of another person (or things or creatures), and its details and degree of organization vary over time and between levels within one subject; they also vary at any one time from one subject to the next. (p. 29)

The relationship between the development of self and object representations involves a complex, reciprocal, oscillating, and ongoing process. It sees continued mutual interaction in the course of development, whether this involves the infant, adolescent, or adult. Sandler (1992) provided a comprehensive account of how self and object systems interface, coexist, and continuously influence one another:

> From the concept of self representation . . . it is not a difficult step to make the further extension to representations which correspond to all the non-self components of the child's world. As the child gradually creates a self representation, so he builds up representations of others, in particular of his important love and hate objects. In the beginning the representations which he constructs are those linked to need satisfaction, but he gradually creates schema of many other things, activities and relationships. He does all of this as a consequence of the successive experiences of his own internal needs and their interaction with his external environment. He gradually learns to distinguish between "inner" and "outer", a distinction which he cannot make in the earliest weeks and months of life, where the main differentiation between experiences must be based on whether they provide pleasure or pain. (p. 397)

Thus, contemporary psychoanalytic theory and research moved to a higher level of conceptualization—one that attempts to arrive at a better understanding of how and why an individual interacts in a certain manner with his or her object world and environment. The newest psychoanalytical lens may or may not incorporate more traditional theoretical models emphasizing drive theory and ego psychology, but the resulting models reveal a paradigm in which the focus involves the investigation of various levels of cognitive–affective structures that define and organize an individual's object representations and relatedness. Since the mid-1980s, parallel developments in psychological test theory also emphasized an increasing focus and concern with the systematic assessment of self and object representations embodied in projective test material.

The impetus for the pioneering and ensuing major developments in the psychological assessment of object representations reflect the seminal and prolific efforts of two main research camps. In the first case, Blatt and colleagues at Yale (Blatt & Lerner, 1983a, 1983b; Blatt & Ritzler, 1974; Blatt & Shichman, 1983; Blatt, Brenneis, Schimek, & Glick, 1976; Blatt, Chevron, Quinlan, & Wein, 1981; Blatt, Ford, Berman, Cook, & Meyer, 1988; Blatt, Tuber, & Auerbach, 1990) relied on an assessment approach that incorporates tenets of developmental psychoanalysis (Freud, 1965; Jacobson, 1964; Mahler, Pine, & Bergman, 1975) and cognitive developmental psychology (Klein, 1976; Piaget, 1954; Werner, 1948; Werner & Kaplan, 1963). This model emphasized definition and understanding of cognitive parameters and the structural aspects of object representations integrating facets of cognitive psychology, contemporary object relations theory, developmental psychoanalysis, and ego psychology.

Equally important and impressive are the contributions and research generated by Mayman and colleagues at Michigan (Krohn, 1972; Krohn & Mayman, 1974; Mayman, 1963, 1967, 1968; Mayman & Krohn, 1975; Mayman & Ryan, 1972; Ryan, 1973; Urist, 1977). In contrast to the previously mentioned efforts, weighted toward investigation and definition of structural aspects of the self and others, this approach tended to stress the concept of *ego state* (Federn, 1952) as a central theoretical organizing principle, along with the theory of psychosexual development. Anchored in ego psychological theories, Mayman's efforts were also influenced by developmental psychoanalysis and reflect Mahler's (Mahler, 1963; Mahler, Pine & Bergman, 1975) and Kernberg's (1966, 1975) theoretical and clinical formulations regarding object relations functioning. Finally, the influence of self psychology provides a central theoretical reference point, as represented by the writings of Kohut (1966, 1971, 1977).

A critical distinction between Blatt's and Mayman's work lies in the emphasis paid to the assessment of the content and affective themes of object representations as embodied in the work of Mayman and colleagues. This emphasis is a deliberate and distinct attempt to move away from a structural approach, gravitating toward one stressing a more humanistic direction by way of the interpretation of object representation material.

Although viewing the construct of object representation through different lenses, these efforts do ultimately converge and complement one another in several respects. As Blatt and Lerner (1983b) summarized:

> Both are interested in the individual's construction and representation of reality as it relates to interpersonal relationships and the attendant mental templates that transform experiences into subjective ideas and meaning. Both approaches also emphasize the thinking that one's object representations mediate and modulate drives and subsequent encounters with the environment. And in both models object representations are seen as originating from pivotal, specific interpersonal experiences and encounters, related to the drives in an epigenetic process which reflects the genesis of new levels of representational schemata in relation to self and others. (p. 236)

Efforts to empirically evaluate object representations in adults, adolescents, and children emphasized the utilization of information generated from psychological test results, and witnessed the development of a variety of scales and approaches, many of them based on Rorschach measures (Blatt, Brenneis, Schimek, & Glick, 1976; Urist, 1977, 1980). Both the Developmental Analysis of the Concept of the Object Scale (DACOS) developed by Blatt and associates (Blatt et al., 1976) and the Mutuality of Autonomy Scale (MOA), another object relations scale, developed by Urist (1977, 1980) and colleagues (Urist & Shill, 1982) represent attempts to define and articulate structural and relational aspects of the self and others. Comprehensive description of the MOA, accompanied by detailed scoring examples with adolescents, is presented in chapter 4.

Recent efforts also witnessed the development of a comprehensive TAT object representation scale that integrates object relations theory and facets of cognitive–developmental psychology. The Social Cognition Object Relations Scale (SCORS), developed by Westen and associates (Westen, Lohr, Silk, Gold, & Kerber, 1986) is outlined and discussed more completely in chapter 4. Briefly, this instrument evaluates four unique aspects of an individual's object representations, with the underlying premise being that one's functioning in this domain of personality is multidimensional—it is related to, and reflects an interaction and integration of, an array of cognitive–affective factors.

RORSCHACH OBJECT REPRESENTATION RESEARCH WITH ADOLESCENTS: IDIOGRAPHIC AND NOMOTHETIC FINDINGS EMPHASIZING THE MOA

The MOA is readily employed in the assessment of the schema or template that defines salient aspects of a child's, adolescent's, or adult's object representations. This scale can be and was used to investigate both nomothetic and idiographic differences in children and adolescents, in clinical and nonclinical populations (Tuber, 1989b).

The work of Tuber (1989a, 1989b, 1992) and colleagues (Meyer & Tuber, 1989; Tuber & Coates, 1989; Tuber, Frank, & Santostefano, 1989) reflects a sampling of the pioneering efforts to utilize the MOA in the investigation and assessment of child and adolescent object representations. Tuber employed both nomothetic and idiographic interpretive approaches to organize and integrate his findings. His research provided cogent clinical and theoretical findings in relation to assessment and treatment, although at this juncture, the findings are more germane to preadolescents and latency-age children. A sampling of selected Rorschach research emphasizing the MOA follows.

Tuber's and others' initial efforts, for example, Tuber (1983), Goldberg (1989), Ryan, Avery, and Grolnick (1985), Thomas (1987) tended to direct their efforts in a more nomothetic approach to the investigation of younger children's object representations and relatedness, with findings suggesting that MOA measures could be utilized as predictors of later object relations functioning and healthy adaptation (Tuber, 1983, 1989b). Specifically, these investigators found that (a) more adaptative MOA scores were positively correlated with ratings of self-esteem, ability to work cooperatively with peers, and academic competency (Ryan et al., 1985); (b) depressed inner-

city girls demonstrated lower MOA scores than did less depressed counterparts (Goldberg, 1989); and (c) children with attentional disorders,
compared to those with borderline personality disorder, produced less
developmentally advanced object representation functioning. In reviewing
these findings, Thomas (1987) cautioned that children with attentional
disorders (i.e., *DSM–IV*, attention deficit disorder with hyperactivity
[ADHD]) may present a clinical population whose manifest neurobiologi-
cal presentation represents an array of object representation and relatedness difficulties. These problems are obfuscated by the behavioral, attentional, and inhibitory control symptoms central to children and adolescents
with this syndrome.

The MOA was also employed in research involving preadolescents
with gender identity disorder (Coates & Tuber, 1988; Ipp, 1986; Tuber &
Coates, 1989). Results emphasized self and object representations that
were less autonomous in the boys with gender identity conflicts, with
indication of significantly more malevolent interpersonal interactions being noted in the protocols of the clinical group when compared to control
subjects.

Additional clinical subjects, for example, boys with separation anxiety
disorder, could also be differentiated from controls when mean and modal
MOA scores were compared (Goddard & Tuber, 1989). The anxious boys
produced four times as many scale point 3 responses as did their normal
counterparts. As the authors noted, the significant congruence between
the manifest symptomatology of the anxious child is impressively mirrored by the clinging, leaning MOA responses—thus illustrating and
providing an important connection between inner object representation
and external relatedness.

Turning toward a more idiographic approach to MOA interpretation,
Tuber (1989a, 1992) also demonstrated the utility of the MOA in the clinical
situation. Again, these efforts primarily reflect findings and impressions
more germane to latency-age children, but they also provide some findings worth considering, as they have obvious clinical implications for
work with adolescent patients. Findings suggest that MOA scale responses
parallel actual interactions with the therapist, thus providing cogent diagnostic information and an obvious theoretical–clinical link between
object representations and manifest relatedness.

Kelly (1996) extensively employed the MOA and the SCORS in evaluating latency-age children with a range of psychiatric disorders, ranging
from more benign adjustment and situational reactions to those emphasizing more severe forms of psychopathology, such as schizophrenia and
borderline states. Findings pointed to the usefulness of evaluating object
representation measures, as they provide vital information in relation to
structural–developmental functioning and guide and direct clinicians in

the development of therapeutic formulations and subsequent treatment directions.

Turning toward research that employed the MOA in the assessment of adolescent object representation functioning, we find a sparse number of studies to review.

MOA object representation measures in sexually abused female children and adolescents (Leifer, Shapiro, Martone, & Kassem, 1991) revealed more disturbed perceptions of interpersonal contact in contrast to the controls. Sexually abused subjects could also be differentiated from controls when the lowest object representation scores (LORS) were compared. When highest object representation scores (HORS) of the groups were compared, they did not differ. The authors concluded that although sexually abused girls are capable of socially appropriate behavior, as suggested by the HORS index, their internal models of relationships show obvious disturbance witnessed by median MOA scores and the significantly disparate LORS score levels.

Greco and Cornell (1992) investigated the object relations of homicidal adolescents employing three object representation measures: the Differentiation scale (Blatt et al., 1976), which categorizes human responses on a 4-point scale; the MOA scale; and an aggressive content measure (Holt, 1975). Results showed that a subgroup of adolescents who committed homicide in the context of another crime demonstrated indication of lower object relations based on Differentiation scale results. Although group MOA differences were recorded, the authors did not provide additional LORS or HORS data to reveal important object representation differences between, and probably within, the clinical groups.

This hypothesis is suggested by a viewing of human content responses referenced by the authors. Of interest are protocols provided by two adolescents. The first is of a 17-year-old female who had a 1-year history of drug and alcohol involvement, and who shot her mother to death following a heated argument. As the authors noted, all human content responses were described in adequate detail and depicted benign images. However, in the second case—that of a 17-year-old male who robbed, raped, and subsequently killed an elderly woman—qualitative inspection of his responses reveals, "primitive, unrealistic object relations, suggesting a pervasively malevolent object world and a potential to relate to others as dehumanized objects rather than living, feeling individuals" (p. 581).

Hart and Hilton (1988) used the MOA in conjunction with other measures to study personality characteristics of adolescents who are at risk for pregnancy. Results suggested that adolescents who used birth control had higher levels of object representation and possessed a clear sense of personal autonomy along with respect for the autonomy of others. Evaluation of the MOA object representation scores of adolescents who were sexually active and did not use birth control measures revealed somewhat variable findings. According to the authors, many of these latter young women also showed high MOA scores, juxtaposed against some who revealed low scores, suggesting that some of these adolescents resembled the birth control users in terms of their level of psychic complexity. Others with low MOA scores appeared more like pregnant adolescents, a group whose object representations suggested developmental arrests and regressive phenomena. In this group, having a baby appeared to be equated with having some purpose in life, realizing a sense of connection, and providing the opportunity for restoring affective ties to lost others.

Finally, Blatt and colleagues (Blatt et al., 1990), in research involving older adolescents with severe psychiatric disturbance, utilized three MOA scores (mean score, HORS, LORS) in an attempt to evaluate the quality of interpersonal relationships. In this case, results suggest that MOA scores might relate more to factors involving aspects of psychopathology (e.g., severity of clinical symptoms, extent of thought disorder), and only secondarily to the quality of an older adolescent's object relatedness.

OBJECT REPRESENTATION RORSCHACH RESEARCH EMPHASIZING OTHER MEASURES

In addition to object representation research utilizing the MOA, other investigators used other Rorschach scales in order to evaluate self and other object representations in adolescents. Efforts reflected nomothetic and idiographic approaches.

Blatt and Lerner (1983b) employed the DACOS (Blatt et al., 1976) in the systematic evaluation of three adolescent patients in order to analyze their unique and distinct object representation configurations. Their intent was to advance the understanding of psychopathology as it relates to impairments in the interpersonal arena, and to address how this information guides formulations regarding therapeutic directions. Results revealed significant differences in personality organization as a function of psychopathology; results also emphasized distinct differences in object representation with clinical vignettes being referenced in what follows.

In the case of a 19-year-old schizophrenic male subject, object representations were undifferentiated, poorly articulated, and lacking in meaning or purpose. Although able to present a superficial impression of intactness, closer inspection of object representations suggested a barren, inaccurate, and inarticulate inner world.

In another instance involving a 16-year-old adolescent female with anaclitic depression, her inner world was portrayed as one in which figures were passive, helpless, vulnerable, needing to be cared for and protected from objects depicted as frightening and ominous. In this case, the image of the mother figure was charged with ambivalent, conflicted, cognitive–affective material, with representations suggesting experiences of adequate care and nurturance juxtaposed against rejection and an overbearing presence.

Finally, in the presentation of a 17-year-old female adolescent with a histrionic personality disorder, impressions are helpful in delineating that she will likely display different patterns of relating with males as opposed to females. Interactions with females are portrayed as cooperative, positive, and reciprocal. But her object representations of male objects connote a sense of passivity and danger. In extrapolating from this material to the treatment situation, the authors posited that disruptions may occur in therapy as she attempts to avoid more painful issues, and when the therapeutic relationship becomes more involved.

In reflecting on the utility of object representation measures, the authors (Blatt & Lerner, 1983a) concluded that this information provides important diagnostic material about different forms of psychopathology, the developmental level of personality organization, and the quality and nuances of interpersonal relationships. In addition, this material is readily translated into indispensable information relating to aspects of the ensuing psychological treatment, for example, transference reactions.

Kelly (1986) also employed the DACOS in evaluating object representation functioning in conduct-disordered, borderline, and depressed female adolescent inpatients. Results revealed that borderlines could be differentiated from both of the other two clinical groups, as they demonstrated significantly lower levels of functioning on this scale. The borderline's human percepts were often poorly articulated, fragmented, and imbued with aggressive and primitive destructive attributes. Borderlines lacked the capacity to initiate and sustain relatedness when compared with the other clinical groups.

In a study of 13 older female adolescent bulimics, Parmer (1991) used measures from the Comprehensive System (Exner & Weiner, 1995) in order to investigate object relations capacity. The bulimic group's test protocols revealed significant signs of object representation impairment reflected in erratic personality functioning suggesting arrest at the differentiation subphase of development. These impressions were suggested by the fact that the bulimics produced significantly more responses involving merging, engulfment, and hatching themes. These results also emphasized the continued need to heed the level of psychostructural development in individuals with eating disorders so as to develop treatments that promote object constancy.

Kocan (1991) studied the Rorschach responses of a female patient over 8 years, beginning when the woman was 15, in order to demonstrate changes in self and object representations. She specifically focused on the reflection response, and was able to illustrate how inner phenomenologi-cal changes transpired over time, and how these were intertwined and connected to specific therapeutic interventions.

Finally, Sugarman and colleagues (Sugarman, Bloom-Feshbach, & Bloom-Feshbach, 1980) extensively employed the Rorschach in idiographic inves-tigations of borderline and schizophrenic adolescents, arriving at several important conclusions in relation to diagnosis and treatment. Integrating psychoanalytic tenets from ego psychology, developmental psychoanaly-sis, and object relations theory, they focused much of their efforts on documenting the considerable difficulty the second individuation period creates for these adolescents.

In describing different subgroups of borderline adolescents, as well as adolescents who are borderline-like, they noted that formal Rorschach material is often colored by self and object representations that are at a part-object level as portrayed by a predominance of quasihuman, *(H)*, and quasihuman detail, *(Hd)* types of responses. Few full human, *H*, responses are noted in the protocols. Thus, representations reveal schema suggesting lack of interaction and an accompanying sense of aloneness with rare evidence of symbiotic content. Responses also convey that self representations are bad, evil, destructive or impaired in some way.

Berg's (1982, 1986) writings on the borderline adolescent similarly emphasized that these patient's object representations reflect few human percepts, with those that are seen revealing strange, unappealing, and distorted depictions, suggesting a limited capacity for relatedness. Other object representations are troubling in that they depict primitive images indicative of deprivation, abandonment, and annihilation. Berg's explicit thoughts on the role of psychological assessment (1982) underscore the importance of test data in the diagnostic and the treatment situation. More specifically, this material is critical as it ensures an initial and accurate taxonomical identification that defines salient ego and object relations information needed to inform treatment options and direction. Thus, treatment is guided and enhanced by an understanding, based on object representation information, of the vulnerability toward particular trans-ference and countertransference scenarios.

TAT OBJECT REPRESENTATION RESEARCH
WITH ADOLESCENTS: IDIOGRAPHIC
AND NOMOTHETIC FINDINGS EMPHASIZING
THE SCORS

Clinicians and researchers traditionally used the TAT in the assessment of object representations by utilizing an idiographic paradigm and heavily relying on the voluminous contributions of Bellak (1993), whose predominant conceptual frame is ego psychology. But as Stricker and Healey (1990) noted, there have been only a few limited attempts to derive TAT-based object representation scales. An exception to this involves the work of Westen and associates (Westen et al., 1985), who integrated aspects of social–cognitive psycholgy, developmental psychology, and object relations theory in their development of a scale to assess self and object representations. The SCORS taps four dimensions of object representations and relatedness: Complexity of Representations of People; Affect-tone of Relationship Paradigms; Capacity for Emotional Investment in Relationships and Moral Standards; and Understanding of Social Causality. More detailed exposition of scoring and interpretive material is provided in chapter 4. Relevant research pertaining to adolescents is presented in the sections to follow.

In contrast to object representation research in general, and Rorschach investigations in particular, the majority of the work conducted by Westen and colleagues involved adolescents, as they evaluated a variety of clinical and nonclinical populations, including borderline adolescents (Westen, Ludolph, Silk, et al., 1990); normal adolescents (Westen et al., 1991), and sexually abused adolescent females (Westen, Ludolph, Block, et al., 1990).

In a normative study using the SCORS, Westen and associates (Westen et al., 1991) investigated object representation functioning and development in 2nd-, 5th-, 9th-, and 12th-grade children and adolescents. Results showed increased development and differentiation when second graders were compared to fifth graders: specifically with regard to adolescents, the 12th-grade student's representations of people suggested more complexity, emotional attributions became more complicated, and the capacity for interpersonal involvement increased. The studies support several conclusions. First, object relations capacity continues to develop through the latency and adolescent developmental periods. Second, these measures, along with the obtained results, appear applicable to the evaluation of an array of relationships in addition to those involving primary attachment figures. Third, results attest to the diagnostic importance of identifying multiple dimensions of object representations rather than viewing object relations as a unitary developmental line.

In utilizing the SCORS to evaluate object relations functioning in borderline adolescents, Westen and associates (Westen, Ludolph, Silk, et al., 1990) found that borderline subjects could be discriminated from both normal and nonborderline, psychiatrically disturbed female adolescents on the basis of their TAT object representations. The results also attested to the clear pathology of the borderlines as their efforts on all four scales of the SCORS revealed more grossly pathological responses, less differentiated representations of others, and eccentric thinking manifest in blurred boundaries between self and others. The borderline adolescents also demonstrated significantly higher levels of functioning on one object representation scale, Complexity of Representations of People, leading the investigators to caution that under certain conditions the representations of borderlines and their attendant relatedness, may be relatively normal (e.g., under conditions of low arousal). In addition, results pointed to the need for clinicians to reconsider the assumption that borderline pathology always has its roots in the preoedipal period.

In a study of adolescent girls who were hospitalized for psychiatric reasons, Westen and colleagues (Westen, Ludolph, Block, et al., 1990) also used the SCORS in order to document the relationship between developmental history variables and different dimensions of these adolescents' object relations. Findings suggest that a number of factors adversely affected object relations development: prolonged separations from the mother in the preoedipal years, maternal neglect, and sexual abuse occurring in the postoedipal years. Results suggest several observations in relation to the developmental course of these adolescents' object relations. First, preoedipal experiences have a critical role in the shaping of object relations, pointing to the central role of the mother, and of disrupted attachment as major factor in the genesis of subsequent pathology. Second, neglect, sexual abuse, and disruptive family experiences transpiring in the postoedipal years may also have an important impact on object relations development. This also suggests the obvious importance of according more investigative attention to a developmental period that has been relatively ignored by psychoanalytic theory.

Other authors began to employ the SCORS in the evaluation of object relations functioning with adolescents who were physically and sexually abused (Freedenfeld, Ornduff, & Kelsey, 1995; Ornduff et al., 1994).

In one instance, Ornduff and associates (Ornduff et al., 1994) found that sexually abused female children, including adolescents, could be differentiated from nonabused counterparts on the basis of SCORS object representation scores. Results revealed lower levels of developmental functioning on all four scales, suggesting that the object representations of the sexually abused children and adolescents were colored by more primitive and simple perceptions of objects. Relations were also perceived as negative and imbued with punitive affective connotations. An inability to initiate and sustain relationships was also indicated. The abused children also were unable to make age-appropriate observations with respect to social causality. Abuse subjects displayed a proclivity for the production of primitive and pathological object representations.

The authors arrived at several conclusions with diagnostic and therapeutic ramifications. The TAT, and in particular SCORS material, may contribute to the diagnosis of sexual abuse as there is a strong indication of a relationship between a history of documented sexual abuse and subsequent impaired object relations. With regard to treatment, implications suggest that the goals of therapy should involve reparation and integration of a poorly defined and unintegrated sense of identity, improved ability to modulate intense and overwhelming affects, and modification of a world view dominated by largely malevolent perceptions. As the authors advised, abuse victims somehow need to recognize and modify patterns of maladaptive past relationships in the hope of steering clear of future repetitious patterns of relatedness emphasizing a cycle of repeated abuse and maltreatment.

Finally, the efforts of Freedenfeld and colleagues (Freedenfeld et al., 1995) showed that another type of abuse (physical maltreatment), also has an adverse impact on a child's object relations capacity as documented by SCORS results. More specifically, 39 physically abused children, many of them adolescents, revealed a more malevolent representational object world when compared to controls. Abused subjects demonstrated a lower capacity for emotional investment in relationships, a less accurate and simplistic understanding of social causality, and ascribed more malevolent and negative affective connotations to relationships. Abused subjects did not differ from nonabused counterparts when it came to the SCORS scale assessing an understanding of the cognitive complexity of representations of people. This finding led the authors to caution that:

> ... different aspects of object relations can be affected by the trauma of abuse, although other aspects may remain relatively unaffected. The multidimensional nature of object relations is important to consider when evaluating the impact of physical abuse. (p. 565)

Implications and caveats for treatment suggest that therapists who work with children and adolescents who were abused should be attuned to working toward specific goals, including helping the patient acknowledge and modify distorted perceptions of self and others, helping them to alter malevolent and illogical perceptions of the world, and assisting them in recognizing the patterns and dynamics intrinsic to abusive relationships. Therapists also need to be particularly sensitive to transference issues. These are likely to present as assumptions and expectations that the therapeutic connection may reflect the anticipation (perhaps conscious as well as unconscious) that relationships are abusive, nonnurturant, punitive, and not rewarding.

The review of the varied object representation research in this chapter suggests that an emerging, impressive, and vast panorama is available when clinicians adopt SCORS and MOA measures in their repertoire of assessment strategies. This is afforded when one applies the tenets of contemporary psychoanalytic object relations theory as the theoretical lens with which to interpret psychological test material. This material easily translates into vital and substantial diagnostic information regarding salient aspects and dimensions regarding the adolescent's personality organization and functioning. Object representation information serves as a guide—informing and directing the ensuing therapeutic course and providing a perspective on what the therapeutic odyssey will be like. Reasonably clear speculations and informed caveats about process factors and nuances of therapist–patient relatedness are possible (e.g., manifestations of transference and countertransference phenomena).

4

Object Representation Scales

This chapter is intended to provide the reader with an introduction to the scoring and interpretation of the two major scales used to assess the object representations of adolescents. The MOA is outlined first. Complete exposition of the scale is presented along with scoring examples of the 7 scale points as they relate to responses produced by adolescents. Next, the SCORS is presented in detail, along with scoring examples pertaining to the four object representation dimensions as they apply to adolescent clients.

MOA

The MOA was originally developed by Urist and associates (Urist, 1977; Urist & Shill, 1982) to evaluate the thematic content of kinetic responses depicted on the Rorschach by rating all human, animal, and inanimate movement responses along a 7-point ordinal scale continuum, ranging from 1 (*positive, empathic, separate,* and *autonomous relatedness*) to 7 (representations of relatedness characterized by *malevolence, overpowering envelopment, fear of incorporation*). The results provide considerable information about an individual's object representations.

Before proceeding with more detailed description and scoring examples of the 7 scale points of the MOA, it is necessary to provide brief commentary on the reliability and construct validity of this object representation device in order to provide the reader with perspective on the empirical rigor of this measure. This is a difficult and still incomplete task in the case of adolescents, as most of the existing reliability and validity reports relate to adults (Urist, 1977) or children (Tuber, 1992), and only a few to adolescents.

Research focusing on interrater reliability with adult subjects revealed fairly consistent results. Urist found (Urist, 1977) that interrater reliability ranged from .52 (for exact agreement) to .86 (agreement within 1 point). Stricker and Healey (1990), in reviewing MOA interrater reliability with adult subjects, reported that most studies found that 1-point agreement was generally reflected by results ranging from .72 to .98. Blatt et al. (1990) in commenting on the issue of reliability with respect to the MOA, concluded that it appears to be a reliable and useful measure with children, adults, and adolescents in both nonclinical and clinical settings.

With respect to children, there is considerable indication of sound interrater reliability in studies emphasizing nomothetic clinical group comparisons. In the investigations of Meyer and Tuber (1989); Ryan, Avery, and Grolnick (1985); and Tuber (1983), the MOA scale was easily applied to children's Rorschachs, and sound interrater figures were reported. Exact agreement figures ranged from .73 to .90, whereas agreement within 1 point consistently yielded results above 90%. Leifer and colleagues used the MOA as one measure to assess object representations in sexually abused latency females (mean age of 8.9) and reported exact agreement figures of 84%. Kelly (1995) reported interrater MOA reliability of .85 in a study that investigated object relations functioning in latency age children who were subjected to chronic, complex trauma, and abuse. The MOA has provided reasonable estimates of reliability in nomothetic comparisons with both normal and clinical groups.

Investigations with adult clinical populations in which the MOA was used as a measure of object representation generally revealed variable findings, although overall, there is ample indication of reasonably good construct validity. Harder, Greenwald, Wechsler, and Ritzler (1984) in a nomothetic study comparing schizophrenic, depressed, and nonpsychotic inpatients, found that MOA results were significantly correlated with ratings of severity of psychopathology derived from checklists and clinical assessments based on criteria related to the *DSM–III*. Spear and Sugarman (1984) demonstrated that two types of borderline patients (i.e., infantile and obsessive–paranoid) could be differentiated from schizophrenics on the basis of their MOA scores. In a study related to assessing object representation changes as a function of psychotherapeutic involvement, Kavanaugh (1985) found that MOA changes were related to ratings of improvement with patients treated by psychotherapy and psychoanalysis. With adolescent patients, Urist and Shill (1982) utilized a variety of direct and indirect measures (e.g., developmental and family history, clinical progress reports), and compared them to MOA scores on the Rorschach in order to assess object relations functioning. Ratings of the clinical case material correlated with the MOA mean and LOR scores. More disrupted Rorschach MOA scores consistently reflected current and past reports and accounts of more problematic and less adaptive interpersonal functioning.

A review of child and adolescent research emphasizing the MOA in a nomothetic capacity is reviewed in the previous chapter, but additional comments in relation to construct and predictive validity are warranted before moving on to a more detailed consideration of the scoring and interpretation of the MOA. Tuber's (1992) review provides ample examples attesting to the sound validity of the MOA as it relates to the assessment of children's object relations capabilities.

The theoretical underpinnings of the MOA rely on the developmental theory of Mahler (1974). Mahler's work provides detailed material in relation to aspects of object relations development, emphasizing the discrete stages of separation and individuation as components of one's object constancy. As Urist (1977) commented with regard to the theoretical underpinnings of the MOA:

> Individuals tend to experience self-other relationships in consistent, enduring characteristic ways that can be defined for each individual along a developmental continuum. This continuum corresponds to the various stages in the development of object relations, ranging from primary narcissism to empathic object-relatedness. (p. 3)

Thus, the MOA can be utilized to assess two separate dimensions of an individual's object relations, the degree of self–object differentiation and the degree of empathic relatedness. In terms of the first dimension, at one end of the continuum, relatively undifferentiated and inarticulate self–object representation is characteristic: self–object boundaries are blurred, there is no sense of autonomy, and imagery suggests possible themes of merger, engulfment, annihilation, and symbiosis. At the higher end of the continuum, representations reveal increasingly separate, defined, and more autonomous self–object definition: The self is presented as a relatively stable, enduring, and unique psychic entity vis-à-vis others.

With respect to the second dimension, that of empathic relatedness, the most primitive and nascent representations of others are cloaked in terms of imagery and percepts that suggest themes of malevolence, and others who are controlling, punitive, and emotionally unavailable. In contrast, at the higher end of the continuum, representations suggest themes of more realistic, mutual, and autonomous relatedness with implicit respect and regard for others, and where the autonomy of the other is tolerated, understood, and appreciated.

The specific and discrete 7 MOA scale points as originally outlined by Urist (1977) are presented, along with scoring examples. The hypothetical responses all represent variations on the same response so that the reader gains a sense of how the emphasis on mutuality changes along the 7-point continuum.

Scale Point 1

This scale point captures the highest and most adaptive level of object relatedness. The reciprocal individuality of figures (human, animal, inanimate) is well-defined. Implicit or explicit reference is made regarding the separateness and autonomy of the figures, yet there is a clear sense of mutuality noted in the relatedness. Words or phrases such as *each other, one another, both of them, together,* are helpful in determining whether or not a response should be scored as a scale point 1, as they connote distinct individuality in the context of a mutually positive encounter. Examples of responses scored as scale point 1 include:

Card II. "Two bears giving high-fives."
Card III. "Two ladies rocking a baby. Each of them taking turns and laughing."
Card IX. "Two witches having a talk."
Card X. "Two spiders carrying a stick together."

Scale Point 2

To receive a scale point score of 2, the figures must be involved in a relationship, but it is explicitly or implicitly parallel in nature. There is no direct or implied mutuality, yet the autonomy of the figures is not distorted. The key to differentiating a score of 1 from 2 requires keeping in mind the reciprocal, mutual nature of a representation scored as 1. With a response scored scale point 2, the emphasis is on relatedness of a less intimate nature, suggesting interest, but without the degree of investment or distinct mutuality. Examples of responses that qualify as 2 include:

Card II. "Two bears dancing around."
Card III. "Two ladies cooking something."
Card IX. "Two witches looking at each other."
Card X. "Two spiders walking up a little wall."

Scale Point 3

Scale points 3 and 4 reveal an emerging loss of autonomy and, as Coates and Tuber (1988) noted, both points imply a need for another figure to allow for a sense of structural cohesion. For a response to receive a scale point 3, figures are depicted as leaning on or supporting one another. There is the stated or implicit sense that the figures require external support. Figures described as *leaning, hanging, catching, holding,* or *grabbing* connote the need for dependence and reliance on another. Examples of scale point 3 responses include:

Card II.   "Two bears leaning on one another . . . drunk maybe."
Card III.   "Two ladies . . . tired, leaning on a rock."
Card IX.   "Witches leaning on a giant crystal ball."
Card X.   "Two spiders sleeping against a dead tree."

Scale Point 4

A scale point of 4 is assigned when one figure is depicted as a reflection or imprint of another. One of the figures exists as an extension of the other, for example, as a shadow. Increasing loss of autonomy and mutuality is conveyed, slightly more so than responses scored as scale point 3. The major difference between scores of 3 and 4 is that in the latter case, only one solid being is present. In the former (i.e., responses scored 3), there is the sense of two distinct beings without the indication that either is less fragile, impaired, or inept than the other. As Goddard and Tuber (1988) emphasized, although both points 3 and 4 share a depiction of self in which narcissistic issues are central, scores of 3 suggest the availability of a mirroring, cohesion-building "other," with more autonomous capacity being suggested than scale point 4 responses, which suggest that object representations reflect a more anaclitic–dependent motif (Urist & Shill, 1982). Percepts involving reflection responses, mirror images, shadows, or footprints would earn scale point 4 scores. Key words and phrases include *identical, reflection, both the same . . . identical.*

Examples of responses qualifying as scale point 4 ratings include:

Card II.   "Bear looking in the mirror . . . yawning and stretching."
Card III.   "Looks like a pendant . . . two women. They are both identical . . . same women."
Card IX.   "A wicked, evil witch looks in the mirror and sees herself. Kinda like Cinderella."
Card X.   "A spider here. Another one. No, really just one looking at reflection in a puddle."

Scale Point 5

For the first time, the theme of malevolent control is documented along with the loss of capacity for separateness. Percepts involving influencing, controlling, manipulating, and coercing are generally indicative of the type of responses earning a scale point of 5. One figure may be portrayed as helpless and under the control of a powerful, malevolent other. Coates and Tuber (1988) provided a helpful clarification in regard to scale points 5, 6, and 7, and the preceding 2 scale points. They noted that the latter are more linked to narcissistic concerns and possible disturbance, whereas the final 3 scale points are distinctly tied to increasingly primitive modes in the experiencing of others. The autonomy of the self is under attack and object representations increasingly reflect emptiness, depletion, annihilation, or destruction. On a cautionary note, responses such as *people fighting* are usually scored as scale point 2 responses because there is no distinct reference to a loss of intactness of either figure. On the other hand, *two people fighting . . . blood all over*, would qualify as a scale point 5 response because there is clear and distinct indication that either one or both of the object's integrity and intactness was violated. Examples of responses scored as scale point 5 are:

Card II.   "Two bears . . . fighting . . . kicking . . . blood there."
Card III.   "Two ladies . . . they've turned someone into a skeleton . . . at the bottom . . . a skeleton."
Card IX.   "Two witches . . . casting evil spells on people."
Card X.   "Two spiders. Shooting poison at each other."

Scale Point 6

Malevolent, one-sided aggression and domination is a major difference between responses receiving a scale point score of 5 and those scored as 6. Not only is there a severe imbalance in the mutuality of relations between figures, but the imbalance is imbued with distinct and obvious destruction. Percepts emphasize a serious and dire assault on the autonomy of the object. Also included within this response category are those documenting a parasitic relationship, wherein one figure exists as a consequence of robbing or severely compromising the integrity and autonomy of the other figure. Scale point 6 responses are illustrated by the following:

Card II.   "Two bears stomping on that dead animal. Because of all the blood there."
Card III.   "Two cannibal ladies tearing apart that animal. Want to drink the blood . . . maybe vampire cannibals."
Card IX.   "Witches . . . shooting lasers . . . this one here explodes. She's the new queen of the witches."
Card X.   "Spiders sucking the blood out of that bird."

Scale Point 7

Scale point 7 responses connote a type of relatedness characterized by total control at the hands of an overpowering, enveloping, and devouring force beyond the control of the individual. As Urist (1977) noted: "Figures are seen as swallowed up, devoured or generally overwhelmed by forces completely beyond their control" (p. 5). The destructive element or force is portrayed as existing outside the relationship of the figures, clearly reflecting the enormity of the power and utter helplessness of the figure or figures. Examples of responses scored as 7 are the following:

Card II. "Two bears ... all burnt up ... just stood up ... stepped on a land mine. Smoke and fire there."

Card III. "Megaforce ... just disintegrated ... nothing left of those two ladies ... burnt to a crisp. Can't even tell who they were."

Card IX. "Evil and bad ... laughing as they set the world on fire .. . explode the trees and kill all those people down there ... looks like dead babies ... down there at bottom."

Card X. "Spiders ... crabs ... people ... big explosion ... maybe plane crash ... arms there ... head ... rabbit ... all dead ... blood. Nothing left ... looks like guy's face ... smushed all up."

Deriving Scores

Following the scoring of the MOA responses (which again involve human, animal, and inanimate relationships), 4 scores are derived from the protocol. The first score is the mean MOA score, which reflects, in most instances, the typical or average level characterizing the most likely and preferred object representation schema or template. It is also helpful to derive the modal MOA score, especially when one specific score predominates that would have important clinical implications, but might be obscured if one were to look at only the mean MOA score. Lastly, the highest object representation score (HOR) and the lowest object representation score (LOR) should be obtained, as these provide important information about the adolescent's range or repertoire of object representation responses, and will ultimately provide valuable glimpses of possible variability in object relations, as is the case with more disturbed adolescents, such as the borderline.

SCORS

The SCORS is a 5-point scale, measuring four dimensions of object relations derived from TAT responses. The four object relations scales are: Complexity of Representations of People, Affect-tone of Relationship Paradigms,

Capacity for Emotional Investment in Relationships and Moral Standards, and Understanding of Social Causality.

The scale, which was originally developed by Westen and colleagues (Westen et al., 1985), underwent several revisions and was employed to assess object relations functioning in both normal children and adolescents (Westen et al., 1991), as well as with disturbed children and adolescents— for example, physically abused (Freedenfeld et al., 1995); sexually maltreated (Ornduff et al., 1994); borderline (Westen, Ludolph, Lerner, Ruffins, & Wiss, 1990; Westen, Ludolph, Silk, et al., 1990); and inpatient adolescents with a variety of psychiatric disorders (Westen, Ludolph, Block, Wixom, & Wiss, 1989).

The results of this research consistently revealed high levels of corrected interrater reliability figures in the range of .83 to .96 (Westen et al., 1991). This compilation of most of the existing research involving adolescent populations attests to the robust construct and predictive validity of the SCORS as an instrument capable of providing multidimensional measures of an individual's object relations functioning (Stricker & Healey, 1990). More extensive information on the validity of the SCORS scales can be found in several sources (Westen, 1990; Westen, Lohr, et al., 1990).

Before proceeding to a description of the four SCORS scales, I note some of the theoretical concerns and assumptions Westen (1990, 1993) addressed in his research with these object representation indices. Concerns about the theoretical underpinnings of several of the basic tenets of object relations theory, coupled with an interest in developing empirical devices that could capture and assess the multidimensional components of an individual's object relations, led Westen and colleagues (Westen et al., 1985) to develop the four object representation scales of the SCORS.

These scales were devised to assess varying dimensions of object relations in children, adolescents, and adults based on data derived from TAT narratives. The SCORS theoretical base is heavily influenced by two theoretical perspectives, object relations theory and research, as well as developmental social cognition.

As Westen's (1991a) conclusions indicated, the theoretical underpinnings of the scales, all of which are yoked to object relations theory and developmental cognitive psychology, ultimately converge to capture the breadth and depth of object relations dimensions in an individual:

> The term object relations actually includes a number of different functions and structures, such as ways of representing people in relationships; interpersonal wishes, affects, and conflicts; ways of attributing causes of other people's behavior; capacity for investing in relationships, and so on. The concept of general levels of object relations is clinically indispensable; however, there is little reason to believe that patients uniformly respond at a single level or that they even respond on a single level on all of these dimensions at a single time. (p. 57)

In integrating tenets from various schools of object relations theory, he observed three theoretical threads serving to connect observations about developmental phenomena. In the first case, as Westen (1990) concluded, the development of object representations emphasizes increasingly differentiated growth throughout childhood and adolescence (Westen et al., 1991), likely well into adulthood. Observations reflect the progressive ability of individuals to make more refined, articulate sense of their own perspectives as distinct, separate, and apart from the representations of others. A related and second major assumption of object relations theories is that one's representations of self and others become more complex and assimilated as a function of maturation. Lastly, object relations theories posit that certain psychological phenomena (i.e., presence of primitive defense structure, poorly integrated self-structure, borderline–narcissistic personality organization), are usually transcended by the oedipal period. The etiology of severe character pathology is entirely related to events occurring very early in the developmental odyssey, before the oedipal period, and usually within the first 3 years. This continues to be a belief held by many adherents of object relations theory.

As a result of a growing and impressive literature emphasizing the SCORS in the assessment of object representations with normal and disturbed children, adolescents, and adults, Westen (1990) concluded that several of the core assumptions widely subscribed to by most object relations schools need to be more closely scrutinized, revisited, and probably modified. His comments, noted here, suggest that the SCORS provides clinicians and researchers with a model pertaining to dimensions, development, and pathology of object relations.

> Object-relations theories share a number of core assumptions that require reconsideration in the light of empirical data. These include the assumptions that (1) a continuum of development is isomorphic with a continuum of pathology, (2) the origin of severe character pathology lies in the pre-oedipal period, (3) certain features of borderline object relations (such as splitting and narcissism) are transcended normatively by the oedipal period, (4) object relations is a unitary phenomenon or developmental line, (5) object-relational stages are culturally invariant, and (6) clinical data from pathological adults are necessary and largely sufficient for constructing and evaluating theories of object relations. Empirical research has begun to clarify the nature of borderline object relations as well as the development of normal and pathological object-relational functioning. (p. 689)

In the sections to follow, the four scales of the SCORS are introduced with some preliminary comments regarding the theoretical rationale underlying each scale. This is followed by description of the actual scale. Finally, adolescent TAT responses provide scoring examples in relation to each scale. For more detailed and comprehensive theoretical underpinnings of the SCORS, accompanied by elaborate and informative scoring examples, the reader is referred to Westen's original manual (Westen et al., 1985).

COMPLEXITY OF REPRESENTATIONS OF PEOPLE

How the adolescent constructs and modifies self and object representations is a matter of some debate, but most object relations theorists agree on several points. First, as Westen and associates (Westen et al., 1991) showed, the development of representations proceeds along a course that documents and delineates clear differences between younger and older adolescents in terms of how they present conceptualizations relating to self and others. Younger adolescents present less articulate and differentiated representations than do older adolescents. Second, the representation of self and others broadens, expands, and becomes more complex, yet increasingly integrated, when younger as opposed to older adolescents are considered. Third, the developmental task of assimilating and integrating disparate affective information regarding self and others reflects ongoing business. Older adolescents in comparison to younger adolescents display a greater and more defined ability to integrate richer, more elaborate, ambivalent, and sometimes disparate affective self–object representations. This finding challenges the more traditional time frame proposed by many object relations theorists who hold that these developmental processes are completed at roughly age 6, the time when the phase-specific oedipal crisis is usually resolved.

This initial object representation scale measures the extent to which the individual clearly defines and differentiates the perspectives of self and others, seeing aspects of self and other as having stable, enduring, and multidimensional qualities and attributes. The scale also evaluates to what extent an adolescent is capable of seeing self and others as psychological beings who possess complex motives and subjective experiences.

At the lowest scale point, Level 1, individuals have great difficulty distinguishing people and perspectives—people are not clearly differentiated and the boundary between self and others is not clear. The individual does not make a distinction between his or her own thoughts and feelings and those of others. Stories indicating boundary confusion are typical of Level 1 responses (i.e., characters are portrayed as sharing the same situation, feelings, or thoughts). The examiner is likely to have difficulty distinguishing one character from another, as responses suggest global reference to *they both, both of them,* and so on. However, an important exception to this guideline should be stressed when the response seems reasonable based on the theme or context of the story. For example, *they are both worried she will not be able to handle the situation.*

Level 2 responses emphasize simple unidimensional representations with the focus largely on behavior and immediate actions, although there is a clear and distinct sense that people have boundaries between self and others. This is a major difference between Level 1 and Level 2 responses. TAT characters are portrayed as mostly unidimensional with respect to their thoughts, feelings, and motives; there is no elaboration of internal motivational states. What the person does, as opposed to why the person does what he or she does, suggests lack of traits or dispositions that would reveal who the person really is. Simple understanding of affective states and intentions is seen, but there is no elaboration of motivational factors, for example, *she seems calm, he feels mad, and that one over there doesn't care . . . don't know how come they feel that way.* As Westen (Westen et al., 1985) advised, "People are seen as unidimensional, existing *in* situations rather than *across* situations" (p. 20).

Level 3 responses represent TAT stories scored according to this central principle: The adolescent begins to show the inclination to make inferences about subjective psychological states in addition to focusing solely on actions or behavior. Still, these inferences are elementary, unidimensional, and lacking in depth. Scoring guidelines emphasize an indication of at least one simple emotion, with respect to self or other, being ascribed to several causes, for example, *she is sad because her boyfriend left her and she does not like to be left alone.* In this case, the adolescent has some emerging and nascent sense of psychological-mindedness with respect to the enduring attributes of self and others. However, these perspectives and hypotheses are general, global, and lacking in subtlety—characters are romanticized, stereotypical, and lack a sense of being imbued with more than superficial and unidimensional traits and qualities, for example, *she's about to leave for school, feels sad because she loves him. He cares about her . . . has to think of his own life, where he wants to go, can't become involved at this time. She's just off in her own thoughts.*

Level 4 responses demonstrate that the adolescent has a clear appreciation of the involved nature of the emotional lives of other people, and of subjective emotional material. The adolescent is demonstrating a more obvious psychological-mindedness. There is still no sign of appreciation that different parts of the personality are part of an interactive system wherein the link between conscious and unconscious is realized. Where enduring personality traits are referenced, there is adequate material to assign a Level 4 score to the response, for example, *he's upset at her for trying to hold him back but he knows that his temper has gotten him into trouble . . . can't just let things go, takes it as a real affront to his ego.* A score of 4 is also given when the individual designates a character as possessing relatively simple traits but with indication of opposite affective valence, for example, *she's got a bad temper but can be kind too.* Lastly, scores of 4 are assigned when the adolescent produces stories that reveal simple conflicting intentions, for example, *he knew he should stick up for him, but he just couldn't get himself to do it.*

Level 5 responses reveal that the adolescent is capable of viewing others in complex and elaborate ways. Clear inferences are made in reference to others' emotional states, motives, attitudes, and unconscious processes. People are viewed as having conflicting feelings and able to express different parts of their personalities according to the demands of varying situations. Guidelines for assigning a score of 5 include: (a) score where stories emphasize that a character's subjective experience is multidimensional and enduring; (b) where there is an indication of clear contrast between the way a character is portrayed in the picture and the typical way he or she usually is; (c) when the characters manifest very complex motives or well-defined mental conflicts not indicative of momentary situational conflict; (d) when traits or attributes with disparate affective valence are seen as describing a character, and where at least one such trait is not global or is qualified, for example, *she's moody, but basically she thinks a lot about people.* The difference between a response scored as 5 and one scored as 4 is that the score of 4 is assigned when characters possess traits with opposite affective valence but there is not the appreciation that the ascribed traits are more than global or unidimensional in nature. For example, *he's nice but basically dumb,* would earn a score of 4, whereas *he's nice, but he sometimes doesn't think things through enough* would be scored 5 because of the embellishment of one of the traits.

Scoring examples of typical responses depicting the levels in relation to the Complexity of Representations of People scale are noted here. All involve stories given to Card 4 of the TAT.

Level 1: "There's a guy there and he's gonna split."

Level 2: "That guy is gonna leave . . . she doesn't want him to go. He goes."

Level 3: "He's gonna leave. She doesn't want him to go because she's afraid he'll get killed in the war, never come back, and she will be alone."

Level 4: "He's gonna leave . . . doesn't want to. She's mad but afraid that he will get hurt."

Level 5: "He's gonna leave . . . has to. He's like his father . . . stubborn, believes in what he's doing. She doesn't want him to go . . . mad but afraid of like what happened long time ago with his dad. Had to go to war to defend his country."

AFFECT-TONE OF RELATIONSHIP PARADIGMS

This second object representation scale of the SCORS was designed to assess the extent to which an individual expects relationships to be destructive, harmful, or threatening as opposed to safe, nurturant, and rewarding. This process, as Westen (1993) observed, involves conscious and unconscious processes in order to retrieve affect-laden representations and to organize experiences of the self in relation to others. The scale measures the affective quality of representations of people and relationships and is based on theoretical material pertaining to psychoanalytic theory (Kernberg, 1966; Klein, 1952; Kohut, 1971; Lustman, 1977) and to cognitive–developmental psychology (Elkind, 1985; Harter, 1977).

In order to appreciate how an adolescent orders his or her object representations in relation to affective valence, it is necessary to consider the concept of splitting, as it can be utilized in the viewing of normal development illustrating how the infant first organizes affectively charged representations of self and others. As Lustman (1977), in commenting on how infants organize early affective experiences of self and others, observed:

> For a time then the splitting process sponsors the slow architecting of self-object representations, throwing into conjunction self-object experiences with similar valence-response qualities. This implies that the building up of representations obeys laws of simple association, that anlagen of self-object representations "coalesce" when they possess similar valences. It is likely that even at this early stage, groups of representations begin to constitute more complex, sophisticated class formations, not only linked internally by valence similarities and increasingly differentiated part properties which exist at sensorimotor and perceptual level of experience, but also by emerging properties which exist at a higher level of conceptualization. (p. 131)

Viewed from this perspective, splitting describes a basic foundation for psychic organization and defense. As development proceeds, the mechanism of repression or *horizontal splitting* (Kohut, 1971) may be seen as a later manifestation of this initial and basic developmental paradigm. As Lustman (1977) noted, it is still possible to observe residuals of splitting in adolescents. It is revealed by the persistence of a distinct binary or dualistic quality characterizing thought organization, and certainly not unfamiliar to clinicians who work with adolescents where there is a distinct tendency to paint representations with "either–or" colors.

Research focusing on the borderline adolescent (Masterson, 1976; Rinsley, 1968) highlighted the central role of splitting in this group. Various part-objects in relation to the self and others are organized and integrated along global, primitive, and basic lines to suggest that affective representations are dominated by a rigid internal division and polarity. Clear lines of demarcation exist between good feelings, which are the outgrowth of positive and growth enhancing self–other interactions, and bad feelings based on negatively charged and frustrating self–other involvements. This ultimately results in distorted and rigid cognitive–affective perceptions of one's object representations. As Rubenstein (1980) observed, "given the unassimilated nature of the part-self and part-object representations, these inner images remain real and are projected or introjected, again depending upon the existing ego state" (p. 451).

Before proceeding to exposition of the various levels of the Affect-Tone of Relationships Paradigm, it is important to consider Westen's (Westen et al., 1985) comments in relation to how individuals with varying degrees of psychopathology display a continuum of responses on this particular scale. Patients with more severe characterological disturbance (e.g., borderlines) manifest overgeneralized or poorly differentiated affective expectations, revealing perceptions of object representations that reflect global and undifferentiated affective expectations in regard to self and others. Although in other instances, where there is less psychological disturbance (e.g., an adolescent who has significant yet encapsulated problems in getting along with her mother, but who has a fairly good relationship with her father), may present expectations of rebuff, criticism, and negativity from female figures. Juxtaposed against this are expectations that relations with male figures will be nonjudgmental, positive, or benign.

Thus, an adolescent's affective expectations of relationships may reveal a situation suggesting a continuum of more or less differentiated and organized representations in relation to the self and others. As noted, relationships may be portrayed as imbued with all-inclusive, negative affective components. In other instances, the adolescent may reveal more indication of differentiated affective expectations in relation to self and other representations. Ultimately, this is a function of several intersecting and converging factors, cognitive and emotional maturation on the one hand, and in the other instance, the presence of individual psychopathology suggesting inherent cognitive and emotional limitations or derailment.

Turning to the specific discrete levels of this object representation measure, at the lowest level, Level 1, subjects portray an expectation that relationships will be almost entirely colored by hostile, destructive, and aggressive transactions, whereas at the higher end of the scale, subjects affix affective connotations to relationships, indicating increasingly positive, satisfying, and nurturing connectedness.

At the lowest scale point, Level 1, the individual views the interpersonal world as globally threatening, dangerous, and painful. Persons are depicted as abandoning, abusive, and capable of destroying others and self with little reason other than lack of concern or malicious intent (Westen et al., 1985). At this level, objects are represented as victims or victimizers. TAT stories that depict themes describing malevolent representations of others, or that suggest caretakers as grossly negligent, are scored as Level 1. Responses to cards where the adolescent introduces and emphasizes gratuitous violence or aggression (suggestion of projection or projective identification) where this is not commonly perceived should be scored as Level 1 responses. Responses depicting fights should not be considered as examples of Level 1 responses unless percepts include material representing more idiosyncratic trauma or malevolence, for example (Card 4 of the TAT), *He's gonna fight him . . . doesn't see that they are there too, waiting on the roof. Just blow him and her away. Good bye, nothing left . . . just wasted.*

Level 2 responses reflect the adolescent's world view as hostile, empty, distant, and lonely but not overwhelming. Others may be represented as unpleasant, unavailable, or uncaring, but are not depicted as engulfing or destructive. Life may be represented as unpleasant, unhappy, and without suggestion that significant others are pleasant or empathic. Themes suggesting a profound sense of loneliness or abandonment are scored 2, as are stories suggesting victimization. Fights and aggressive encounters without qualification regarding motives are also examples of stories that would earn a score of 2.

Level 3 responses start to herald a subtle yet significant shift in terms of the adolescent's affective self–object representational schema. Stories begin to suggest acknowledgment of a range of emotional perceptions. People are sometimes portrayed as loving, caring, and nurturant, although social interaction and object representation is viewed through a mildly negative lens. Examples reflect the following themes and stories scored as Level 3: arguments between characters, stories suggesting affectively mixed representations where the predominant tone is negative, escape from danger via the help of benevolent others, and where there is no interaction between actors and the affect-tone is neutral.

Responses that show that the individual has an inner schema suggesting a range of object representations and interpersonal expectations are scored as Level 4. Objects are portrayed as being able to love and be loved and are quite capable of caring for one another. Overall, however, the prevailing affect-tone suggests a neutral and somewhat bland valence; but this is in contrast to Level 3 responses, which connote a mildly negative affective tone. Principles regarding whether or not a response should be scored as Level 4 include: (a) score for minimal affect involved in the story and where the predominant tone is essentially neutral; (b) score if the characters are somewhat bland, perhaps coexisting, but not opposed to being involved; and (c) score if relationships are satisfying and not particularly imbued with negatively charged affective representations, but a certain richness or special quality is lacking.

Level 5 responses, according to Westen and colleagues (Westen et al., 1985), suggest that the individual's responses on the TAT denote representational schemas portraying a range of affectively charged object representations and interpersonal expectations. On the whole, the affect-tone valence is decidedly positive, in contrast to Level 4 responses that load on a more neutral affective valence. Scoring guidelines include: (a) score 5 where there may be indication of a mix of affects, but with indication that the predominant feeling tone is positive in nature, (b) where people are portrayed as happy, content, and optimistic in their transactions, and (c) when stories depict individuals as doing for one another and responding to others' needs and wishes.

Scoring examples for the five levels of the Affect-tone Object Representation Dimension of the SCORS follow and they all represent adolescent responses given to Card 4 of the TAT.

Level 1:   "He's just standing there. Turns around and beats her up . . . knocks her down. Nothing."

Level 2:   "He's gonna' go after that guy and beat him up cause he called her a name . . . didn't like what he said. Don't know. Bad name. She's just crying."

Level 3:   "He's just standing there, wants to go. She's just looking. I don't know. How am I supposed to tell?"

Level 4:   "They are in love. Get along. Feel O.K. . . . they care about one another and will probably get married."

Level 5:   "He looks somewhat upset, like maybe he lost his job and she wants to help him, listen to him. They know things will get better because he's a good worker. He listens to her because he loves and trusts her. Happy with one another."

CAPACITY FOR EMOTIONAL INVESTMENT IN RELATIONSHIPS AND MORAL STANDARDS

This scale was designed to evaluate the extent to which relationships with others are portrayed as ends rather than means, where relationships emphasize mutuality as opposed to need gratification. Moral standards and beliefs that guide behavior and influence relationships, reflecting the nuances of conscience and one's value system, are also evaluated. Relationships are experienced as meaningful, fulfilling, and enduring.

The theoretical tenets underlying the development of this scale reflect a developmental model that integrates facets of object relations theory, ego psychology, and developmental psychology, as it captures the maturational process by which an individual achieves a status wherein mature relatedness is realized. It is important to clarify why this scale combines what may seem to be disparate constructs and theories (i.e., object relations principles and social–cognitive theories relating to empathy and moral development). Westen and colleagues (Westen et al., 1985) succinctly underscored why it is essential to consider these tenets as central to the development of this scale for three major reasons.

In the first case, the investigation of the moral development of the child and adolescent cannot be seen as separate and isolated from the study of object relations development. Morality encompasses the regulation of relations between individuals, particularly between self and others. It may be the case that cognition about morals may ostensibly proceed independently of investment in others, but the ultimate development of investment in morals cannot proceed without a sincere concern and empathic connectedness with others. Clinicians are all too familiar with patients who know the rules of the game, but cannot apply them to the interpersonal arena; the most obvious example is the antisocial or prepsychopathic adolescent who is quite capable of saying why certain behaviors are wrong and why they are hurtful to others, but who repeatedly displays a modus operandi suggesting that knowing what to say does not translate into what one should do to function appropriately in the world.

In the second instance, as Westen noted, it is all but impossible to differentiate a need-gratifying interpersonal orientation from a need-gratifying moral orientation. Freud (1966) and Piaget and Inhelder (1969) referred to the importance of empathy for the feelings and thoughts of others as central in the development of morality. Hoffman (1984) stressed the importance of guilt and other emotional aspects of morality as emanating from the capacity for empathy with the trials and tribulations of others, with this first evident in the first year of life, but becoming more articulated with the advent of the ability to take roles in the third year. Dunn's (1987) research provides an important link between relationship and morality, as her efforts revealed that 2-year-olds who were well-adjusted and had good object ties were able to demonstrate indication of shared fantasy activity involving the feelings of others. This indicated a capacity to understand and practice how to conform to rules and rudimentary social expectations. Other researchers employing a social–cognitive lens to evaluate constructs such as empathy (Bruchkowsky, 1989; Case, 1988) and social perspective taking (Selman, 1980) developed sequential stage models that highlight increasingly differentiated levels of functioning and more refined levels of adaptation as the child progresses thorough adolescence. These efforts attest to the shift from an egocentric, need-gratifying perspective to one emphasizing a more altruistic, mature object relations perspective in the moral domain.

The underlying structure or conceptual thread that connects and emerges across many domains of child development and clinical research involving investigations of empathy, morality, and prosocial behavior, is that development and emotional investment in the social world proceeds from need-gratification to investment in independent others (Westen et al., 1985). Thus, it becomes virtually impossible to separate true and empathic concerns for the needs of others from moral concerns. Gilligan (1982) found that young adult women's orientation toward moral issues emphasized care, responsibility, and relatedness, whereas others found that adolescent and young adult males subscribed to a world view of morality based more on justice, rights, and individual autonomy (Colby & Kohlberg, 1987).

Thus, the theoretical impetus underlying the development of this object relations scale reflects the rapprochement of two theoretical positions: object relations theory, and various theories subsumed under the rubric of social cognition. As Westen (1991b) succinctly commented:

> The measures for assessing capacity for emotional investment reflect a developmental model aimed at integrating cognitive-developmental research with object relations theory and theories of superego development. It attempts to assess investment in relationships and values that regulate relationships, rather than only reasoning about them. (p. 446)

General observations regarding the scoring of this scale were offered by Westen et al. (1985). At the lowest levels, others are viewed primarily as means to ensure one's gratification and pleasure. At the more intermediate level, Level 3, relations are valued but appear superficial; rules are respected but moral beliefs reflect a rigid and concrete quality. At the higher levels, the individual possesses the capacity to initiate and sustain deep, enduring relationships in which there is indication of true empathy, and others are valued for their individual qualities. People are concerned with doing the right thing, of adhering to societal rules, but also critically reflecting on belief systems and not blindly following social dictates if they are harmful to an individual.

Level 1 responses indicate that the individual is primarily concerned with his or her own gratification. Responses may depict acts of extreme aggression or violence without any apparent sign of remorse. A score of 1 is given when:

Stories portray people pursuing their own needs without regard for others.

Where one character takes action of some type that impacts others but where there is no apparent concern for what happens to the other.

Stories focus on a single character and exclude others.

Stories suggesting that others are represented as mirrors or tools for gratification and where there is substantial self-preoccupation suggestive of narcissism.

Where the individual displays egocentric qualities by placing the self or someone he or she knows into the story.

When the story represents characters as loners.

Where people coexist without any sense of emotional connection.

Where people are grossly devalued or maligned.

Where there is no ascertainable response or depicted reaction to a major interpersonal trauma.

Level 2 responses suggest that, although the individual has some emerging sense of potential conflict between his or her needs and those of others, ultimate themes still depict self-serving motives and pursuit of individual needs. Attachments are possible but relationships suggest a self-absorbed quality. The sense of morality reflects a fairly elementary sense of right and wrong (i.e., actions are bad not because of the impact on others, but because punishment is the consequence, again suggesting an egocentric perspective). The following represent instances where stories would be given scores of Level 2:

Stories that depict persistence of interpersonal problems without resolution of conflict.

Stories that depict antisocial acts without remorse or guilt.

Stories that hint at grandiosity where it appears inappropriate to the story.

Stories containing impulsive aggression with some attendant remorse but without appreciable guilt.

Stories that suggest superficial relationships or simple participation in mutual activities.

Stories that reveal defiance of authority in order to express autonomy, or where themes suggest false accusations and implicit externalization.

Stories that portray extreme masochism or victimization in relation to severe abuse or trauma.

Level 3 responses suggest that the individual thinks of the needs and wishes of others. The motivation to please others, of being liked and behaving in accordance with societal rules and conventions, displaces a self-interest orientation noted by Level 1 and 2 responses. The overall quality of relationships is still not deep, although relationships are valued. The person now demonstrates clear signs of guilt for transgressions, not just transient remorse. The representation of moral rules and codes is still rigid and inflexible, with stories emphasizing a sense of duty or blind obligation. Guidelines for scoring stories at Level 3 include:

Stories that emphasize concern for others and disapproval of bad actions because they are not right.

Stories where people are attached but where there is little elaboration as to the history of their connection, suggesting a somewhat superficial and stereotypic relatedness.

Stories that clearly portray guilt for immoral or antisocial actions.

Stories that emphasize caretakers, superficial altruism, performance of social roles or obligations.

Stories that depict internalization of parental wishes.

Stories in which there is a sense of unconventionality, where social rules are dismissed and there is a minimal sense of connection to others.

Level 4 stories suggest that the individual is capable of forming and sustaining meaningful, rich, and committed relationships with others, with this often supplanting personal needs and wishes. Values, moral beliefs, and modes of conflict resolution reflect conventional themes. Individuals want to do the right thing in relation to societal expectations or authority figures, and they may reference more abstract and altruistic narratives. The stability, permanence, and intimacy of relationships is emphasized. Guidelines for scoring Level 4 emphasize:

Stories where long-term, committed, and deep relationships are described.

Instances where there is clear indication of mature empathy, not simply sympathy or simple, unelaborated compassion.

Stories that indicate an appreciation and enjoyment of another's qualities or self-attributes.

Stories that represent conflict but where one of the characters is able to surmount the impasse and still display concern for the other.

Stories that suggest obedience and compliance with moral codes based on concern for others, not simply emanating from a perspective suggesting unilateral respect for authority.

Level 5 responses suggest that the person is interested in the development of relationships that result in the happiness of both the self and other. Attempts to acquire an autonomous identity reflect a sincere, mature, and committed involvement in relationships. Conflicts are depicted as being dealt with via compromise respecting the needs of others. Authorities and societal rules are viewed with respect and there is strong indication of a higher moral and ethical sense that is attuned to and respectful of the rights and needs of others. At times, existing rules and societal values are questioned when, for example, the rules or rights of others are significantly violated or infringed on. Several guidelines for assigning Level 5 scores are:

Themes indicating flexible problem solving in the way of compromise or mediation of conflict, suggesting the parties recognize the importance of conflicting–competing interests, beliefs, or attitudes, but are able to work things out.

Themes that depict conflict and tension between social norms and beliefs of the individual where there is evidence that the individual's motivations and actions are tied to obvious empathic concerns in relation to others, and there is not the hint of ulterior self-serving intent.

Stories that stress the goal of self-development, mastery, autonomy occurring within the context of a mature, loving, and committed relationship.

Some brief examples of adolescent TAT responses to Card 4 illustrate various types of responses found on the developmental levels of this scale.

Level 1: "This is a man who is looking . . . thinking about leaving and he just goes away. Not sure, maybe to the city."

Level 2: "They are having a fight, that guy and her. I don't know why they are. She just yells and screams and he's bummed . . . just leaves."

Level 3: "They are . . . like you know . . . really in love. Have a big fight. Make up I guess. Probably get married I guess."

Level 4: "They are . . . these two here are in love. She's worried that he will do something stupid . . . talks to him, concerned about him. Doesn't want him to do something he will regret later. Calms him down. They go home . . . everything's cool."

Level 5: "They are fighting . . . she's really pissed. Talk it out . . . listen to one another. He can see her point . . . knows he was wrong and doesn't want to hurt her. They have different ideas, but work it out and get along better in the future."

UNDERSTANDING OF SOCIAL CAUSALITY

The ability to attribute complex, logical, accurate, and psychological definition to behavior, motives, thoughts, and emotions reflects the individual's understanding of social causality. The Understanding of Social Causality scale was developed in order to assess the working representations that shape and guide information processing and behavior in relation to an individual's ability to demonstrate logical, complex, and accurate causal attributions and intentions (Westen, 1993).

The theoretical underpinnings of this scale also reflect the influence of two theoretical camps: object relations theory and research in developmental–social cognition, although the former reflects less empirical research than the latter. A brief review allows for some sense of how the integration of these two theoretical positions resulted in the development of an object relations scale that provides another dimension and measure of the individual's functioning in this domain.

The development of this scale reflects clinical and empirical findings that suggest that adolescent patients with severe personality disorders tend to make highly idiosyncratic, illogical, and inaccurate assumptions about others' intentions. Westen and colleagues (Westen, Ludolph, Lerner, Ruffins, & Wiss, 1990; Westen, Lohr, et al., 1990) found in several studies looking at the social–cognition object relations of borderline adolescents, that these patients' cognition tended to reflect several deviant perceptual styles. In one instance, the causes of others' behavior, thoughts, and emotions were interpreted in idiosyncratic ways reminiscent of preoperational causality; in other instances, impaired social causality reflected distortion and interference from motivational and defensive processes.

Another study with hospitalized adolescent girls (Westen, Ludolph, Block, et al., 1990) investigated the relationship between social cognition and object relations as assessed by the SCORS and developmental history. Results emphasized that the adolescent group whose mothers were either neglectful or literally absent had considerable difficulty in making sense out of why people behave in certain ways, and also displayed obvious idiosyncratic and primitive attributions vis-à-vis their social cognition understanding and processing. Results also indicated that adolescents raised in chaotic and disorganized households also display difficulty understanding and making sense out of the social arena. Findings provided strong support for the documentation of the serious impact of early disrupted attachments and disruptive family experiences on subsequent social functioning.

Downey and Walker (1989) also found that the social cognition of adolescents was adversely influenced by early maternal neglect, maternal separation, and intrafamilial disorganization and dysfunction. Here again, a cluster of mother–child factors loading on unavailability and absence are ultimately reflected in deficits wherein the adolescent manifests underdeveloped cognitive capacity, making it difficult to translate and comprehend others' behavior and intentions.

Research investigating social cognition in children was extensive (Baron-Cohen, 1993; Beardslee, Schultz, & Selman, 1987; Damon, 1975, 1981; Dunn & Munn, 1987; Hay, 1994; Selman, 1980). It suggests a developmental course in which stages and levels reflect increased complexity and differentiation. With increasing age, thought organization in this domain reveals shifts from outer to inner; thinking proceeds from the focus on the external, concrete, and physical properties of the object or situation to higher developmental levels emphasizing cognitive organization based on internal conceptual properties. This results in the ability to generate hypotheses and inferences about self and other with regard to social situations and problems.

An illustrative example of one type of structural model outlining the stage development sequence of social perspective taking was illustrated in Selman's (1980) efforts. In the earliest stages, ages 3 to 6, the child's concept of social causality and people shows little differentiation between objective–physical and subjective–psychological. Concepts of relationships are colored by egocentric representations wherein the child attributes his or her own perspective to the other person. At higher levels, ages 6 to 12, the child manifests the ability for cognitive mediation and can see his or her own thoughts, feelings, and actions from another's perspective. Attributions about others now reflect some uncertainty because the other is acknowledged to have an inner life separate and distinct from one's own. Higher developmental levels witness the development of a cognitive perspective that allows for a clearer view of the mutuality of individual perspectives and a vantage point from which one can simultaneously coordinate the perspectives of all parties in interaction (e.g., self, other, and the greater social system). At the highest developmental level, age 12 to adulthood, there is still more differentiated and complex mental processing of relationships involving the self and other. At this stage, the concept of a personal unconscious emerges. Understanding of relationships and social events reflects a highly differentiated perspective in which the individual's representations indicate coordination, convergence, and balance between self, other, and the greater environment.

Thus, the construction of the Understanding of Social Causality scale is yoked to research and clinical material emphasizing the understanding of social causality and functioning. This scale of the SCORS specifically evaluates the logic, complexity, and accuracy of causal attributions (Westen, 1993). At the lowest levels, causality is illogical, egocentric with disorganized or inappropriate attributions. At intermediate and higher levels, the individual's understanding of social causality is colored by representations that indicate increased appreciation and understanding of how thoughts, feelings, and actions are linked to compex conscious and unconscious psychological operations. In the sections to follow, the five levels of the scale are presented with examples of adolescent TAT responses appropriate to each.

Level 1 responses indicate that the individual has a markedly impaired or absent sense of causality as applied to the social domain. The individual does not seem to need to understand why feelings, behavior, or thoughts are relevant to interpersonal situations. Or, if explanations are proposed, they are grossly illogical. More specifically, scores of 1 are assigned when (a) stories are noncausal or where causality is only physical, (b) stories emphasize unexplained affect, (c) stories are bizarre and illogical, and (d) stories reveal the inappropriate or peculiar attribution of motives.

Level 2 responses indicate that the individual has some basic or rudimentary sense of social causality. Actions are portrayed as responses to environmental stimuli. Behavior, feelings, and interactions are explained in a manner that may hint at mild illogical thinking. Scores of 1 are given to stories that suggest that actions and feelings result from environmental stimuli or in response to impersonal forces. There is no indication that cognitive–affective mediation plays a role. Score for incongruity between thoughts, feelings, and actions. Scores of 1 are also given to stories in which (a) thoughts result in action but there is not a causal connection between the thought and the deed, (b) stories depict action resulting from simple intention and where people respond appropriately to simple emotions, and (c) stories emphasize that magical abilities of omnipotent authority figures are responsible for the attainment of some type of goal.

Level 3 responses suggest that the individual can logically and accurately decipher social situations and problems, but there is still the representation of an external locus of causality. These stories show the individual has some sense of causality, represented by minor elaboration of psychological causes around a context that focuses on behavioral or environmental causes. Score 1 when a story depicts complex mental states on the individual's part, but where this does not result in any subsequent action or behavior. Scores of 1 are also assigned to responses where (a) stories suggest that the individual has a fairly sophisticated understanding of causal processes by making ad lib comments that are not reflected in the actual TAT narrative and (b) stories in which the individual makes reference to how the greater social system impacts thought, behavior, or feelings.

Level 4 responses reveal that the individual displays an increasingly clear sense of the role psychological factors play in determining actions. At this level, cognitive involvement is the intermediary between stimulus and the individual's subsequent reaction. Causality is incomplete or applied inconsistently. More specific criteria used to assign Level 4 scores involve instances where (a) stories that reflect that a character's actions are a result of complex psychological causes, (b) stories where the individual demonstrates that one's feelings, thoughts, motives differ from those of others based on how a situation is viewed, (c) stories in which one of the characters responds to the perceived wishes of another, and (d) stories that indicate several characters' actions are guided by psychological processes, although these ultimately connote basic and simple representations of causality.

Level 5 responses suggest that the stories are imbued with complex thoughts, feelings, and actions, indicating that the individual has the ability to understand self and others' behavior as caused by psychological factors. The person makes complex hypotheses and inferences about the psychology of others. Score where the story references that multiple figures' actions and behavior are guided by rich and elaborate perceptions, thoughts, emotions, wishes, or conflict. If the motives of one of the characters indicates complex internal phenomena and another character displays internal but not complex motivation, the story is still scored 5. However, if motives are internal but not complex, a lower score should be assigned. Score 5 if one of the characters in the story acts on the basis of his or her perceptions in relation to another's thoughts or perceptions, but only where there is indication of complex mental mediation. Other examples of responses scored 5 would involve (a) cases where action is based on introspection, reflection, insight into one's psychology; or (b) stories that indicate unconscious motivation as the impetus for action.

Examples of the five levels of the Understanding of Social Causality scale of the SCORS are illustrated by adolescent TAT responses given to Card 4.

Level 1:   "This guy is mad, hurt his arm I guess. Don't know why it happened. He gets better."

Level 2:   "That guy is mad. He hurt his arm. She helps him. She bandages his arm."

Level 3:   "This guy feels messed up . . . hurt and mad . . . sad. She wants to help . . . understands . . . went through the same thing."

Level 4:   "He is really mad . . . wants to end the relationship because he feels it's not going anywhere . . . feels trapped but doesn't want to hurt her . . . like he was hurt. Doesn't want to do that. He needs to be on his own at this point in his life."

Level 5:   He is mad . . . sad too, but does not want to hurt her. Knows that he has done this before . . . really eats at him . . . thinks about why he can't stay in relationships without messing them up. He cares a lot about her . . . needs space to think. She's sad but knows it's better to take a break . . . sees it's best to let things cool down. She knows he cares and is having real struggle, can sense his pain."

At this point, the reader should have some sense of the two major object representation measures utilized in the assessment of adolescent Rorschach and TAT data. More detailed and elaborate guidelines for scoring are available and should be reviewed in order to ensure additional familiarity and scoring competence. For the MOA, the following sources are recommended: Tuber and Coates (1989) and Urist (1977). Sources that provide more detailed scoring guidelines for the SCORS include the original manual (Westen et al., 1985), as well as other references (Westen, 1991a, 1991b).

The next chapter illustrates the application of the MOA and SCORS scales to Rorschach and TAT material provided by normal adolescents of varying ages. The intent is to provide a sense of developmental changes between younger and older adolescents in addition to demonstrating the utility of these object representation measures as they inform and attest to functioning in the external world.

5

The Assessment of Object Representation in Normal Adolescents

Any discussion of what constitutes normality in adolescence has to take into consideration the need for close scrutiny and evaluation of many oscillating dimensions involving aspects of internal and external change and functioning. As Hauser and colleagues (Hauser, Borman, Powers, Jacobson, & Noam, 1990) observed, the initial and early stages of adolescence are marked by pervasive concern and preoccupation with immediate physical feelings and biological changes, a belief in external control, an egocentric view of the world, and a limited ability to connect and be empathic. Intermediate and later adolescent development sees a shift toward a more internal locus with an increased ability to see differences between self, others, and events, and finally, by an increasing ability to establish and maintain intimate and collaborative relationships.

Yet, even when these transformations are taken into account, or viewed as benchmarks from which to survey the adolescent journey, the attempt to define what is normal is akin to trying to arrive at an agreed definition of what constitutes normal New England weather in April. Depending on where one lives, there is likely to be considerable difference of opinion. Likewise, it is almost impossible to arrive at a universally acceptable definition of normality in adolescence, as it must involve considerable latitude and take into account the dramatic transitions and transformations repeatedly taking place during this period.

Three basic areas serve as diagnostic reference points, and should be of considerable benefit when one is confronted with questions regarding whether or not a given adolescent is demonstrating a relatively normal passage or adjustment. They refer to both internal and external factors. These three areas of focus are by no means all-inclusive, and the reader may well embellish or dismiss them, but they are worth considering as they do provide some parameters in relation to questions and concerns regarding the issue of defining normality for a given adolescent.

These areas of concern may be translated into three essential proposals: (a) adolescence is a period of marked transition dictating that any attempt to define normality needs to attend to the adolescent's current adjustment to a given environment or context; (b) adolescence is a period wherein there is constant attention directed to addressing the mastery of various developmental tasks; and (c) adolescence is a period where the concept of synthesis assumes a critical mediating role, providing the clinician with important diagnostic information that can be utilized to formulate and buttress structual developmental assessments, and to provide indispensable information regarding therapeutic direction.

Context and developmental task define external environmental and internal factors, referring to the "what" in the assessment equation. Specifically, the former defines the external parameters of the immediate psychosocial, interpersonal environment and the greater societal world to which the adolescent is reacting. Who the child lives with, where he or she resides, under what circumstances, and what are the particular stressors comprising the adolescent's daily existence, are some of the facets serving to define context.

Developmental tasks connote particular internal demands or problems in relation to different areas of psychological and interpersonal functioning. Cohen and Weil (1972), drawing upon the earlier work of Erikson (1959) and Gardner (1960), enumerated many of these and developed a formal assessment device, the Tasks of Emotional Development, to evaluate how children and adolescents address and confront these emotional developmental tasks. Some examples include: socialization within the peer group; establishment of trust in people; acceptance of limits from adults; establishment of a conscience with respect to the property of others; and separation from the mother figure.

Similarly, Bryt (1979) observed that adolescence is a period requiring increasing ability to meet critical and more complex demands for personality integration involving the mastery of select tasks. These include: emancipation from childhood; development of a more reliable sense of identity and individuality; clarification of vocational interests; preparation for intimacy in interpersonal relationships; organization of genital activity; and crystallization of a personal and social role, including the consideration of moral and ethical issues. Lastly, the global task of separation–individuation (Mahler et al., 1975) constitutes another example of an obvious source of potential conflict. It is also a psychological task, being universally addressed as adolescents proceed on their developmental course.

The process of *synthesis* refers to "how" factors, or to organismic variables defining the psychological means and resources the adolescent brings to bear in his or her attempts to cope and master. Conversely, it can refer to those resources being ineffectually deployed in an attempt to arrive at some reasonable adjustment. These adaptational mechanisms involve ego resources and object relations. Some authors (Sugarman et al., 1980) defined synthesis in a somewhat different manner, as they considered this phenomena to be a developmental task in its own right, in contrast to a definition emphasizing a functional role or construct involving a mediating and organizing process. Specifically, they described synthesis as the major task of adolescence, commenting that adolescence involves the resolution of an array of dimensions—psychosexual, psychosocial, cognitive, object relational, structural, and moral.

In summary, the adolescent passage allows for the viewing of an ever-changing vista that witnesses the unfolding and powerful intertwining of interpersonal (external) and biological (internal) forces giving rise to the general paradoxical situation of adolescence: to move on, separate, and become one's own person while connecting and relating to self and others in a new way. The clinician is often asked to address how this process is proceeding, although the questions and concerns are often more urgent and couched in pathological terms with reference to aberrant relationships or self-injurious behavior. How does the clinician arrive at some sense of closure as to whether or not the adolescent sitting before him or her is coming to some reasonable resolve with this general mandate?

This question suggests the need to come full circle and return to the more basic question raised previously, that is, what is the definition of normality as it pertains to adolescence? It is possible to make reasonable observations relating to some of the previously mentioned points of reference (e.g., context, task, synthesis), when one ponders how a particular adolescent is faring at a particular point in traversing the developmental expanse of adolescence.

Exner and Weiner (1995) provided a thoughtful and helpful perspective, emphasizing that any definition of normality should consider evidence of internal and external effectiveness or adaptability when deciding whether or not a given adolescent is manifesting normal adjustment. Noting that the concept of normality provides at best a vague reference point, it does constitute an important framework for detecting unusual or abnormal functioning.

Related to these concerns and observations, the introduction of psychological test material can be of indispensable diagnostic assistance in the assessment or viewing of the inner domain for reasons discussed earlier and at greater length in chapter 2. Results from the TAT and Rorschach (in particular, object representations information) may be utilized in either an idiographic or nomothetic manner to more fully elucidate factors in relation to the inner adaptational resources the adolescent brings to bear in his or her struggles with developmental demands. The contemporary work of Exner and Weiner (1995), as well as earlier efforts by Ames, Metraux, and Walker (1971) provided informative nomothetic normative material as to how normal adolescents present on the Rorschach. And more recently, Westen and colleagues (Westen et al., 1991) began to introduce normative material in relation to how normal adolescents of different ages respond to the TAT, and how their object representations and object relatedness are portrayed therein.

In the remaining sections of this chapter, the reader is introduced to six adolescents, three females and three males, all of whom are doing relatively well in their lives. Two of them have exhibited some difficulties, but overall the reports of their teachers and parents attest to the fact that they are moving on and not manifesting significant intra- or interpersonal difficulties. None of these children were involved in psychological treatment, nor was there compelling indication they should be. They all seemed to be moving along—some perhaps slower than others—but they are well-connected and comfortable with themselves and with others. They were all doing relatively well in school and most were involved in activities or extracurricular pursuits, which bolstered their sense of self-worth, provided important outlets for emotional and impulse discharge, and connected them with their peers.

Thus, in an attempt to gain an additional glimpse of their adaptational resources, the presentation of projective material is provided in order to acquaint the reader with normative MOA and SCORS material obtained from a limited sample of adolescents deemed as doing fairly well by those who know them best: their parents, peers, and teachers. All of the adolescents were administered the Rorschach and TAT as part of a longitudinal study in which they served as control subjects.

CASE 1: KEITH, A 13-YEAR-OLD MALE

The first nonpatient protocol is of a 13-year, 4-month-old male. Keith was in the eighth grade when he was seen, and he was doing well academically, receiving mostly A's and B's. He expressed that he generally liked school and especially enjoyed social studies and geography. He was getting along with his peers, had one close friend with whom he spent time after school, and did not feel he had difficulties in the interpersonal peer arena. He liked sports and participated in junior varsity soccer and baseball; he also liked to ski and snowmobile during the winter months. Additional interests included swimming, riding his dirt bike with friends, and listening to his stereo. He also mentioned that he enjoyed taking care of his pets, two dogs and a cat, and that he might like to be a veterinarian when he grew up. He did not reference major problems in getting along with his parents or his older 15-year-old sister, although he did mention that he and sister did occasionally fight. He helped out around the house and assisted his father in taking care of a wood lot.

When seen for evaluation, this young adolescent was quite cooperative, pleasant, and easily involved. He related in a quiet, subdued, and pensive manner, giving considerable attention and thought to his answers. He impressed the examiner with his sincere and thoughtful presence.

TABLE 5.1
MOA and SCORS Responses for Case 1

TAT object representation measures

Card 2: "Looks like a daughter going to school or maybe she's a teacher, and the father or brother are plowing the fields. And the mother is leaning against a tree. Looks like she's kinda sick or tired. They live back in the old days . . . the prairie. Few hills around them and they have a big house. They feel lonely . . . they have only the house and their family around. All they have are themselves. Looks like it's summer cause guy has shirt off and can see the sun. I think it's the morning cause the girl will go to school and the lady . . . looks like she's pregnant. So she'll go in and sew or cook lunch. She might just stay out, too. Man keeps working for a while."

Scores

Complexity of representations of people—Level 2
Affect–tone—Level 4
Capacity for emotional investment and moral standards—Level 3
Understanding of social causality—Level 2

Card 4: "Looks like the 60s or the 70s cause of hair and clothes. Looks like they're in a restaurant or on a street cause people behind them. The girl is kinda hugging him or holding him back. He's looking at something . . . maybe she's holding him back cause he wants to fight someone. I don't think he fights him cause the girl, wife, or girlfriend holds him back. Tries to make eye contact so he won't look at the other guy. They love each other. Will probably talk about it . . . and then go home."

Scores

Complexity of representations of people—Level 3
Affect–tone—Level 4
Capacity for emotional investment and moral standards—Level 3
Understanding of social causality—Level 3

(Continued)

TABLE 5.1

(Continued)

Rorschach object representation measures	
Card III.	"People . . . looks like they're stirring something in a pot. Looks like a mirror image to me."
MOA score:	4
Card IV.	"Looks like a figure tilted on a piece of wood. Wood is holding it from falling backward."
MOA score:	3
Card VI.	"Looks like somebody holding something up in the air. Looks like a torch or a club."
MOA score:	3
Card VII.	"Looks like silhouettes of two people. That's all."
MOA score:	2
Card VIII.	"Looks like a hummingbird sucking pollen from a flower."
MOA score:	5
Card X.	"Looks like a coral reef . . . fish swimming all around it . . . here, here, and here."
MOA score:	2
	"Wolves . . . there. They're attacking the animal in the middle . . . nothing else."
MOA score:	5

Highest MOA score:	2
Lowest MOA score:	5
Mean MOA score:	3.43
Mode MOA score:	2.50

Keith's SCORS and MOA responses are presented in Table 5.1, with impressions of the material following.

Impressions

His SCORS responses reflect an even and fairly well-developed object relations capacity. His responses to Card 2 tend to depict relatedness as tinged with conflict, hinted at by themes suggesting loneliness and sickness, but this is juxtaposed against material on both cards that indicate a young adolescent who can be thoughtful, empathic, and well-connected to others. He generally portrays relationships in a positive manner, albeit in a cautious way. People are close, depend on one another, and there is a projected sense of trust and positive affiliation.

Keith's MOA responses show a range of responses with the clear sense that he can connect and relate, although on a level somewhat less intimate and mutual than can many older adolescents and adults. There is a quality of being connected in a more dependent way, indicated by the several distinct scale point 3 responses, although this is hardly a major concern as he is a younger adolescent and still quite emotionally involved with parental figures. In general, his ability to initiate and maintain ties to others reflects that he views relationships as nurturing, satisfying, and not imbued with malevolence or threats to his emerging sense of individuality.

This young adolescent's object relations functioning is proceeding along in a positive manner, with indication that his sense of self and others is beginning to show signs of subtle and perceptible shifts, indicating a more differentiated and mature way of thinking and feeling about himself and others. There is obvious convergence and agreement between the object representation measures and reports attesting to the adequacy of his relatedness at home and in school.

CASE 2: SUSAN, A 14-YEAR-OLD FEMALE

The second protocol is that of a 14-year, 6-month-old female. Susan was in the ninth grade and reported that her adjustment was generally going well. She liked her classes and her teachers. Teachers found her to be inquisitive, bright, responsible, and involved. She said she particularly enjoyed social studies and English courses and was unsure of what she would do in the future, although she mentioned college as a goal. Several extracurricular activities took up hours after school: band, track, and the school newspaper.

Susan revealed she was close to her parents and younger 9-year-old sister. Her father worked as a teacher and her mother was a registered nurse. She related to a small group of friends and often spent time at her own or others' homes watching videos or just "hanging out." Other interests included softball, swimming, reading, and watching television.

The examiner found Susan to be a bright, warm, and very personable young woman. She was easily engaged in the assessment procedure and gave considerable thought to the material before arriving at her response. She seemed quite self-assured and confident in her productions and was upbeat and positive about her involvement in the study. Her SCORS and MOA responses are noted in Table 5.2, followed by impressions and comments in relation to the object representation material.

Impressions

In viewing the SCORS material, the immediate impression is that this young woman possesses very well-developed object relations capacity. Her representations of self and others indicate the ability to ascribe complex motives and subjective states in her narratives. She tends to have positive expectations of the social world, even though the stories also portray adversity and struggle. People tend to be reasonably content and successful, with this being tied to the ability for them to work things out.

TABLE 5.2
MOA and SCORS Responses for Case 2

TAT object representation measures	
Card 2:	"This girl looks like a teenager going off to school . . . early in the day but could be summer. The father's got his shirt off already . . . probably hot. Her mother looks pregnant . . . kind of relaxed. The daughter is sort of concerned because the baby is due soon . . . wants to be there to help out. Will go to school . . . knows things will be all right because father is right there working. She's kinda glad cause she'll have brother or sister . . . will make family closer cause they are pioneers and don't have neighbors that are nearby."
Scores	Complexity of representations of people—Level 4 Affect–tone—Level 5 Capacity for emotional investment and moral standards—Level 4 Understanding of social causality—Level 3
Card 4:	"Not sure . . . looks like he's pulling away from her. Maybe they had a fight or argument or he's trying to get someone. She's concerned that he'll do something stupid and make things worse . . . but he's all worked up . . . can't stop self. Doesn't do it. He listens to her . . . she's scared and screams at him, and he stops . . . goes back home with her and they talk about it. Guess that they are pretty close and care about each other . . . don't know. Guess they're glad that it's over."
Scores	Complexity of representations of people—Level 3 Affect–tone—Level 4 Capacity for emotional investment and moral standards—Level 3 Understanding of social causality—Level 3
Rorschach object representation measures	
Card I.	"Two people sort of holding hands. They have some kind of hats on. Looks like some kind of skirts on. Not really anything."
MOA score:	1
Card II.	"Looks like two people playing 'pattycake' . . . no, you know when you play together . . . a game, have on big red, floppy hats."
MOA score:	1
	"Could be two bears. Shape, black, head, and arms up."
MOA score:	2
Card III.	"Two people with high heels on . . . looks like they're stirring something in a pot."
MOA score:	1
Card VI.	"Don't know what this one looks like. Guess it looks like side view of two people . . . looks like ladies there cause you can see their hair and just looking at one another."
MOA score:	2
Card VII.	"Oh. Looks like two Indians doing a dance. Feathers in their heads . . . moving their arms."
MOA score:	2
Card VIII.	"Two bears climbing up a mountain. It just does. Don't know just looks like they're going straight up."

(Continued)

76

TABLE 5.2
(Continued)

MOA score:	2
Card IX.	"Looks like two witches . . . have witches' hats on. Arms out and looks like they're casting a spell."
MOA score:	5
Card X.	"Two little black bugs looking at each other with antennas."
MOA score:	2
	"Two seahorses there and there . . . just there . . . swimming around."
MOA score:	2
	"Two people, the blue . . . right there . . . holding hands."
MOA score:	1

Highest MOA score:	1
Lowest MOA score:	5
Mean MOA score:	1.90
Mode MOA score:	2

Her capacity for investment suggests that she sees relationships as enduring and committed, based on love and concern for others.

Additional support for the initial impressions of solid, consistent, and increasingly differentiated object relations capacity is seen when MOA material is examined. Susan produces a large number of MOA responses, 11 in all. With one exception, these are all of high quality, as reflected in the mean and modal scores. The presence of several scale point 1 responses, along with a predominance of scale point 2 answers, suggests that she is quite able to initiate and sustain gratifying relationships with others. There is the distinct sense of increasing individuality and mutuality when the overall protocol is considered. Her sense of relationships connotes expectations of mutual, positive, productive, and benevolent relatedness.

There is every indication that this young woman's object relatedness with peers and adults represents an adaptive and untroubled adjustment. Themes of nurturance, trust, dependence, and empathic concern readily define the way she presents her representational world. The reports of her teachers and observations of her parents offer additional considerable credibility to the projective material, suggesting the picture of an adolescent who gets along fine, who cares about others, and who generally has positive and optimistic expectations about the social world.

CASE 3: JUSTIN, A 15-YEAR-OLD MALE

The third adolescent is a 15-year, 6-month-old male. This adolescent was in the 10th grade when he was evaluated. He reported that he liked school and generally did well, citing that he received mostly B's for grades. He liked science courses, admitted to having some problems with English and related language arts subjects, feeling that he needed to spend more time on these. He derived considerable satisfaction and enjoyment from his extracurricular pursuits, including participating in the varsity soccer and baseball teams. When not in school, he also enjoyed skiing, fishing, and "hanging out" with a small circle of friends. Reports from his teachers emphasized that he was a quiet and serious, reserved student who was respected and liked by peers and teachers.

Justin lived with his parents, younger 9-year-old sister, and 7-year-old sister. His father worked as a sales representative and his mother was a teacher. At home, he generally reported a positive relationship with both parents, although he tended to be somewhat closer to his mother. He generally got along well with his younger siblings, but sometimes felt that his parents were partial to them when arguments or disagreements created conflict. In general, he did not reference major problems in his dealings with parents. He felt support and encouragement from them and respected their opinions and beliefs on most matters, and felt comfortable turning to them when he was confronted with major concerns or periodic problems. By his report, he was not experiencing any real problems at this point in his life.

When seen for evaluation, this adolescent impressed the examiner as quiet, somber, and thoughtful, quite in keeping with the observations of his teachers. He tended to be rather reticent and subdued in his relatedness and was pleasant and obviously involved with the tasks before him. His object representation responses are presented in Table 5.3, followed by impressions and observations in relation to his object relations functioning.

Impressions

Consideration of the SCORS material reveals consistent efforts in relation to the way that he views relationships, the depth of his relatedness, his ability to comprehend social causality, and his emotional reactivity to others. He appears thoughtful and concerned, although tentative and cautious in his interpretations about the underlying motives, feelings, and emotions of others. Although he does not portray relationships as pervasively negative or imbued with severe conflict, there is some hint of a mixed emotional tone as he creates his stories. In the final analysis, relationships are seen as providing nurturance, comfort, and understanding.

His MOA productions tend to converge with TAT object representation material to suggest that, although he seems capable of relating and becoming involved, he does so in a measured, tentative, and reserved manner. This is indicated by the preponderance of scale point 2 responses.

TABLE 5.3
MOA and SCORS Responses for Case 3

TAT object representation measures

Card 2: "Maybe Pennsylvania. A girl coming home from school. Father working in the field. Mother leaning against the tree . . . 1800s. Looks like mountains there. Hot cause he's got his shirt off. Not happy cause working too hard. The girl is not happy, looking away . . . not sure . . . might be walking away. Someone in the background. Maybe they are cultivating the field. Looks like she will leave [woman against the tree] . . . goes home and starts dinner. He works in the fields late and then comes home and has dinner. Relieved that the stress of the day is over . . . get feelings out when talking over dinner."

Scores

Complexity of representations of people—Level 3
Affect–tone—Level 4
Capacity for emotional investment and moral standards—Level 3
Understanding of social causality—Level 3

Card 4: "Looks like time period of one of the world wars. This girl is hugging husband. Lady in the background. He looks rugged . . . got a type of shirt . . . maybe he works in a factory. During the war. In love maybe cause hugging but he's looking away. Maybe she asks him a question and he's looking away trying to figure it out. Then gives her the answer."

Scores

Complexity of representations of people—Level 3
Affect–tone—Level 3
Capacity for emotional investment and moral standards—Level 3
Understanding of social causality—Level 3

Rorschach object representation measures

Card II. "Two people trying to kick or hit . . . no, giving high-fives. Looks like blood from hitting shins. Don't look too happy."

MOA score: 2

Card VII. "Two indians looking at each other. Feathers. Nope."

MOA score: 2

Card VIII. "Looks like a fox here. Two fox walking. Or could look like a fox walking along side a lake on rocks . . . reflection in the water."

MOA score: 4

Card X. "Flowers . . . flowers blowing in the breeze . . . way they're bent."

MOA score: 2

Highest MOA score:	2
Lowest MOA score:	4
Mean MOA score:	2.50
Mode MOA score:	2

This adolescent's object relatedness projects a somewhat reserved and cautious approach to his interpersonal world. Results do not suggest conflicted or troubled involvements and there is some indication that he struggles with deciphering and integrating affectively charged material, but appears capable of getting along, as there is perseverance and determination to make sense out of conflict. His relatedness is somewhat shy or introverted although there is not the suggestion that he is intimidated or repulsed by relationships. Again, the observations and evaluations from his teachers and parents are generally supported by object representation material, which serves to provide a fairly comprehensive sense of how he construes his thoughts, feelings, and impressions of significant others, and how these serve as a barometer of his actual relatedness.

CASE 4: JOHN, A 16-YEAR-OLD MALE

This 16-year-old male was in the 10th grade when seen. He conveyed a positive attitude toward school, but admitted that he struggled with his studies and hinted that excessive socializing had probably been a factor that interfered with more productive achievement. He received mostly C's for grades in his major subjects. He was actively involved in varsity athletics, playing soccer, basketball, and baseball. John said he would like to attend college on completion of high school and mentioned career options, including being a trainer, physical therapist, or coach of some type. In his spare time, he enjoyed being with friends, both male and female, and had a steady girlfriend. Reports from his teachers stressed that he was quite personable, outgoing, and perhaps too much caught up in the social scene, with this detracting from his academic efforts.

John's parents divorced when he was 6 years of age, and he subsequently lived with his mother and younger sister. John saw his father on a fairly regular basis, as he lived nearby. His mother was a psychiatric social worker, and his father was a dentist. His mother portrayed her son as kind, thoughtful, personable, but stubborn. She related feeling that it was necessary to be firm and consistent with John, as he sometimes needed a close rein given his tendency to test her rules and regulations. She cited instances of not keeping his curfew and a few episodes of alcohol experimentation as sources of concern. John said that some of his mother's concerns had merit (e.g., his grades and socializing), but overall he tended to minimize and discount major problems in their relationship. He voiced that he got along well with his father, although there was some suggestion of estrangement. John had many friends but offered that he could be his own person and was not unduly influenced or led by his peers. He reported being self-assured and confident in his dealings with others.

He presented as a bright, articulate, and forthright young man whose manner seemed to belie an underlying nervousness and anxiety mostly reflected in heightened motility and restlessness. Initially somewhat constricted when presented with test material, he gradually became more relaxed and composed and increasingly displayed the self-assured and comfortable side he felt was most characteristic of him. John's object representation material is presented in Table 5.4, followed by comments in regard to interpretive perspectives about his object relations functioning.

Impressions

The SCORS material suggests that John is beginning to ascribe increasingly complex attributions and subjective states to himself and others, although there is still a superficial quality to his self and object representations. His representations of relationships also indicate a mixed affective tenor with expectations that things will finally turn out for the best in the end. There is some sense that he is able to realize that negotiation is necessary to resolve conflicts involving one's own interests and concerns and the wants and issues of others. The themes of both stories graphically portray a dominant interpersonal theme and concerns in relation to conflicts centering around separation and individuation issues, with this being especially the case on Card 2, where the central figure is taking leave to be on her own.

The MOA material also suggests that his object representations are essentially positive in nature as indicated by the mean and modal scores. The presence of one scale point 4 response and the additional scale point 5 response suggest lingering issues involving occasional instances of perceived or compromised loss of autonomy with this hardly atypical in adolescents his age. This converges with SCORS material, which suggested obvious conflicts in relation to separation and individuation. The reports of John's mother attesting to his strong-willed, stubborn demeanor, and his periodic defiance lend credibility to MOA and SCORS material.

This adolescent is manifesting every indication of moving along in his developmental odyssey despite the indication of some "ups and downs" referenced by his mother. The situation at home would hardly be atypical as most adolescents at some point or another differ with their parents around what is good for them, how much freedom they should be allowed, and what rules and regulations are reasonable or appropriate. John's SCORS material suggests that the dominant interpersonal themes certainly revolve around separation and individuation, and there is every indication that he possesses the requisite resources to negotiate, compromise, and entertain others' points of view as he makes his own needs and

TABLE 5.4
MOA and SCORS Responses for Case 4

TAT object representation measures

Card 2:   . "A girl likes to read . . . in a pasture . . . Colonial times. She looks intelligent, thoughtful, but worrisome look on her face. Her mother looks like she's kind of mad at something . . . kind of turning head away from her. Guy is just doing the horses. Probably keep . . . just walks away, goes to class. Looks like she's on her way out . . . you know, getting ready to leave. Feels all right . . . it's time for her to go . . . like be on her own."

Scores

Complexity of representations of people—Level 3
Affect–tone—Level 4
Capacity for emotional investment and moral standards—Level 3
Understanding of social causality—Level 3

Card 4: "Something out of a move I guess. Looks like a movie. An actor and actress playing parts. Looks like advertisement for a movie. Looks like he's leaving and she's trying to hold him back. He'll go back to her . . . realizes he cares for her. Her eyes don't look desperate . . . his don't either. He turns back to her. Listens to her I guess."

Scores

Complexity of representations of people—Level 3
Affect–tone—Level 4
Capacity for emotional investment and moral standards—Level 3
Understanding of social causality—Level 3

Rorschach object representation measures

Card III. "Could be two people talking to each other or could be mice cause of the nose . . . looks like they have tails . . . off the end there. Just kind of talking."

MOA score: 1

Card VII. "Two maybe babies or cartoon characters talking to each other. Could be standing on rocks. Just talking about something."

MOA score: 1

Card VIII. "A bear or some kind of animal climbing up the side of a mountain or a tree . . . or could be more like . . . looking at reflection off the water."

MOA score: 4

Card IX. "These two guys could be witches or sorcerers. Could be fighting or casting spells."

MOA score: 5

Card X. "Two . . . maybe ants dancing together on the top there."
MOA score: 1

"Two spiders . . . just walking around . . . those blue guys. Nothing."

MOA score: 2

Highest MOA score: 1
Lowest MOA score: 5
Mean MOA score: 2.33
Mode MOA score: 1

---

wishes known. Finally, this adolescent, like his previous counterparts, manifests essentially intact and even object relations functioning when material is integrated. In this instance, the accounts of adults in his world tend to portray his relatedness in a similar vein to what is gleaned from psychological data.

CASE 5: CATHY, A 17-YEAR-OLD FEMALE

This 17-year, 1-month-old female adolescent was seen for follow-up evaluation as part of an ongoing longitudinal study involving the TAT and Rorschach. She had originally been seen some 2 years earlier and was familiar with the evaluative process.

Cathy was in the 11th grade when evaluated. She was doing well academically, as her grades were mostly B's. She was tentatively thinking of college and mentioned possible careers involving health care, specifically physical or occupational therapy. Her teachers depicted her as a serious student who was an active contributor in her classes. They also mentioned she was kind, caring, and fair, noting that she served as a peer counselor and tutor. She admitted to liking the sciences and her mathematics courses and expressed less interest in social studies areas. Cathy was involved in varsity athletics, playing soccer and basketball. Outside of school, she enjoyed spending time with her friends and being involved with interests such as watching sporting events, going to the movies, and working part time. Cathy had a boyfriend with whom she had been going out for almost 2 years. She described the relationship as having its ups and downs and was uncertain where it would go when she left high school.

Cathy lived with her mother and 18-year-old sister. Her parents had divorced when she was 9 and she saw her father on a fairly regular basis as he lived nearby. She did not feel particularly close to her stepmother but did not allude to major conflict. She felt close to her parents but depicted differing relationships with mother and father. She said she felt closer to her mother and would confide in her, whereas she felt she could not share upsets or concerns with her father, whom she respected but saw as having a hard time listening. Her mother did not have major concerns about Cathy, although she mentioned periodic arguments and differences of opinion around issues such as curfew, household responsibilities, and disrespect. Her mother saw Cathy as more reserved and quiet than her slightly older sister and mentioned that her daughters, although occasionally having fights and differences, were close and stuck together when the situation required it. She felt they had become closer because of their parents' divorce.

When seen for the evaluation, Cathy impressed the examiner as reserved, sincere, pensive, and gentle. She was easily involved in the evaluative process and remembered the material from the initial time she was seen. She was polite, demure, and fairly taciturn, not particularly given to small talk or conversation but did allow that she was fairly happy with how things were going for her. She did not reference significant problems in her life and really did not feel that she would like to see things change. She expressed some concern about the future but seemed clear that she would attend college after high school. Object representation material and results are noted in Table 5.5, followed by interpretive comments.

Impressions

Regarding the TAT object representation measures, Cathy's cognitive representations of relationships tend to be characterized by fairly minimal elaborations in relation to emotions, thoughts, and intentions, although there is not the suggestion of substantive overriding conflict or clear malevolence. Her descriptions of interpersonal encounters suggest a range of subtle attendant affective states: contentment, concern, blandness, and anger. Cathy's capacity for investment suggests a somewhat tentative, reserved tenor as her narratives in relation to enduring relationships still have a shallow quality, possibly suggesting some concerns that things will not go right, with this being suggested by her response to Card 2, where there is a decided lack of closure or resolve, even though the situation calls for it.

The MOA results suggest likely variability in her object relations functioning as she gives a limited number of responses (four), with the highest scale point response being a 2, along with one 4 and two 5s. Her representations would raise some questions about her sense of self and others with the possibility that her self representations are still less differentiated than those of other adolescents her age. Results hint at possible conflicts in relation to dependency. At times, she allows for some fleeting feelings of vulnerability and is likely to perceive that others are controlling and domineering, possibly like her father; at other times, there is the inkling of more mutual and autonomous relatedness, as suggested by the aforementioned scale point 2 response.

The results of the object representation material do not suggest convergence between the SCORS and MOA, with the latter raising some possible concerns about future problems given what appears to be an uneven quality vis-à-vis her self and object representations. More specifically, there is the hint that she feels periodically vulnerable and perhaps intimidated or threatened by more intimate connections. There is also the suggestion of this on the TAT where in one instance there is a halting

TABLE 5.5
MOA and SCORS Responses for Case 5

TAT object representation measures	
Card 2:	"A woman with two books sort of gazing off at something. Barn and a field. Woman relaxing and looking off . . . leaning up against a tree. A horse doing some kind of work . . . a stone wall there. Mountains and trees and a lake in the background. Man is looking off in the same direction as the woman against the tree. They sort of feel relaxed, just taking things in. Woman with the books is pondering something . . . I don't know. Looks like she could be considering . . . the beauty. Woman with the books is heading off to school . . . dressed that way. Don't know about the woman . . . she could be pregnant . . . thinks about her husband who is working in the fields."
Scores	Complexity of representations of people—Level 3
	Affect–tone—Level 4
	Capacity for emotional investment and moral standards—Level 3
	Understanding of social causality—Level 3
Card 4:	"Man and a woman. Woman seems shook up. Something caught his attention. Woman seems concerned and worried about the man . . . I don't know. Probably because she cares for him . . . doesn't want him to do something. I don't know. Guy looks kind of angry. He's somewhere else. Two possibilities. Woman could hold him back and keep him from . . . would worry if he did go somewhere."
Scores	Complexity of representations of people—Level 3
	Affect–tone—Level 3
	Capacity for emotional investment and moral standards—Level 3
	Understanding of social causality—Level 3
Rorschach object representation measures	
Card III.	"Looks like a dog . . . can see two dogs. Just standing there."
MOA score:	2
Card IV.	"Some sort of big creature. Got arms out like raging or something. Like reminds me of a big figure cartoon. Sort of like casting a spell or upset about something."
MOA score:	5
Card VII.	"Not much. Looks like a needle going into something."
MOA score:	5
Card VIII.	"Looks like lizards or could look like wolves climbing on rocks or trees. Water there . . . reflected in the water."
MOA score:	4

Highest MOA score:	2
Lowest MOA score:	5
Mean MOA score:	4
Mode MOA score:	5

and incomplete story, possibly reflecting emerging anxiety or tension. This may be related to the residual of earlier conflict with her father and could be playing out in her relationship with her boyfriend, as she hinted in the interview. But juxtaposed against this is the more calm and less conflicted, albeit somewhat tentative, material generated by Card 1. Also, by her self-report and the accounts of others, she is not faring all that poorly in her major relationships.

The examiner did discuss the results with Cathy who acknowledged some current discomfort with her relationship with her boyfriend, mentioned that they fought more than she would like, but did not reference major concerns about her father, whom she depicted as less vocal and abrasive than in the past. Her current strengths and resources were reinforced with the suggestion that she might like to consider the option of sharing concerns with a counselor if the need presented itself.

CASE 6: ELIZABETH, AN 18-YEAR-OLD FEMALE

This 18-year, 2-month old adolescent was seen for follow-up evaluation as she, too, had been an earlier control subject in a longitudinal investigation involving the TAT and Rorschach.

Elizabeth, or Beth as she preferred, was in her last year of high school and was in the initial stages of applying to colleges. She was unsure of what she would study but did lean toward the sciences, given her mathematical and scientific aptitude and interest. She was also a very competent artist and had received formal recognition for her efforts. Beth was a capable student receiving mostly B's for grades, and her teachers described her in a most positive light but emphasized that she needed to participate more in class discussion. She maintained a busy schedule, playing three varsity sports (softball, basketball, and field hockey), acknowledging that she hoped to continue with softball at the college level. Aside from her athletic schedule she spent much of her leisure time with her boyfriend or, increasingly, with her classmates as she felt tightly connected to a small group of peers, most of whom were teammates. Gravitating toward peers had created some strain in her relationship with her boyfriend who was already off at college.

Beth lived with mother and father. Her 23-year-old sister was no longer at home. She appeared to get along fairly well with her parents, although she saw her father as sometimes autocratic and dogmatic. She felt more connected to her mother, who was a lawyer; her father was a self-employed cabinet and furniture maker. Beth did not reference significant problems with her parents: she felt supported, encouraged, and respected by them. Her mother offered that Beth was not, and had not been difficult to parent, but did cite that she could be quite strong-willed, somewhat moody at times, and tended to be resolute and self-assured, not liking to bend to adversity and sometimes too quick to blame herself when circumstance did not warrant it.

When seen for evaluation, Beth impressed the examiner with her friendly, sincere, and enthusiastic manner. She recalled the material from the previous evaluation and seemed eager to be of assistance. Her stance toward the testing revealed a businesslike, serious, and reflective approach. She was not particularly given to idle talk and carefully weighed her responses before answering. She was a pleasant and conscientious young woman. The SCORS and MOA material is presented in Table 5.6, followed by interpretive comments.

Impressions

Beth's representations initially reveal a tendency to describe self and others in a spare, minimally elaborated manner with no reference to either internal states or enduring dispositions. This does change, however, as she also portrays other relationships as somewhat more complex, although still somewhat stereotypical. Her world view does not appear especially negative or conflicted—she sees herself as independent and perhaps enters relationships with some reserve and trepidation, with this being suggested by her story to Card 2. The predominant affective tenor is difficult to ascertain as there is a neutral and bland quality defining both stories, but she does not appear all that discontented with her relationships.

Her MOA object representations all suggest that she possesses a robust sense of individuality and mutuality in her dealings with the world. All responses are either scale point 1 or 2, with the modal score being 2. This again suggests a somewhat measured, slightly reserved nature or basic temperamental style she brings to bear in her dealings with others. There is no suggestion that self or object representations are imbued with less than positive connotations.

Beth might best be described as a young woman whose temperament reflects a slow to warm up quality (Chess & Thomas, 1984), suggested by sequential analysis of her reactions and responses to the projective material. She does not immediately jump into relationships, although when she feels more comfortable, she is able to maintain positive connections to others, with this being more suggested by MOA material than the SCORS results. She obviously has much on her mind at this point: gradually approaching separations and loss as she readies to leave home, friends, and security, and is very much caught up in the pressures of later adolescence. Also, one has to wonder how pressured and conflicted she feels about the status of her current relationship with her boyfriend, and to what degree this is a source

TABLE 5.6
MOA and SCORS Responses for Case 6

TAT object representation measures

Card 2: "Well ... Don't know what to say. Looks like in ... somewhere in Europe. Don't know why, just does. And ... this girl is waiting for a ride to the library. She has books she needs to return. And this is her sister who is resting against the tree with her eyes closed. The brother is in the middle working on the farm. Family, I guess ... two sisters and a brother ... they all look young. I don't know ... just looks like a regular day. Going about regular business. I don't know ... other things around the farm."

Scores
Complexity of representations of people—Level 2
Affect–tone—Level 4
Capacity for emotional investment and moral standards—Level 3
Understanding of social causality—Level 3

Card 4: "Man is trying to go after something or someone. She has a calm look but he looks angry or ... well, maybe not angry ... don't know ... kind of determined to do something. He's kind of determined to do his own thing and she's kind of calm, trying to calm him and keep him from going where he's moving towards. Woman is ... either he goes through with what he's going to do or he doesn't. Looks like scene from an old movie."

Scores
Complexity of representations of people—Level 3
Affect–tone—Level 4
Capacity for emotional investment and moral standards—Level 3
Understanding of social causality—Level 3

Rorschach object representation measures

Card I. "Looks like woman there ... don't know ... two figures there look like angels ... with figure in the middle ... dancing about."

MOA score: 2

Card II. "Looks like two people ... squatting down with their hands together ... no."

MOA score: 1

Card III. "Two people ... carrying ... picking up object in the middle."

MOA score: 1

Card IV. "Lying on the ground and looking up at a big monster ... looking ... just looking down on you."

MOA score: 2

Card VII. "This one has two heads ... profiles. Girls with ponytails ... two girls. Nothing ... no bodies ... just their profiles ... standing there."

MOA score: 2

Card VIII. "This one is ... two animals climbing on some object ... a tree. Kind of looks like ferrets without tails ... or maybe it's hidden."

MOA score: 2

Highest MOA score: 1
Lowest MOA score: 2
Mean MOA score: 1.66
Mode MOA score: 2

of conflict, hinted at by SCORS material. This young woman's situation reveals a somewhat unsettled, multifaceted inner vista, although there would be every reason to suspect she will continue to move along and realize a productive adjustment over time.

SUMMARY

This chapter attempts to provide the reader with how a wide range of adolescents, seen as doing reasonably well in their lives, present their inner object representational landscapes. As psychologists, we often lack the opportunity to spend time with children or adolescents who are doing well. There is a dearth of normative material pertaining to both the MOA and the SCORS as these are applied to adolescents. Thus, the present findings could be construed as cautionary or tentative if viewed from a nomothetic perspective. Changing the lens in order to incorporate an idiographic perspective does allow for a more valid and individually tailored interpretive approach that renders the SCORS and MOA material more immediate, relevant, and sensitive to a particular adolescent's developmental position.

In the current cases we witness how external observations and comments about a given adolescent's object relatedness converge with and reinforce psychological data, thus lending support for the contention that MOA and SCORS material ultimately translates into observable behavior (i.e., object relatedness). It is also possible to witness how object relations functioning is hardly a unitary or global construct, that it contains multiple facets, and that there is an indication of intrasubject variability when different dimensions are considered. In most instances, there is more intrasubject consistency than variability, which is more likely to be the case with individuals who do not present major psychological disorders.

In the majority of instances, MOA and SCORS material is fairly convergent, as opposed to divergent, leading to the conclusion that both scales are useful and appropriate measures of an adolescent's object representational world. The SCORS is more sensitive to capturing nuance and subtle details not obtained when one looks solely to MOA material, which appears to assess a more global, yet integral, measure of an adolescent's object relations functioning and capacity.

6

Introduction to
Clinical Case Illustrations

This chapter is divided into three sections. In the first, three clinical cases of younger adolescents are introduced in order to illustrate instances of less disturbed object relations functioning, and to document examples where more disturbed developmental adaptation is manifest. In the second, three clinical illustrations of youngsters in middle adolescence are presented in order to again contrast adolescents' Rorschach and TAT responses. Object representation material (e.g., MOA and SCORS results) is translated into impressions about adolescents' object relations functioning, and clear and informative directives regarding therapeutic planning are given. The final portion of the chapter provides clinical material of three older adolescents. Case material serves to highlight aspects of disturbance relating to self and others and the utility of object representations data in regard to directing and informing clinical treatment directions and parameters.

The nine case illustrations emphasize brief exposition of demographic and clinical material followed by the MOA and SCORS data. This provides for inspection and evaluation of the adolescents' object representation schemata, with this information then transformed into observations and diagnostic formulations vis-à-vis the adolescents' object relatedness. Finally, this material is used to generate hypotheses and guidelines in relation to the treatment course, with particular focus on articulating which treatment modalities seem indicated, what transference phenomena should be anticipated, and what additional areas of concern need to be explored and addressed in light of object representational material.

EARLY ADOLESCENCE CLINICAL ILLUSTRATIONS

Case 7: Kimberly, Adjustment Difficulties in a 14-Year-Old

This adolescent was seen for outpatient consultation at the request of her parents, who cited several referral concerns: a recent history of acting out, including shoplifting, lying, excessive testing of limits at home, one incident of running away, cannabis experimentation, and sexual involvement with a 15-year-old foster sister who had been living with the family for the past 3 years. This latter concern provided the impetus for the referral. Her parents also related that Kim and her foster sister had become obsessed and infatuated with a local female rock group, attended all of their concerts, and dressed and acted like them much to the consternation of Kim's parents, who felt this to be an unhealthy and excessive preoccupation.

Kimberly lived with her mother, stepfather, 9-year-old half-brother, and her foster sister, Gale. She had no contact with her biological father, whose whereabouts were unknown; her parents had divorced when Kim was an infant and he had no subsequent contact with the family. Her mother noted a fairly unremarkable developmental history save for the referral concerns, which had all emerged within the past year. Kim enjoyed a reasonably good relationship with both her mother and stepfather up until the past year.

At school, she displayed a more positive adjustment as she was described as doing well by her guidance counselor. She was achieving good grades, played the saxophone in the school band, and was also a member of the varsity basketball team. Well liked by peers and teachers, she seemed not to be having difficulties in this arena.

When seen for evaluation, she presented herself as a neatly attired, tall, young adolescent who related in a relaxed, candid, and pleasant manner. She sheepishly discussed the problems she had been having and seemed somewhat at a loss to explain what had been going on. She did not feel she had significant problems, but did say her acting out had resulted in definite parent–child tensions. She was a willing and involved participant in the evaluation and showed excellent perseverance showing no indication of unusual behavior or altered relatedness. Her object representations material is outlined in Table 6.1, followed by interpretive analysis and comments.

Impressions and Therapeutic Recommendations. Observations based on SCORS material suggest that her sense of complexity of representations is predominantly defined by a sense that there are articulated boundaries between self and others, but she does not yet understand how her feelings,

TABLE 6.1
MOA and SCORS Responses for Case 7

TAT object representation measures

Card 2:   "It's a pregnant woman watching her husband plow the field. She's
                           watching the daughter leave for school. Mother goes in to cook lunch
                           for her husband. They're poor. Because they have a small house and
                           not much fields. Don't know what happens . . . just do their work.
                           No."

Scores
                           Complexity of representations of people—Level 2
                           Affect–tone—Level 4
                           Capacity for emotional investment and moral standards—Level 2
                           Understanding of social causality—Level 2

Card 4:   "Looks like an old movie. And the lady is trying to tell him not to
                           go. And he's refusing . . . has to go he tells her. That's all. Don't
                           know what happens. He just goes."

Scores
                           Complexity of representations of people—Level 2
                           Affect–tone—Level 3
                           Capacity for emotional investment and moral standards—Level 2
                           Understanding of social causality—Level 2

Rorschach object representation measures

Card I.   "Looks like a picture of an angel. Put up against a mirror so you
                           can see two images . . . two angels."
MOA score: 4
Card II.   "Looks like two people playing pattycake."
MOA score: 1
Card VII.   "Looks like two rabbits singing to each other."
MOA score: 1
Card VIII.   "Looks like a tiger walking along and reflected in the water. That's
                           all."
MOA score: 4
Card X.   "Looks like a bunch of small animals or critters just running all
                           around. No."
MOA score: 2

Highest MOA score:	1
Lowest MOA score:	4
Mean MOA score:	2.40
Mode MOA score:	2.50

motives, and thoughts are consequential in relatedness. She does not
appear to have more than a rudimentary sense of what motivates others
and how they might feel. Kim does seem to sense that relationships are
not imbued with a negatively tinged affective tenor, although there appear
to be bland or unelaborated feelings projected onto relationships. She
appears capable of forming attachments, but these still appear secondary
to her own somewhat self-serving interests and motives. In general, the

profile is not all that atypical for what would be expected from a younger adolescent. Significantly derailed or aberrant relatedness would not likely be the case with Kim.

Based on her MOA responses, one is likely to see some variability in her relatedness, although not to a pathological extreme. She certainly has an innate capacity to connect and relate; she is capable of initiating and maintaining close relationships, as there is indication of strong autonomous capability and interest in others. At other times, one still will witness dependent and less individuated relatedness, suggested by the exaggerated narcissistic quality, indicating a more anaclitic–dependent flavor (Coates & Tuber, 1988) implied by several scale point 4 responses. Are the two reflection responses of diagnostic concern? Also, is there the indication of developmental arrest or derailment, where Kim's representations signify a need for her mother's participation in a reactivated mirroring capacity (Kohut, 1968) in order to bolster her narcissistic enjoyment and thus confirm her self-esteem?

The two reflection responses connote a somewhat self-centered side to this adolescent, but when they are juxtaposed against the other high level MOA measures, the SCORS material, and her overall adjustment, they are probably more indicative of phase-specific developmental phenomena that will alter with increased maturation (Exner & Weiner, 1995).

Kim's parents were advised that their daughter was not in immediate need of individual psychotherapy. Although acknowledging the seriousness of the situation at home, her parents were advised that the psychological findings generally supported their observations and those of her teachers. She was, in essence, doing rather well in her overall adaptation with this suggested by solid and enduring relationships with teachers and peers, academic accomplishments, varied and satisfying extracurricular pursuits, and the absence of significant psychopathology. Moreover, she did not present object representation material of significant concern. To the contrary, she exhibited consistent strength and adaptability in her dealings with the interpersonal world.

Her parents were advised that a therapeutic course of action should involve two or three parent interviews to review diagnostic findings and address their referral concerns in relation to Kim and her foster sister. These sessions would also provide the opportunity to enable Kim's parents, particularly her mother, to discuss her own adolescence and to evaluate whether or not Kim's entry into adolescence had reactivated unresolved developmental issues in her parents. Also, these sessions were seen as critical in allowing for suggestions and recommendations in relation to modifying parental perceptions and expectations regarding normal versus abnormal early adolescent behavior and to discuss what parental interventions would be indicated. It was suggested that a trial of family psychotherapy could be considered in order to focus on parent–child communication with the goal of ameliorating the acting out and allowing the parents and adolescent to realize a more adaptive relatedness. The goals for family psychotherapy included (a) inspecting mutual issues and concerns, thereby allowing for improved respect for each others' opinions and positions; (b) productive discussion of differences and areas of disagreement in order to emphasize and elucidate distortions and examples of projective identification; (c) create a climate where affect-laden material can be be outlined and discussed and in which some closure can be realized in order to dispel underlying assumptions that things will not or cannot change.

Case 8: Wes, Severe Conduct Disorder in a 13-Year-Old

This 13-year, 6-month-old adolescent male was seen for psychological evaluation shortly after he entered a residential treatment center following a 2-month stay on an inpatient psychiatric unit. The hospitalization was precipitated by serious and escalating acting out at home, including fire setting, stealing, assaultive behavior toward his mother and sisters, and killing the family cat. At school, he was doing poorly in both academic and interpersonal areas. He was failing most of his courses, was verbally abusive to his teachers, and was becoming more and more involved in physical altercations with his peers.

Prior to being hospitalized, he lived with his mother, stepfather, and two older sisters. His developmental history was remarkable for multiple incidents of abuse and neglect. Wes had been physically abused by his alcoholic father up until age 4, at which point his parents separated and his father had no subsequent contact with the family. Starting at age 9, and continuing for a 3-year period, Wes was sexually abused by a 17-year-old male cousin, resulting in criminal proceedings.

His brief tenure in residential treatment had already reflected initial concern. He was mostly aloof, detached, and isolated, but did seem inclined to gravitate toward adult staff. Problematic behavior in the way of stealing, lying, and fighting marked his early stay. In school, he was no longer posing problems, although his teacher said that he had become more withdrawn and isolated in the past several weeks. The cottage staff described him as manipulative and provocative with peers. They also noted he had trouble sleeping and had confided to staff that he was having dreams involving Satan and directives to kill his sister.

When seen for evaluation, Wes presented as pleasant, cooperative, and chatty, telling the examiner that things were going well for him. He steered clear of any discussion of problems. He appeared guarded and reserved in his relatedness despite his ostensible friendly posture. He showed little indication of affective upset, not manifesting significant signs of irritation, anxiety, or dysphoria. He did not reference odd or unusual thoughts or concerns, minimized the aforementioned dreams, and denied any suicidal or homicidal fantasies. Toward the end of the interview, he did launch into a lengthy and somewhat unexpected discourse about his interest in cats and small animals, saying that he liked to draw cats and hoped to perhaps be a veterinarian when he grew up. He appeared nonplussed when the issue of the family cat was raised. He also minimized problems in getting along with his peers, tending to externalize blame onto others. His interests and extracurricular activities emphasized solitary pursuits: collecting Matchbox cars, comic books, and marbles. Wes' object representation measures are summarized in Table 6.2, followed by interpretative comments.

Impressions and Therapeutic Recommendations. Based on TAT findings, this adolescent's cognitive structure of object representations consistently suggests a simple and unidimensional motif with minimal hint that he construes self and others as possessing internal or emotional attributes. People coexist and interact in perfunctory ways, although there is not the impression of significant or profound conflict. Subtle indications of tension and discomfort are hinted at in both TAT stories, but he tends to ward off this affective material by retreating and ultimately producing sparse stories without clear closure. Wes' capacity for connectedness suggests a limited and shallow quality with some indication that closeness and intimacy pose a threat to him, and that he tends to respond defensively by manifesting an avoidant, detached style of attachment and relatedness. Overall, although the material does not portray striking indication of developmental arrest, representations of self and others are colored by themes emphasizing superficial definition and relatedness, with this paralleling accounts and descriptions of his actual object relatedness.

MOA findings raise concerns about inner disturbance as well as suggesting that object relations functioning is likely to reflect a variable and, at times, quite problematic clinical picture. He would seem to possess some inherent ability to connect based on the two scale point 2 responses, but even here there is an absence of human percepts. Indications of more primitive representations (e.g., two scale point 4 and 6 responses) raise questions about an increasing loss of autonomy with underlying expectations that relationships can be quite destructive, malevolent, and damaging. His comments, "not whole anymore," and "person trapped in there" convey a sense of loss of control, desperation, and diffuse anxiety in relation to his safety and integrity. These latter scale point 6 responses are of particular concern, as they are usually not encountered unless there

TABLE 6.2
MOA and SCORS Responses for Case 8

TAT object representation measures

Card 2:   "An old western picture of a farm type place. Saying goodbye before she went to school. Mother going to have a baby. Father said goodbye to the daughter. Looks like a hot day. She could be going away for a while because things are hectic or she could be worried about mother having a baby. Don't know . . . looks like they live in the mountains or toward the ocean."

Scores

Complexity of representations of people—Level 3
Affect–tone—Level 3
Capacity for emotional investment and moral standards—Level 2
Understanding of social causality—Level 2

Card 4:   "Kind of looks like an old movie. Looks like she's trying to get husband to believe what she's saying. Could be a play. Or the husband is trying to leave and the wife tells him to come back. He stays and listens and finally figures out what she tries to tell him. Don't know . . . can't really say what they're feeling."

Scores

Complexity of representations of people—Level 2
Affect–tone—Level 3
Capacity for emotional investment and moral standards—Level 2
Understanding of social causality—Level 2

Rorschach object representation measures

Card IV.   "Looks like two carnivores guarding something. Resting, trying to sleep with feet up. Leaning against a tree possibly."

MOA score: 3

Card VI.   "Reflection of a iceberg. Here's the ice and its reflecting in the water. Little island."

MOA score: 4

Card VII.   "Two dogs eating something . . . like two dogs eating their dinner."
MOA score: 2

"Two elephants standing on their hind legs."
MOA score: 2

Card VIII.   "Reflection in the water of a mountain lion climbing over things."
MOA score: 4

"Digestion of a fish inside of a fish. Starting to rot . . . not whole anymore."
MOA score: 6

Card IX.   "A mountain with different colored trees . . . inside of a mountain with a person trapped in there. Can see the eyes."
MOA score: 6

"Looks like something a witch would have. Crystal ball. Looks like two witches there and they are casting spells of some type."
MOA score: 5

Highest MOA score:	2
Lowest MOA score:	6
Mean MOA score:	4
Mode MOA score:	4

is faltering personality development or significant psychological problems (e.g., borderline organization). The combination of several reflection responses raises the possibility of a narcissistic clinical picture, not simply excessive self-absorption because of the additional aforementioned representational material being more indicative of significant object relations problems.

When the percepts involving extreme malevolence, destruction, and serious threats to the self are also considered, the clinical picture becomes more troubling. At best, Wes' relatedness will take on a superficial quality and he will show his most adaptive efforts when low levels of affective arousal characterize the environmental tenor. Capable of more regressive and fragmented connectedness, this could emerge when he perceives the environment as attacking, potentially harmful, and malevolent.

In Wes' case, it is possible to see convergence and similarity between overt functioning and adjustment, his relatedness, and the object representation material. At best, a superficial and tentative connection to others characterized his best side. At other times, he was seen as more fragile, needy, and vulnerable. At his worst, he could be estranged, provocative, sneaky, and wary. Converting these diagnostic impressions into treatment formulations focused on his individual treatment and on the greater therapeutic milieu in school and cottage. He was to be seen for individual weekly psychotherapy in addition to being actively engaged in milieu treatments, that is, social skills group and activity therapy (sports or recreation opportunities) in addition to being involved in weekly family psychotherapy.

With respect to his individual treatment, his therapist was advised to initially engage him in an approach combining activities of his choosing in conjunction with the opportunity for verbal therapy initially designed to encourage relatedness. This would eventuate in a mutative experience if he could learn to trust. Based on the psychological material, the possibility of distinct transference reactions or responses were posed: initial compliance and a somewhat variable neediness (perhaps even impatient demandingness) juxtaposed against passivity and an avoidant stance if he felt threats or perceived malevolent intent from the therapist. In the intermediate phase of treatment, when more affectively charged material becomes part of the treatment (material generated by problems while in residence, historical conflict material possibly relating to abuse) Wes may retreat and become more passive, or he may assume a more verbally contentious, contemptuous, and devaluing posture. Given his fragility and diffuse fears of harm, it was suggested that an active approach should be initially adopted (e.g., feedback, advice, clarification, structuring, and "mirroring") to help contain as well as ease his anxiety in order to foster relatedness.

Case 9: Rob, Borderline Personality Organization
in a 13-Year-Old

This 13-year, 3-month-old adolescent was referred to a multidisciplinary child assessment team in order to address mounting concerns in relation to his behavior and overall adjustment both at home and in school. His mother specified a variety of concerns: playing with matches, sexual contacts with an 8-year-old male, extreme defiance, lying, stealing, assaultive behavior with siblings, and possible inhalant abuse. She described her son as lonely, mean to his siblings and peers, destructive, disobedient, and unhappy. He was extremely difficult to parent and his mother felt she or husband were unable to discipline him effectively. Diagnosed as having attention deficit disorder with hyperactivity, he was maintained on a regimen of Ritalin, 10 mgs., t.i.d. daily with mother and teacher questioning the helpfulness of this intervention. He had also been involved in weekly psychotherapy for the past 6 months, reportedly looking forward to his regular meetings with his male therapist. Information relative to his therapeutic progress was not available at the time he was seen.

School personnel were concerned about this youngster for several years, with reports indicating fighting, provoking peers, and being disruptive in class. At least one previous teacher had raised the question of whether or not he was being physically abused by his parents, although no formal report was made to the appropriate authorities. Rob's teacher highlighted his notable difficulties in getting along with his classmates, citing that he was provocative and unpredictably assaultive and had no friends. He was placed in a self-contained class for children with emotional and behavioral disorders and in this setting his teacher commented that he appeared wary and fearful, was disruptive in class, could be secretive, and often did not complete his work. Despite these problems, he was generally at or close to grade level in most of his subjects, but he did have problems with organization and written output. He was not learning disabled.

Rob lived with his mother, stepfather, and 4-year-old half-sister. His parents had divorced before he was born and his biological father's whereabouts were unknown. His developmental history was unremarkable for early problems. Rob was described as a "good" baby and toddler. At age 5, he began to display encopresis and recurrent abdominal pains. Medical evaluations failed to confirm a physical basis for the problems and the encopresis ceased shortly after his sixth birthday. His mother raised the possibility that his maternal grandmother may have sexually abused Rob when he was approximately 3 years of age, although this was never substantiated, and Rob never disclosed incidents of inappropriate sexual involvement with his grandmother, whom he sees on an infrequent basis.

His mother noted that Rob began to have problems in school when he was in the second grade and that these were manifest in learning and behavioral areas. He struggled with graphomotor output, but most of his problems were in the social–emotional domain. He was depicted as having problems with rules, could not stay out of trouble, and interacted with peers in a manner emphasizing a predominantly provocative and aggressive modus operandi resulting in rebuff and rejection.

When seen for evaluation, Rob presented as impulsive, restless, and distracted. Superficially cooperative, he frequently complained and whined about the difficulty of the tasks, but usually completed them when firm directives were enacted. He tended to deny that he had problems at home or in school, displaying a total inability to entertain any possibility that he was troubled or in trouble of any kind. At one point, he unexpectedly announced that he was a troublemaker, but that he had a lot of friends. He mentioned that he liked to play basketball, watch television, and play Nintendo. He did not reference fears, upsets, or unusual thoughts. He denied being depressed, anxious, or angry. His relatedness, at best, suggested a superficial and avoidant quality, and the examiner felt he established a limited connection with her. Information regarding Rob's object representation material is presented in Table 6.3, with clinical impressions and therapeutic recommendations following.

Impressions and Recommendations. Initial observations with regard to SCORS object representations highlight significant and pervasive developmental derailment. All scores are at Level 1 and all responses are imbued with idiosyncratic, illogical, and malevolent themes. His cognitive representations of self and others indicate profound boundary disturbance and lack of any differentiation. He conceptualizes relationships as grossly malevolent, destructive, and annihilating. There is little sense that he is capable of initiating and sustaining more than cursory or superficial connections to others, peers as well as adults, with involvement predicated on primitive and basic need gratification. His sense of how people relate, why they do the things they do, and what is correct or incorrect in a given situation suggests a highly personalized, eccentric, and illogical pattern of ordering his impressions and responses to his world. The dominant interpersonal concerns reflect across-the-board themes of victimization, diffuse violence, and apprehension of severe harm.

Similarly, the MOA responses raise a most ominous flag. All of his responses are scored as scale point 6, suggesting that there is a severe imbalance in the perceptions of self and others indicative of marked boundary disturbance. Of concern is the fact that this adolescent is on constant alert to the possibility of harm, intrusion, and, in the worst-case scenario, has some dim expectation of dire environmental assault. His

TABLE 6.3
MOA and SCORS Responses for Case 9

TAT object representation measures

Card 2: "Looks like a storm . . . the girl carries school books, gets dragged into a tornado. Mother gets pulled in with her. The man's driving his horse. Then they're in another tornado, a meteor hit . . . there's no more world. Picking her up with a sponge."

Scores

Complexity of representations of people—Level 1
Affect–tone—Level 1
Capacity for emotional investment and moral standards—Level 1
Understanding of social causality—Level 1

Card 3BM: "A guy. He shot himself . . . that's the gun there. He hated his wife, then haunted her house. She called (unintelligible). He got terminated. She was mean, hated his wife."

Scores

Complexity of representations of people—Level 1
Affect–tone—Level 1
Capacity for emotional investment and moral standards—Level 1
Understanding of social causality—Level 1

Rorschach object representation measures

Card III. "Figure with blood coming out of him . . . red is blood . . . figure is dead, legs broken."

MOA score: 6

"Weird bug with two pincers and two long legs. Has butterfly it's eaten in its stomach."

MOA score: 6

Card VI. "Guy stuck in a hole, in a crack in the earth. Two executioners at the top throwing slugs down and leeches to eat them up. Two people at bottom of hole."

MOA score: 6

Card IX. "Boll weevil cut in half (gestures). Someone just sliced it . . . Boll weevils have snout. Rest is the body."

MOA score: 6

Card X. "Big scary face . . . monkey man from Mars. Two bugs . . . no, crabs grabbing onto him . . . biting his face."

MOA score: 6

"Alligator head with jaws going together something . . . small animal . . . here's the bones.

MOA score: 6

Highest MOA score:	6
Lowest MOA score:	6
Mean MOA score:	6
Mode MOA score:	6

sense of self and others is blurred, poorly articulated, and it is unlikely that he is able to decipher how he feels versus understanding how others feel and relate. His object relatedness is undoubtedly impaired and coun-terphobic defensive maneuvers (e.g., retreat or acting out) will be keys to sensing environmental pressures or excessive arousal that stimulate maladaptive behavior.

There can be little doubt that this is a very disturbed young adolescent whose current intrapsychic and interpersonal adjustment is quite compro-mised. Whether or not his current developmental status suggests faltering personality development (Exner & Weiner, 1995), or is indicative of an organizational level of adaptation suggesting prominent borderline per-sonality attributes (Chethik, 1986; Kelly, 1986; Petti & Vela, 1990; Pine, 1974) is moot as his adjustment to early adolescence has gone awry. Based on his mother's report, the current problems are not of recent origin, as Rob increasingly displayed, over the course of the past 3 years, an insidious and increasingly maladaptive developmental course. The situation now calls for urgent and immediate implementation of a multiplicity of therapeutic programs and specific interventions designed to stabilize his functioning and to begin addressing his overt and obvious severe inner difficulties. Aggressive treatment is warranted given the fact that the youngster with this constellation of symptoms does not appreciably improve with adoles-cent maturation. The sequelae is increasingly problematic, more often than not eventuating in a variety of crystallized personality disorders and attendant dysfunctional functioning in later adolescence and early adult-hood (Lofgren, Bemporad, King, Lindem & O'Driscoll, 1991).

Initially, there must be immediate attention directed toward assessing how capable his mother and stepfather are of parenting him. His mother's frustration in containing and protecting him suggest things are not stable at home. The previous reference to possible abuse raises some concern about whether or not an alternative living situation should be considered. His therapist needs to evaluate this and there needs to be a concerted evaluation of whether or not he should remain at home in light of his escalating acting out. In the event he cannot stay with his parents, several options could be considered.

An initial option, perhaps the most appropriate, would involve referral for time-limited residential treatment, as this intervention is often cited as resulting in a more positive eventual prognosis (Bentivegna, Ward, & Bentivegna, 1985). This would result in environmental stability and con-tainment, and would open the door for more intensive mutimodal thera-peutic work within the context of a milieu that could tolerate and translate pathological relatedness and acting out into potentially mutative and abreactive experiences. Within the context of this therapeutic experience, Rob would receive individual, group, and family psychotherapy.

Psychopharmacological treatment options should be reviewed given current concerns that the stimulant medication was not particularly helpful. Although specific guidelines for medication of children with borderline organizational functioning have not been delineated (Petti & Vela, 1990), it was suggested (Rogeness, Hernandez, Macedo, Amrung, & Hoppe, 1986) that a combination of neuroleptics and methylphenidate or sometimes imipramine alone, may be helpful in allowing children like Rob to realize a more adaptive level of functioning outside of a hospital setting. In addition, lithium, a psychoactive agent with antiaggressive properties, has also reportedly been effective, particularly with affective types of aggression similar to this case (Campbell & Cueva, 1995).

Another scenario might well involve this child remaining at home with this being dictated more by fiscal constraints than clinical realities, a situation increasingly confronting clinicians. In this case, the caveat of concerted multimodal interventions would still prevail. Interventions would likely include strong consideration of placement in a therapeutic day school in order to provide Rob with the requisite external environmental stability, supervision, and small group containment. This would allow him some opportunity to experience predictability, safety and structure within the context of a therapeutic milieu also offering structured socialization, behavior management, and individual attention. If he is to be at home, the family will require support in the way of ongoing family treatment, possible opportunities for respite care and the option for brief hospitalization.

Individual weekly psychotherapy should be provided with every effort being made to find a therapist who will be available for extended work and who has demonstrated experience in treating children like Rob. The psychotherapeutic work will be difficult and fraught with an array of oscillating transference reactions, running the gamut from possible physical acting out and assaultiveness on the one hand, to parasitic-like clinging, demanding, and highly petulant relatedness. The ultimate goal will be to provide this youngster with a mutative experience that will gradually allow him to develop a sense of trust, relatedness, and will ultimately help him to realize a sense of object constancy.

MIDDLE ADOLESCENCE CLINICAL ILLUSTRATIONS

Case 10: Linda, Borderline Personality Organization in a 15-Year-Old

Linda is a 15-year, 6-month-old adolescent who was seen by a multidisciplinary child evaluation service at a medical center. The referral was initiated by her mother who referenced a variety of concerns in relation to her daughter's faltering adjustment at school and her escalating acting out at home. More specifically, Linda was failing most of her courses at school and often was truant. At home, she was defiant and oppositional, stayed out past her curfew and had, on several occasions, absented herself from the home for several days. Her mother was unsure of her whereabouts, wondered about possible drug involvement, and had sought the assistance of the juvenile probation department in order to provide some external leverage. Her mother also related that Linda had trouble sleeping, often roamed the house at night, and, in her opinion, was both angry and depressed.

Linda was an only child and lived with her mother. She never knew her father, who abandoned the family before she was born. Her mother worked as a teacher but was recently laid off from her position in an elementary school. Linda's developmental history was remarkable for early social adjustment problems in preschool and her mother kept her out of school in order to mature. In the elementary grades she was a competent student but had difficulty getting along with her peers; she tended to be shy, avoidant, and preferred the company of adults in the school setting. At home, she played infrequently with a small, select group of neighborhood children but spent much of her time by herself. Her mother did not portray her adjustment as atypical but felt her daughter was on the quiet side and struggled with peers.

At the time of the evaluation, Linda was beginning the ninth grade and was off to a poor start, suggesting a continuation of the problems she demonstrated in the eighth grade. School reports noted excessive absences, erratic academic performance despite normal ability, and no suggestion of a learning disorder, difficulty in getting along with peers, and labile and unpredictable mood and behavior. The school guidance counselor described her as "alienated, angry, insecure, and rebellious." Questions were raised by her mother and school personnel as to whether or not a regular public school setting was the most appropriate place for Linda, or if, given her significant problems in that setting, an alternative school was indicated.

When seen for psychological assessment, Linda presented as a thin, pale, tall young woman attired in tattered jeans with a bandana covering her hair. She was rather easily engaged in the interview and spent a considerable amount of time talking about the difficulties she was experiencing in relation to school. She also talked about her interest in theater and acting, mentioning that she was involved in pursuing the study of theater and acting lessons under the auspices of a local theatrical organization. Despite problems with school, she was an avid reader and was focusing on world literature, mentioning several classic novels she was reading. She was forthcoming about the fact that she had not been attending school, and that she did not care at all for her peers or the courses she was required to take. She felt she was different from her classmates and really wanted to be off somewhere with the older crowd with whom she associated through her theater involvement. She mentioned not really liking any of her teachers or the school psychologist, whom she had seen on several occasions.

Linda then launched into a lengthy discourse about her relationship with her mother, whom she also said she did not like because they had major differences of opinion most of the time. As she gradually depicted her sense of the mother–daughter relationship, it became increasingly apparent that estrangement characterized the status quo. Linda did not see her mother as a source of support or intimacy and portrayed her as a focus of wrath and anger.

As the interview proceeded, the psychologist became increasingly concerned about Linda's shallow and suspect judgment vis-à-vis her nocturnal activities. She mentioned staying with "acquaintances," partying with new friends, and hitchhiking in the early morning hours. She appeared to possess little insight into her problems, became periodically guarded and defensive when queried about areas where she was having problems, and tended to offer explanations couched in denial, rationalization, and minimization. Her mood and affective response to the interview and subsequent projective testing suggested mild variability. Initially apprehensive, this gave way to a more loquacious, comfortable, and animated presentation in which she seemed reasonably at ease. This did change with the introduction of projective material, where she manifested more variable functioning. At times, Linda appeared able to modulate her emotions, appearing calm and composed; at other times, she appeared more upset, distracted, disorganized, and almost overwhelmed. Her mood revealed a more even quality: serious, somber, and, at times, pensive and reflective. In rare instances, there was a fleeting suggestion of irritation and anger, but this was contained and did not herald more regressive shifts.

Linda's TAT and Rorschach object representation material is presented in Table 6.4, followed by comments relating to diagnostic as well as therapeutic concerns.

Impressions and Recommendations. Inspection of SCORS material indicates that Linda's representations of self and others are almost entirely imbued with egocentric and undifferentiated attributes. There is the strong hint of diffuse and poorly defined boundaries between herself and others. She appears to have little appreciation of the fact that relationships possess emotional substance or depth: people seem unempathic, empty, almost nonexistent—simply coexisting. She appears uncomfortable with the pos-

TABLE 6.4
MOA and SCORS Responses for Case 10

TAT object representation measures

Card 2:
"I see . . . reminds me of the *Grapes of Wrath*, a little farm and a horse and a guy plowing. Not proportioned . . . nothing is proportioned right. She may be fat or pregnant. Daughter there, her books, . . . pensive maybe. I don't like it. I don't know . . . I don't care how they feel. I don't know."

Scores

Complexity of representations of people—Level 1
Affect–tone—Level 3
Capacity for emotional investment and moral standards—Level 1
Understanding of social causality—Level 1

Card 4:
"I feel like this one . . . a 50s movie. And I do like this woman, one leering in the background. I think. Let's see what's the story here. Some really attractive young couple . . . just a very silly couple . . . looks ridiculous. They're all serious and it looks funny. I don't know . . . I am being serious! I don't know."

Scores

Complexity of representations of people—Level 1
Affect–tone—Level 4
Capacity for emotional investment and moral standards—Level 1
Understanding of social causality—Level 1

Rorschach object representation measures

Card I.
"Flying pigs . . . two flying pigs . . . ears, snouts, body and the legs."

MOA score: 2

"Well . . . two people. No looks like one person cut in half so you have two people who look exactly the same. Here and here."

MOA score: 4

Card II.
"Someone disemboweled someone else and their heads blew up and they're giving each other high fives. I don't know . . . I just like the word [disemboweled]."

MOA score: 6

Card III.
"Two monkeys with erections playing bongo drums and there's like . . . don't know. Blood splattered on the wall. Don't know."

MOA score: 2

Card VI.
"Looks like has four whiskers but I don't see anything else. Wait . . . could be road kill. It's just flattened . . . splattered . . . can kind of make out a cat that just got mangled. Can't really make out anything else."

MOA score: 6

Card VIII.
"Kind of looks like two figures climbing up something . . . they both look the same . . . looks like they could fall . . . they both look like . . . identical . . . not sure. Don't know."

MOA score: 4

Highest MOA score: 2
Lowest MOA score: 6
Mean MOA score: 4
Mode MOA score: 5

sibility of intimacy or emotional closeness and becomes more disorganized when asked to embellish on her own or others' internal feelings or motivations. There is indication of an increasingly avoidant and distancing style of relatedness. Her sense of social causality also reveals a decidedly eccentric and tangential cognitive perspective. Her representations load heavily on illogical, noncausal themes with unexplained transitions and, at best, are poorly articulated, peculiar, and without integration of affect and impulse. Dominant interpersonal concerns revolve around themes suggesting alienation, isolation, and impoverished relations.

An additional reason for concern about faltering and oscillating object relatedness arises when examining the MOA material, which shows four of the six responses in the scale point 4 to 6 range. The only hint of genuine relatedness, her two scale point 2 responses, still indicate, at best, a parallel and superficial quality. And more importantly, the percepts are odd and infused with idiosyncratic ideation (i.e., "flying pigs; monkeys with erections playing bongo drums"). Beyond this fragile and tentative facade, one is likely to see more disorganized relatedness and inner vulnerability suggested by the reflection responses, which indicate a self-absorbed quality and attempts to assuage her diffuse anxiety and discomfort. Finally, more variable relatedness is suggested by the two MOA scale point 6 responses. The focus on body damaging, destructive, and malevolent interaction depict the same wary, avoidant, and aggressively charged nature of her transactions at home and in school. Taken as a whole, accounts of her actual relatedness suggest clear convergence with the MOA results, which portray a most disturbed, disorganized, and derailed sense of herself and others.

In the final summary and disposition conference, Linda's mother met with the team who conducted the assessment of her daughter. School personnel were present, but Linda refused to attend this meeting. A multimodal treatment program was proposed and endorsed by her mother and school officials, and consisted of the following components: referral to an alternative high school program, after school attendance at an adolescent day treatment program, tracking and monitoring by an agency providing ancillary "parenting," and individual psychotherapy for Linda. It was also recommended that her mother seriously consider psychotherapy for herself in order to address her own long-standing psychological problems and difficulties, for example, depression, chronic despair, and upset with her own life situation, as well as serious problems in parenting her daughter.

Several comments and prognostic observations about Linda's likely response to individual and milieu therapies (i.e., day treatment) are possible by revisiting the SCORS and MOA material and then extrapolating to the treatment situation.

Linda expressed strong negative opinions about being seen by a male therapist when the issue of psychotherapy was posed to her by the psychiatrist who met with her. It is hardly the case that being seen by a female will be a panacea, given additional TAT material that does not indicate that the gender of the therapist will have major implications for what is likely to emerge in her transference reactions. Linda could initially be a reluctant participant in treatment with some assurance that avoidance, retreat, and passivity will mark her relatedness. Initial interventions should emphasize an active, structured, and reality-based focus in which the content is directed toward helping her to process and examine problems at home, in school, and in the day treatment settings. An approach emphasizing more expressive treatment would be premature and contraindicated; it would do little to allay her mistrust, and could result in perceptions of assault and threats to her already fragile sense of integrity and cohesion.

At some point, she will probably evidence a more variable and predictable regressive shift in her transferential connection, with this being indicative of increasing unrest and anxiety about the nature of her therapeutic involvement. Again, it will be necessary to continue a more reality-focused approach to reinforce what relatedness may be developing, as well as to contain and structure her in order to minimize the emergence of more primitive diffuse fears (e.g., destruction, harm, malevolence). With adolescents like Linda, it is inevitable that problems will develop. She may suddenly disparage and devalue, avoid treatment, and request someone who is more competent. Experienced clinicians will recognize this as an important indicator of an increasing unpleasant and conflictual situation in which the individual's assumptive world is being challenged. The end result is that tension-ridden, unpleasant, and poorly integrated emotional experiences are being transformed into relatedness and emotional reactivity, eliciting a "this does not fit the situation" perception on the part of the therapist. At this juncture, it will be important to reflect and focus on her maladaptive representational schema in an attempt to provide her with the opportunity to examine her feelings and dire apprehensions in relation to the therapeutic situation in order to initiate the critical work of altering and her stunted and underdeveloped object relatedness. In this case, the therapeutic emphasis must be directed toward the creation and maintenance of a mutative emotional experience (Blatt & Ford, 1994) with this preempting any attempt at the more insight-oriented work that should eventually follow, provided this young woman is able to establish a working alliance with her therapist. The combination of an array of interventions is critical in cases like Linda's, and perhaps provides the last opportunity to have some impact on a situation that will only become more problematic if less concerted or symptom-oriented approaches to treatment are advocated as the preferred way to address her situation.

Case 11: James, Conduct Problems
and Depressive Disorder in a 16-Year-Old

This 16-year, 8-month-old adolescent was seen for a multidisciplinary evaluation at the request of his father on the recommendation of school personnel who advised that increasing behavior problems at school were of mounting concern and were starting to take their toll on his grades. He displayed a mixture of behavior and attitude difficulties: rebellious-ness, breaking-and-entering, stealing from siblings, lying, defiance, verbal tirades, and periodic suicidal threats. He was under the supervision of the juvenile probation department with this being related to his conviction for the above breaking and entering incident in which he stole money from a neighbor's home. Jim lived with his father, stepmother, and his 4-year-old stepbrother. He reportedly quarreled with his stepmother and often picked on his younger brother.

His developmental history was remarkable for his parents' divorce when James was 6 years of age. He subsequently lived with his mother and 4-year-old sister for an 8-year period, seeing his father on a regular basis. His mother remarried when James was 8 and he did not have a positive relationship with his stepfather, who was reportedly a heavy drinker and verbally abusive to him. James felt that this man favored his sister and younger stepbrother. James began to manifest learning prob-lems involving language processing and written expressive output in the third grade. He received tutorial assistance. He did not manifest behavior problems in the elementary grades, but was noted to be moody, impulsive, and occasionally oppositional according to reports of his parents and teachers. He reportedly demonstrated the ability to get along reasonably well with peers and was an active participant in various athletic activities, like baseball, soccer, and ice hockey.

James was in the 10th grade when seen for assessment. School personnel felt his learning needs were being appropriately addressed and expressed more concern with his escalating behavior and attitudinal difficulties. He was depicted as contrary, oppositional, demanding, and inconsistent in completing assignments. His guidance counselor saw him as unhappy and somewhat isolative, but noted that he could be engaged and fairly well-con-nected when he spent individual time with teachers. His compromised academic situation was making it likely that he would be ineligible to compete in interscholastic athletics.

When seen for psychological evaluation, James presented as a reserved and somewhat downcast adolescent who rarely initiated conversation but did readily answer questions, albeit in a terse manner, in relation to home and school. Although he agreed things were not going well at home or in school, he seemed at a loss to explain why and tended to minimize and rationalize his involvement in problematic situations. He mentioned that he definitely preferred living with his father and felt he enjoyed a reasonably good relationship with his father and stepmother. He was not inclined to offer much about his mother or stepfather, but did mention the latter's mistreatment of him, which he now said he could ignore as it "was his problem." He mentioned liking to hang out with friends as a preferred activity and alluded to periodic alcohol experimentation, but felt that he had no problems with this. He said he sometimes felt "bummed" but cited no specific precipitants, although in passing he did mention recently breaking-up with his girlfriend of 1 year. He denied suicidal ideation or intent, but did acknowledge he had had suicidal thoughts in the past.

His relatedness suggested a cooperative, pleasant, and even manner. He exhibited solid selective and sustained attention with no real suggestion of distractibility or heightened motility. His mood appeared somber and serious for the most part and he retained this demeanor throughout the evaluation. He also exhibited a constricted range of emotions, occasionally appearing somewhat anxious about his efforts. He did not present as oppositional, unpleasant, or particularly angry. Unusual ideation was not in evidence.

The results of James' object representation material is presented in Table 6.5, followed by interpretive comments and treatment recommendations.

Impressions and Recommendations. With respect to SCORS material, one initially observes that this adolescent's cognitive structuring of object representations reflects unidimensional and minimal elaboration of his own and others' feelings, concerns, and motives—quite reminiscent of the observations of teachers, parents, and the psychologist who evaluated him. At other times, he seems more inclined and able to make tentative and perfunctory inferences about subjective states as witnessed by his comments to Card 4 of the TAT: "Feels bad when he doesn't get attention . . . feels like she don't care for him." But on the whole, there is minimal capacity to make much sense out of how his or others' feelings and internal lives impact on relatedness. The predominant attendant affective tone raises the question of depressive issues and possible conflict. The themes of both stories converge around loss. In one case, there is actual loss and subsequent hardship. In another instance, there is perceived loss of affection and nurturance. James has difficulty tolerating this unpleasant material and his scenarios are abrupt, terse, and defensively benign, suggesting avoidance, retreat, and minimization as he attempts to ward off upsetting affective material. His capacity for emotional investment suggests an underdeveloped ability to sustain object ties as he seems mostly inclined to become wrapped up in his own needs and looks to

TABLE 6.5
MOA and SCORS Responses for Case 11

TAT object representation measures

Card 2: "Looks like back in the old days. She owned the farm ... owns the corn and sugar fields and is very rich. Her mother gets pregnant and mother dies through pregnancy. Girl takes the baby ... has to sell the farm to support her needs. Lives happily ever after."

Scores

    Complexity of representations of people—Level 2
    Affect–tone—Level 3
    Capacity for emotional investment and moral standards—Level 2
    Understanding of social causality—Level 2

Card 4: "Looks kind of like a movie. She's trying to get his attention but he won't give it to her because he's mad at her. He finally gives her his attention. Feels bad when he doesn't get attention ... feels like she don't care for him ... feels bad. Don't know. Guess they go out ... maybe go out to dinner and dancing."

Scores

    Complexity of representations of people—Level 3
    Affect–tone—Level 3
    Capacity for emotional investment and moral standards—Level 2
    Understanding of social causality—Level 2

Rorschach object representation measures

Card II. "Looks like a bird that got shot ... head, wings and here's the hole where he got shot ... blood here and here."

MOA score: 6

Card III. "Looks like two people fighting over something. Heads, body. Something is there that they're fighting over. Trying to pull it away ... going in different directions and looks like they're gonna fall."

MOA score: 3

    "Two women doing exercises ... looks like they're bending over to touch a ball or something."

MOA score: 2

Card VI. "Looks like a leaf that got all burnt ... just black and like ... crinkled ... like ... could be paper too. Looks like that."

MOA score: 6

Card VIII. "Those two there could look like squirrels I guess ... both look the same. Just climbing."

MOA score: 4

Card IX. "Looks like could be two deer here at the top. Here's the heads and here's the antlers."

MOA score: 2

Card X. "Two guys at top. No, maybe looks like two little creatures leaning up against a pole. Can see how they are shaped ... like just leaning. Can see their legs and tails."

MOA score: 3

Highest MOA score: 2
Lowest MOA score: 6
Mean MOA score: 3.71
Mode MOA score: 3.60

---

others as sources of gratification, or as positive objects who can provide him with self-soothing and mirroring.

His MOA profile also suggests that object relatedness is likely to be colored by variable connections with others. At best, there is an interest in involvement, albeit fleeting and tentative. At other times, a more self-absorbed and need-gratifying picture seems to depict his connections. The two scale point 6 responses are more concerning as they raise several possibilities relating to self and other representations. In one instance, he seems to feel quite vulnerable, defective, and damaged, with this indicated by percepts relating to the burned leaf and the bird that was shot. On the other hand, there is the hint that these may be split-off aggressive and destructive parts of self that gain expression via his recent antisocial ventures and passive–aggressive presentation. The former interpretation is more plausible, when one juxtaposes MOA results against SCORS material, which connotes a more narcissistic and self-absorbed clinical picture. Again, the observations of others regarding his overt behavior at home and in school provide strong testimony to the clarity of object representation material in defining nuance and dimensions of his internal self and object world.

The psychologist and clinical social worker who evaluated James and his family felt strongly that a combination of individual and family psychotherapy was indicated. In the final disposition conference, in which James was present, his father, stepmother, school personnel, and juvenile probation officer were advised of the need to provide continued supervision under the jurisdiction of the juvenile court, and also to continue with the implementation of special educational assistance and monitoring at school.

In this meeting, the psychologist provided James with a formulation that framed his conduct and behavioral problems as surface manifestations that belied his internal distress and unhappiness, and conveyed a sense of urgency and request for help. She suggested that he coped via holding things in, but that this strategy eventually did not work out. She emphasized the emergence of an ominous pattern in which he would experience tension and feel devalued, then respond via acting out and becoming negative and oppositional, with this eventuating in predictable punitive, environmental responses. She continued that this only served to reinforce his negative world view and his damaged sense of self, as well as providing a tension discharge function and distancing him from unpleasant affective material. Although not enthusiastic about beginning psychological treatment, he did accede to the recommendation for a trial of individual psychotherapy acknowledging that things had gone awry at this point in his life, and that things needed to change.

What will be this adolescent's likely response to individual psychotherapy, and how should his therapist initially proceed? Again, object representation material may be referenced to provide some form and direction relating to the treatment course, as well as informing us about possible transference reactions and phenomena.

James will find it difficult and potentially painful to discuss his problems and difficulties, as they connote frailty, weakness, and worthlessness. He will initiate therapy with either mirroring, avoidant, or possibly idealized transference reactions. Early confrontation or interpretation of these clearly defensive transferential behaviors is contraindicated and would either trigger underlying part-object aggressive units (Masterson et al., 1992), or possibly result in a retreat from treatment. The emphasis must initially focus on the development of a working connection, which will hopefully allow for eventual exploration of the reasons for James' narcissistic vulnerability, pain, and depression. These feelings may be related to the period in which he apparently endured ongoing insults and emotionally abusive treatment from his stepfather, along with empathic failures of his mother. Complementing the treatment recommendations, his therapist would be initially advised to structure and contain treatment by focusing on James' current problems at home and in school, offering advice, support, clarification, and an interpretative focus in regard to his narcissistic vulnerability. If he is able to make some type of connection, the focus would then evolve into a more supportive–expressive mode in which James and his therapist would use the time to help James focus on conceptions of himself and his accompanying feelings about self and others.

Case 12: Marla, Acute Affective Psychotic Reaction in a 16-Year-Old

This 16-year, 2-month-old adolescent was seen for evaluation 1 week after she was admitted to an adolescent psychiatric unit. She had recently begun attending a nearby boarding school and her adjustment in that setting was of increasing concern according to information provided by the school physician who initiated the referral. During the month preceding her hospitalization, she became increasingly hypomanic and disorganized. Staying up late, she listened to music and wrote poems and letters. She missed classes, began to lose weight, and talked of leaving school to go to New York City where she would pursue a career in dance or writing. She had no previous psychiatric history according to initial brief information provided by her parents.

Her developmental history was fairly unremarkable for major difficulties or earlier problems. An only child, Marla had lived with her parents up until the time she enrolled in boarding school 3 months earlier. She had attended private schools all of her life and was a capable and bright student according to the reports of her mother. She was an accomplished musician, playing the flute, saxophone, and clarinet. She had always been interested in dance and began ballet lessons when she was in elementary school. She had friends at her school, but generally preferred to spend time by herself. Her mother did not offer that Marla presented significant problems in the latency years, but did relate that the past few years had seen her become more strident, contentious, and somewhat secretive about her comings and goings. Her parents wondered about possible involvement with cannabis or hallucinogens given discussions with teachers who expressed concerns about Marla's association with certain students who were suspected of being drug involved. Marla disclaimed any involvement with drugs and occasionally became involved in heated arguments with her mother who disapproved of her new boyfriend. Aside from these periods of tension, her mother reported that things generally went well at home, although she and her husband, both busy professionals, often worked late and spent minimal time with their daughter. Marla's decision to transfer to her current boarding school, a girls' school some distance from her home, was based on the fact that she liked the geographical area and was impressed with the school when she was initially considering high school options.

When seen for the psychological consultation, Marla presented as a tall, slim, and appropriately attired adolescent who looked her stated age. She initially seemed irritated and impatient with the examiner's questions and offered that she thought people were making too much of her recent behavior and that she did not belong in a psychiatric facility, although she quickly announced that she had made many new friends. She denied and minimized the problems that necessitated her hospitalization, revealing a more contrary and angry posture, as she suggested that school personnel were intolerant of individuality and that school rules were too strict. She denied drug involvement aside from some cannabis use 2 weeks prior to admission, and a drug screen failed to detect evidence of illicit substances. She liked some of her classes, particularly art and drama, whereas she found others boring and irrelevant. She did not like her roommate and thought she would prefer to live alone, but did mention having some friends. She said that some of her classmates were real "geeks" and "snobs"; others were definitely "sluts." Marla did not offer that she had problems prior to her current difficulties. She said that she did not particularly miss her parents or her ex-boyfriend with whom she had broken up before starting at her new school. With respect to her relationship with her parents, Marla offered that her mother could be overprotective and nagging, and that her father was generally critical and prone to isolate himself from the family. She offered that she did not think her parents got along well most of the time. It was difficult to ascertain just how close she felt to her parents, as she had professed difficulty in recalling specifics of her earlier childhood. Marla initially balked at becoming involved with projective assessment, saying she would be missing her art therapy session. With firmness she did accede to participate and subsequently became appropriately involved in the evaluative process, displaying adequate attention and perseverance. Her responses often suggested a somewhat pressured, intense, affect-driven quality with answers being given in a rapid, staccato, and somewhat dramatic manner. Her relatedness was fairly even, subdued, and superficial; on occasion, she seemed irritated with the interview, although this was usually replaced with a more self-absorbed, indifferent, and reserved demeanor. Unusual or bizarre ideation was not referenced; there was no suggestion of delusional thinking, and she denied any type of hallucinatory experience.

Marla's object representation material is presented in Table 6.6, followed by interpretive comments and therapeutic recommendations.

Interpretations and Recommendations. Marla's object representations of self and others suggest a distinctly fluid, poorly articulated, and affect-driven description of her object world. Her SCORS material is strikingly intense and egocentric reflecting focal yet exaggerated conflicts in relation to separation–individuation, fidelity and intimacy, with these manifest themes belying an affect tone that suggests her relationships are empty, disappointing, and frustrating. At worst, they are envisioned as malevolent, painful, and malicious. Marla's capacity for emotional investment in relationships is currently quite compromised. She finds it almost impossible to understand and comprehend the needs, feelings, and inner worlds of others except as they exist as projections or extensions of her self and inner concerns. There is possible grandiosity in her initial TAT story to Card 2 where she presents herself as the savior of the family, but this is replaced by a scenario where the central character is doomed to a a life of unhappiness, suggesting her underlying fears that she, too, will suffer disappointment and failure in her future endeavors. Her sense of social causality suggests an exaggerated concern with global "badness" of the self, in which severe retribution for one's actions and behavior (i.e., suicide) is the only option as a result of moral failings and unfaithfulness. Overall, she shows indication that relatedness will be variable. In more superficial encounters she may be able to maintain fairly adaptive connections. This will shift under the press of affective arousal (i.e., more intimate connections), in which Marla will manifest a more vulnerable, variable, hostile–dependent, and avoidant level of relating. She is likely to reflect a marginal capacity to integrate her emotions and feelings in relation to poorly organized diffuse and intense conflicts involving themes of malevolence, harm, and compromised integrity.

TABLE 6.6
MOA and SCORS Responses for Case 12

TAT object representation measures

Card 2: "It's a family. Brother in the field. Brother is young and handsome. Looks like a farm. Looks like a girl there, a schoolgirl . . . she goes to school. She learns about the world. Wants to reform her brother, father and sister. Comes home . . . tells them about the world outside. She's a budding young woman . . . 16 or so. She is pregnant . . . very happy and ignorant. She . . . brother and the sister remain ignorant all their lives. They're happy I guess. The sister wants to learn something about life . . . she'll never be happy or have . . . will be unhappy all her life."

Scores

Complexity of representations of people—Level 3
Affect–tone—Level 2
Capacity for emotional investment and moral standards—Level 2
Understanding of social causality—Level 2

Card 4: "Woman is trying to keep the man from killing someone else. He found out the guy had made a pass at his girlfriend. Mad and jealous. She's trying to stop him . . . 'he's just a friend . . . don't hurt him.' In the end he kills him. She kills herself because of the affair with the guy . . . was really having an affair with him. Can see it in her eyes that she's lying to this man."

Scores

Complexity of representations of people—Level 2
Affect–tone—Level 1
Capacity for emotional investment and moral standards—Level 2
Understanding of social causality—Level 2

Rorschach object representation measures

Card I. "Two people dancing . . . person on each side looking at each other. Seems so symbolic. Looks like trying to pull apart a headless girl in the middle. Inside the girl . . . a little girl without a head. These two things trying to pull her but the girl is holding on to these two people. Still holding on to them."

MOA score: 5

Card II. "Two people again and they're at odds. Praying together but their knees are bleeding. Crowding, talking . . . yelling at one another. Not getting through. Melting hearts at the bottom."

MOA score: 5

Card III. "Two more people again . . . I don't believe. Bending over, ripping, really hurts . . . looks like an animal. They are in agreement to rip it apart to share it. They're females . . . I suppose. I don't know . . . get the impression they are. Heads are deformed . . . look like dog heads."

MOA score: 6

Card IV. "I see a frog . . . dead frog. Looks like dissected it, left it there . . . took away parts of the inside. Looks like just the shell . . . scooped out the insides . . . just there."

(Continued)

TABLE 6.6
(Continued)

MOA score:	6
Card VII.	"Two people . . . big difference . . . huge gorge. Little monster at the bottom. Walking away from each. Monster at the bottom. Already talked. Monster at the bottom waiting for them to fall in. Shape of it . . . looks dark, slimy . . . between these two pieces of rock . . . living in water."
MOA score:	5
Card VIII.	"Oh, these look like wild animals climbing up the big skull of an animal or buffalo . . . these things are climbing up it. Looks like wolverines or maybe mountain lions. Looks like on top of a cliff . . . from underneath the earth. Skull is the gray thing."
MOA score:	2
Card IX.	"A face . . . looks like a giant burning skull . . . head is on fire. Smoke coming out of nose, and mouth is bleeding. Aren't dead yet. Yelling help . . . mouth is screaming . . . too far gone. Like a light bulb. An electric skull or something."
MOA score:	6
Card X.	"Horses here, leaping down a mountainside . . . chasing after sheep that are falling off the cliff."
MOA score:	5
Card X.	"These two are more blue monsters . . . no bulls . . . big and stab the bulls, carry them on their nose like a rhinoceros."
MOA score:	6

Highest MOA score:	2
Lowest MOA score:	6
Mean MOA score:	5.10
Mode MOA score:	5.50

The MOA material is more ominous, suggesting obvious inner disarray and highly conflicted, affectively charged object relatedness commensurate with a borderline level of organization and adaptation. The predominance of scale point 5 and 6 responses is only encountered in extreme clinical situations where there is acute or severe inner disturbance and the likelihood of psychosis, as would appear to be the case here, or severe personality disorder. This former situation is certainly the case. Self representations are imbued with projected feelings of vulnerability, frailty, and compromised integrity. Object representations depict the environment in a most ominous vein: potentially malevolent, harmful, unpredictable, and ultimately destructive. Marla has little sense of security or comfort in her dealings with a world she senses as frightening, unsafe, and foreboding.

Despite the indication of severe psychological disturbance, the object representation material provides some salient information in relation to personality functioning and informs the treatment direction based on several considerations. Her SCORS material suggests that object related-ness will be reasonably good when affective arousal is low and when Marla does not feel pressured in relation to closeness or intimacy. It is somewhat difficult to say how she arrived where she is, and this bears further concerted investigation. The MOA material suggests she is currently demonstrating a fragmented and variable level of connecting to her world. Imagery is malevolent, destructive, and vigilant with expectations that real or imagined harm is a distinct possibility when one entertains thoughts of closeness or intimate connection. Her recent manic presentation and increasingly disorganized adjustment provides testimony to an urgent clinical situation, whereas the object representation material strengthens the concerns of school personnel and provides a cogent and sweeping dynamic portrayal of this young woman's highly disorganized and fragmented inner world.

The first order of therapeutic intervention is to provide structure, containment, and safety so that stabilization and some initial integration can begin to transpire. She would obviously benefit from inpatient treatment because of the high risk for self-injurious behavior given her manic-like, disorganized presentation. An integral part of the initial inpatient treatment will involve more extensive family interviewing in order to ascertain whether or not extended family members have histories of psychiatric problems—in particular, affective disorders or borderline personality disorder, because some research suggests a relationship between the two (Bleiberg, 1991).

With respect to the initial stages of her treatment, one facet will involve psychopharmacological treatment in order to expedite reintegration and set the stage for psychological therapy. Lithium would be the appropriate drug of choice given the overall clinical picture, which strongly suggests a major affective disruption. It is likely Marla would demonstrate a positive response to this regimen given reports (Carlson, 1979; Petti & Vela, 1990; Ryan, Meyer, Dachille, Mazzie, & Puig-Antich) suggesting that older adolescents who manifest a severe affective component as part of their psychiatric disturbance, as well as those with definite bipolar disorders, respond favorably to this medication and do so within a short period of time—usually within 1 month.

Beyond this, the prospective therapeutic course becomes more tentative. It is appropriate to expect that individual psychotherapy and adjunct parental work will be the disposition. Is it reasonable or possible to speculate on Marla's response to treatment? To what extent can object representation material be relied on to inform and direct aspects of her psychotherapeutic work? Is the obtained material a valid reflection of her premorbid object representational schema, or does it more appropriately reflect her current psychotic level of adaptation and organization? These are reasonable but difficult clinical and theoretical questions that would tax the acumen of most clinicians. But it is possible to provide speculative and tentative hypotheses about initial psychotherapeutic interventions, with these being yoked to object representation material.

Initial individual work would be directed toward the establishment of an alliance emphasizing a structured, supportive, and active stance on the part of Marla's therapist. Given the results of the projective material and aspects of the history, it is likely that she will benefit from eventual supportive–expressive work that gradually helps her to explore her conflicts in relation to separation–individuation and to address her faltering development, particularly with regard to the fragmented and poorly integrated aspects of her self and object representations. It is difficult to predict transference phenomena, but she may oscillate and exhibit marked relatedness based on both SCORS and MOA material. Again, an approach emphasizing the establishment and maintenance of relatedness, a mutative interpersonal experience (Blatt & Ford, 1994), should be the overriding therapeutic goal, with this preempting any attempts at more insight-oriented work until more cohesion, stability, and integration is realized.

LATE ADOLESCENCE CLINICAL ILLUSTRATIONS

Case 13: Terri, Anorexia Nervosa and Depression in an 18-Year-Old

Terri is an 18-year, 2-month-old female adolescent referred for psychological evaluation by her female psychotherapist who emphasized concerns about whether or not she was depressed and why she was making little progress in her individual psychotherapy after approximately 4 months of treatment. She was also involved with several members of a medical center eating disorders team, being seen for nutritional counseling, and having regular meetings with her family physician who monitored her weight. Her weight at the time of referral had remained stable for about 2 months.

Her developmental history revealed a fairly uneventful course. Significant problems were not noted by Terri in early childhood or early–middle adolescence, with her mother corroborating. Terri lived with her parents and 20-year-old sister, with whom she reported a somewhat strained relationship, but did not elaborate. Terri also reported she had periodic difficulties in getting along with her parents, especially her father, reportedly a heavy drinker who would become belligerent and critical of family members when drinking. Her mother depicted Terri as very moody, quick to anger, and capable of becoming involved in heated exchanges with family members, especially her father. Her mother noted that concerns in relation to Terri's weight had gradually emerged over the course of the past year and seemed to surface following a bout of influenza. She apparently did not use laxatives or diuretics.

Her adjustment to school indicated that she was a competent student who generally received B's. She had already decided to attend a local community college following her imminent graduation from high school, but was unsure of a future course of study. She was involved with a small circle of close friends, male and female, and dated occasionally but did not have a regular boyfriend. Teachers saw her as pleasant, quiet, and perhaps somewhat shy. She did not participate in any extracurricular activities.

Terri's therapist felt Terri was maintaining a passive–avoidant commitment. She had missed several sessions, appeared constricted and somewhat depressed. She tended to gloss over and minimize any problems and implied that therapy interfered with her busy schedule. She appeared to bristle and would become indignant when confronted with the fact that she seemed to be working hard to avoid looking at her problems. Sessions were often characterized by long silences followed by terse responses to her therapist's comments and interpretations.

When seen for psychological evaluation, Terri presented herself as a small, slight young woman who appeared tense and giggled somewhat inappropriately. She initially seemed fearful of disclosing much in the way of personal information and expressed some concern about what projective results might reveal about her emotional status. She told the examiner she was not having significant problems in relation to her weight and that she generally did not feel hungry. She did admit to problems with concentration and attention, offering that she often spaced out in class and had a difficult time retaining information. Reference to mood disturbance was made by comments such as: "I act like I'm happy, but I'm really not." She said that her mood was "blah" much of the time but she could not, or would not, elaborate on possible precipitants. She denied suicidal intent or ideation, although she did say she thought about suicide in the past and had talked about it with friends who, according to her, admitted to similar feelings.

She alluded to tensions at home, feeling that her mother was obsessed with her weight and too intrusive. She also referenced an ambivalent tie to her father: "I'm like him . . . I have his temper and can go off." And in the same breath, "He doesn't get off my case . . . he's . . . I just try to stay away from him." Her relatedness suggested a reserved, superficial, wary, and measured involvement. She rarely initiated conversation and when the testing was completed seemed relieved, but again seemed concerned about test results as she made the point of asking the examiner what had been revealed about her.

Terri's object representation material is outlined in Table 6.7, followed by impressions in relation to diagnostic impressions and treatment recommendations.

Impressions and Recommendations. The SCORS material suggests that her portrayals of self and others are elaborated in a cursory, minimal, unidimensional, and global fashion, offering little initial sense about her inner representational world. In considering other SCORS dimensions, it becomes apparent that her self and object schema is influenced by affectively charged material that translates into global self-attributes involving a sense of being bad, under scrutiny, and burdened with diffuse feelings of anger. Because of the sparseness of her responses it is difficult to glean a clear sense of her capacity for emotional investment. In some instances she appears aloof, isolated, and caught up in her own despair, suggested by her avoidant representations as well as the distinct irritated defensive posture gradually emerging over the course of the interview. At other times, there is the inkling of the capacity for a more conventional sense of involvement, although it is defined by a template connoting a sense that ties to others are at best superficial and at other times conflictive. Two themes emerge in relation to her dominant interpersonal concerns. First, she feels disappointment with herself and others. Second, and more importantly, she tends to depict themes of people struggling with global and poorly defined affective states. People are angry but she is unable to embellish as to why she or others feel this way. She appears susceptible and vulnerable in the face of this material, and unfortunately has obvious difficulty integrating and modulating her inner feelings and emotions. Again, formal test material as well as highly defensive avoidant behavior tend to converge around this observation.

Terri had five MOA responses, with these increasingly revealing compromised object representations suggesting a lack of cohesion and autonomy. The scale point 6 response in conjunction with the three scale point 4 responses raise questions about an inner vulnerability that results in a pronounced self-soothing quality, and her final leaning, imbalanced response (Card X) connotes an inner sense of diffuse neediness and fragility. The two scale point 2 responses suggest the potential capacity for connection and involvement, but even here there is the sense of a passive, parallel, less intimate type of relatedness similar to what her therapist and psychologist observed and expressed concern about.

Overall, there are obvious issues relating to primary concerns about self-articulation and definition, a focus that appears to preempt, but obviously influences, her interpersonal relatedness. The object representation material suggests a faltering developmental situation emphasizing a depressive type of introjective disorder (Blatt, 1990, 1995) in which Terri's

TABLE 6.7
MOA and SCORS Responses for Case 13

TAT object representation measures	
Card 2:	"She goes to school . . . coming home and that's her father . . . or someone working hard to make money. Just plowing the field. That's her mother and she's pregnant. She's [girl with books] is mad because she did bad on a test [laughs] and, . . . don't know really. I don't know."
Scores	
	Complexity of representations of people—Level 2
	Affect–tone—Level 3
	Capacity for emotional investment and moral standards—Level 2
	Understanding of social causality—Level 2
Card 4:	"This is a lady and she's trying to . . . he's upset or mad at someone. And she's trying to make him feel better. I really don't like doing this. I don't know. She makes him feel better because she cares about him . . . I don't know."
Scores	
	Complexity of representations of people—Level 2
	Affect–tone—Level 3
	Capacity for emotional investment and moral standards—Level 2
	Understanding of social causality—Level 2
Rorschach object representation measures	
Card II.	"Two dead bears . . . don't know . . . just the blood I guess. Look like they're dead . . . got shot."
MOA score:	6
Card III.	"Two people and there's a butterfly between them. Don't know . . . hands, legs bodies. Just standing there."
MOA score:	2
Card VII.	"Two people's faces . . . look like little kids . . . just looks like it . . . don't know . . . just looking at each other."
MOA score:	2
Card VIII.	"A bear and he's on something and this looks like water. There . . . and he can see his reflection."
MOA score:	4
Card IX.	"Two moose. Head . . . two animals . . . both look the same. Don't know."
MOA score:	4
Card X.	"Two birds (top) . . . just birds and like a tree or something. I'm just guessing. They're in a tree, like just hanging onto a branch or something."
MOA score:	4

Highest MOA score:	2
Lowest MOA score:	6
Mean MOA score:	3.66
Mode MOA score:	4

concerns highlight establishing and maintaining a distinct and viable sense of self, establishing a basic stance of separateness and autonomy, and struggling with issues in regard to self-worth and control. Issues of anger and aggression, a central concern in these patients' lives, are obvious in the projective responses that reference difficulties in the integration and modulation of diffuse and poorly integrated anger and frustration.

Extrapolating from these findings, it is possible to make several recommendations to her therapist. First, therapeutic work must still place a premium on the establishment of a working alliance, with this being the critical initial focus and essential to setting the stage for subsequent supportive–expressive work directed toward helping Terri understand her anger and disappointment in relation to self and others. Initially, her therapist should assume an active role in attempting to forge a therapeutic connection that allows for the initial interpretation of her disappointment and diffuse feelings of vulnerability and fragility, attempting to connect them to her avoidant defenses.

Second, subsequent treatment would emphasize moving her toward a position where she could appreciate and realize a more differentiated integrated sense of herself and others. Connecting with her will not be an easy task. The SCORS and MOA material suggest this and dictate that active mirroring and support provided within the context of explanation, feedback, structure, and clarification could be effective in establishing an alliance and allow her to feel some sense of control and participation in her treatment.

Third, given the obvious indication of an affective disorder, it would also be important to refer Terri for a psychiatric consultation in order to evaluate her for a trial of antidepressant medication, possibly Prozac or a related serotonin reuptake inhibitor. This is an appropriate recommendation given the fact that she does describe symptomatology consistent with a clinical picture of a mild depressive syndrome. A medication trial might ameliorate her affective symptoms and create a situation where she would become more available for psychotherapeutic work.

Case 14: Sheri, A Neglectful and Abused 18-Year-Old Adolescent Mother

This case involves an 18-year, 9-month-old adolescent mother. She was referred for psychological assessment as one part of an extensive, court-ordered care and protection investigation regarding whether or not this young woman and her husband were capable of caring for and parenting their 14-month-old infant son. The social worker who initiated the referral emphasized that Sheri and her husband were involved in a most tumultuous relationship and that this had been the status quo since they were married approximately 1 year ago. They fought frequently, ultimately culminating in a serious episode of domestic violence in which Sheri's husband, Tad, assaulted her. A criminal complaint was filed and charges of neglect were lodged against both parents.

Sheri and her husband continue to reside together, although there are increasing signs that he is planning to leave in the near future. They receive a variety of supports: parent aide assistance provided by an outreach nurse who is assigned to them because of the at-risk status for neglect; family counseling provided by a social worker who also sees them in the home, given their lack of transportation and rural living situation; and weekly visits from their social worker who assumes a monitoring and case management function.

Sheri's developmental history is remarkable for an upbringing emphasizing intermittent physical abuse (father), at least three episodes of sexual abuse during latency (undisclosed relatives), and chronic neglect and family dysfunction. Her mother and father were reportedly heavy alcohol abusers and the family moved frequently. This resulted in marginal school performance, and Sheri eventually dropped out of school in the 11th grade when she was 16. In elementary school, she apparently had problems getting along with teachers and was seen as a behavior problem. She began to see therapists when she was 9.

With the advent of puberty, her problems escalated. At age 12, she began using drugs (i.e., cannabis, alcohol, hallucinogens, and amphetamines) and became sexually active. Her relationship with her parents became increasingly volatile and was marked by increased defiance and acting out. She stayed away from home, failed to go to school, would not keep appointments with her therapist, and eventually found herself, at age 15, under the supervision of the juvenile probation department. Her adjustment remained highly unstable; she made many suicidal gestures, continued to abuse substances, and was placed in foster care when she was 16.

In her foster placement, she became pregnant by her husband and married shortly after she turned 17. Her rationale for marriage was apparently based on her desire to extricate herself from the confines of foster care, although she professed to be in love with her husband, an 18-year-old man with a history and upbringing mirroring Sheri's. He grew up with alcoholic parents, a physically abusive father, and a chaotic household in which several older siblings had been removed from the home when they were younger. Tad also had an extensive drug and alcohol history. He exhibited a pattern of fairly serious antisocial conduct problems, having been involved with the juvenile court for larceny, assault, and truancy in earlier adolescence.

When seen for evaluation, Sheri presented herself as a casually attired, somewhat disheveled and unkempt older adolescent. She was easily involved in the interview and proved to be animated and talkative as she discussed various aspects of her present and past. She appeared estranged and isolated from feelings about the reality of her situation. She seemed neither distressed nor upset about the fact that Tad was abusive and that she again found herself involved with the state agency that had supervised her in foster care. She demonstrated a Pollyannish quality as she recounted her history, glossing over the serious problems that colored her relationship with parents. She felt in retrospect that she had more problems in getting along with her mother and offered that she had been closer to her father, not referencing the fact that he had severely abused her through much of her childhood. She felt she was a good mother and seemed attached to her son, steadfastly denying any problems with parenting. She appeared to resent the fact that she and Tad were mandated to meet with the outreach therapist and social worker, although she did offer that some of the recommendations about child care and parenting had been useful.

The psychologist who conducted the assessment commented on Sheri's specious and obsequious relatedness and on the disparity between her narrative and the reality of the actual situation. That is, the portrayal of a marital relationship that was idealized, loving, and without major problems was juxtaposed against reports from the social worker who referenced domestic abuse, impoverishment, and the possibility that her infant son would be placed in foster care because of neglect.

Sheri's object representation material is summarized in Table 6.8, followed by interpretive comments and recommendations in relation to SCORS and MOA material.

Impressions and Recommendations. Her representations of self and others are banal, unembellished, and limited to a description of superficial attributes, traits, and behaviors confined to the immediate situation. There is little sense Sheri sees herself or others as having an emotional history or inner perspective that motivates or explains why people feel and behave the way they do. There is the strong hint that relationship paradigms are colored by mild to moderate negative affective components reflected in the two stories depicting emotional connections as empty, superficial, and bland, at best. On other occasions, relationships are imbued with aggressive attributes and conflicts are the focal point for connectedness—a situation that obviously calls to mind the situation with her husband.

On another SCORS measure of object representation it is possible to see some variability in her capacity for emotional investment, although this is problematic when viewed more closely. Her capacity for emotional investment is limited, with a prevailing perspective being that relationships are shallow and people go about their business satisfying their own

TABLE 6.8
MOA and SCORS Responses for Case 14

TAT object representation measures

Card 2: "Plowing a field . . . heading off to study. And the other lady is daydreaming. Looks like even though their jobs are tedious, they know they have to do them. This woman against the tree always thinks about the future . . . don't know."

Scores

Complexity of representations of people—Level 2
Affect–tone—Level 2
Capacity for emotional investment and moral standards—Level 1
Understanding of social causality—Level 2

Card 4: "Well . . . looks like might be a problem with the man because the woman looks concerned. He's trying to leave. Woman turns man around and tells him to sit down . . . and tries to work out problems. He probably gives some resistance but gives in to the woman. Don't know after that."

Scores

Complexity of representations of people—Level 2
Affect–tone—Level 3
Capacity for emotional investment and moral standards—Level 3
Understanding of social causality—Level 2

Rorschach object representation measures

Card I. "Actually looks like two elephants on the outside . . . trunks, ears, and the tail. Both look just the same."

MOA score: 4

Card II. "Two clowns . . . both look same again. That's all."

MOA score: 4

"Two bears . . . look identical. Why do they . . . are they all the same?"

MOA score: 4

Card III. "These two look like waiters . . . just kind of bending over, like bowing. I can't tell what the the center is."

MOA score: 2

Card VII. "Two old ladies looking at each other."

MOA score: 2

Card VIII. "A rat or a rodent walking along like a pond. Can see reflection here and here."

MOA score: 4

Card IX. "Looks like witches here. Both at top . . . can see them. Guess they're casting spells. That's what they do mostly."

MOA score: 5

Card X. "Can see two crabs here at the top . . . the blue ones. Just kind of walking along the sand I guess."

MOA score: 2

Highest MOA score: 2
Lowest MOA score: 5
Mean MOA score: 3.36
Mode MOA score: 4

---

needs without concern or regard for how this impacts on others. This is juxtaposed against another representational schema in which relatedness is defined by a more tumultuous, conflictual, and problematic portrayal of Sheri's relationships. She views herself as a caretaker, protector, and the adequate other in her dealings with the world, with this probably reflecting the role that she plays with her husband according to reports provided by her caseworker.

On another dimension of object relatedness involving Sheri's understanding of social causality, her representations reflect that her own and others' behavior is predominately guided by immediate external factors and events. She lacks the sense that actions and behavior might be connected to either greater societal norms or be reflective of internal values, beliefs, and standards.

Other object representation material (MOA responses) also suggest some probable variability in her object relatedness. A clear schemata emerges and is defined by the four scale point 4 responses and one scale point 5 response. This indicates representations of self and others increasingly defined by compromised autonomy and mutuality. Her self representations reflect an excessive degree of self-absorption and narcissism translating into an inordinate need for attention from others, as well as pronounced dependency on others for nurturance and gratification. Her two scale point 2 responses reveal some indication of more mature relatedness, although even here the engagement connotes a less than mutual type of involvement, perhaps superficial, with the implication that a more intimate and reciprocal level of relatedness might be possible.

The central referral question is whether or not this young woman is capable of parenting her infant; more specifically, does she manifest substantive psychological problems that would raise concerns about her mothering? Obviously, psychological test material comprises only one source of information of use in addressing this difficult yet central and critical referral issue given the history of a family milieu revealing neglect and domestic abuse—hardly an environment conducive to the optimal development of a child. Nonetheless, it is appropriate to give serious weight to psychological test data in assessing the referral concerns, for as Levine and Tuber (1993) observed, "From our earliest relationships, we construct representational models that guide subsequent relationships, especially those with our children" (p. 69).

Returning to the object representation measures and using these to provide a reference point and beacon for subsequent therapeutic action, the MOA and the SCORS material converge to suggest that Sheri's object relatedness is consistently defined by an orientation and adaptation characterized by an anaclitic–dependent organizational configuration (Blatt, 1991; Urist & Shill, 1982). In Sheri's case, the exaggerated and distorted preoccupations with interpersonal relations (emphasizing trust, caring, dependability, and intimacy) are focused on her husband and herself, and designed to provide her with a sense of integrity and worth that is obviously lacking. Her situation reflects the sequelae of earlier relational experiences that failed to provide her with a more coherent, defined, and positive sense of herself and others.

The issue of whether or not individual psychotherapy is indicated must be weighed against findings that raise questions about the efficacy of this modality in treating patients with anaclitic–dependent forms of psychopathology (Blatt, 1995; Blatt, & Felsen, 1993; Blatt & Ford, 1994). Others (Kocan, 1991) provided material attesting to the fact that patients of this type can ultimately be helped by a mutative psychotherapeutic approach. This allows for the gradual examining of needs and weakness within the context of a therapeutic frame that accentuates mirroring and interpretive support, and that is ultimately designed to create a sense of being understood, valued, and validated as a unique and worthwhile person. Sheri has been unable to examine and connect her childhood experiences to her present situation where she is again being abused. At some point, this will have to assume a central part of individual psychotherapy lest she repeat an abusive pattern with her own child, or in an equally concerning scenario, continues to find herself entangled in abusive relationships with male partners.

The therapist who provided the family treatment, which largely emphasized a psychoeducational approach intended to strengthen the mother–infant attachment, was advised that a more concerted trial of individual treatment should be undertaken with Sheri, allowing for the possibility that her response and involvement would be mirrored by her object representational material (e.g., aloof, superficial, distant), dictating the need for the type of therapeutic orientation already briefly noted. Individual psychotherapy is certainly not the only intervention that should be considered; in reality, it is one modality implemented to complement an array of other intervention strategies. In addition, it would be important to continue with multimodal interventions designed to provide extensive support: parental guidance designed to help Terri to attach and connect in a manner that would promote optimal developmental functioning in her infant son, protective monitoring, well-baby education, medical monitoring as well as birth control counseling, and referral to a young mothers' support group.

Case 15: Tyler, Acute Psychotic Reaction in an 18-Year-Old

This 18-year, 7-month-old adolescent was seen for psychological assessment 21 days after being admitted to a psychiatric unit. His parents advised that he was currently in his freshman year at a northern New England college and had apparently become increasingly paranoid over the course of the past month. He thought his roommates were stealing his clothes and other possessions and that his parents were not supplying him with adequate clothing. He subsequently left school rather abruptly and decided he would "head for Bermuda" so that he could be warm. After stealing a car and proceeding to put his plan into effect, he was detained by police in a large city, being lost, disoriented, confused, and agitated.

The developmental history suggested minimal problems in early childhood according to information provided by his parents. Tyler was a happy youngster who enjoyed a variety of sports and was an adequate student. His parents recalled that he was somewhat shy but had little difficulty in getting along with others. They reported no significant problems in parenting him and mentioned that he enjoyed an essentially positive relationship with his brother who was 2 years older.

His parents stated that they began to have concerns about their son when he was a junior in high school, feeling that he was becoming depressed and manifesting symptoms including hypersomnia, mood swings, poor concentration, and lethargy. These symptoms continued into his senior year of high school and were accompanied by anhedonia, faltering grades, and withdrawal from peers. Teachers advised Tyler's parents of their concerns and outpatient psychiatric consultation was recommended, but Tyler refused this, offering that he did not have problems. His parents advised that conversations with former friends revealed that their son had become involved with drug experimentation and episodic use of hallucinogens, cannabis, and alcohol. Tyler had expressed reservations about commencing college, telling parents he wished to defer and instead travel for at least a year. His parents had not felt this was advisable and insisted he begin his college education without taking a break from his studies.

Further review of the history suggested that Tyler had no previous history of psychological or psychiatric treatment, although this had been highly recommended at least 1 year prior to his current hospitalization. His family history was remarkable for a significant psychiatric disorder in the maternal grandmother, who had reportedly been hospitalized for intermittent psychotic episodes. His mother also referenced a history of "mild depression," had been involved in psychotherapy in the past, and was currently taking antidepressant medication (Zoloft), which she found helpful.

When seen for psychological evaluation, Tyler presented himself as a tall, thin, appropriately attired adolescent who appeared his stated age. He looked tired and somewhat wary, asking why he needed to be seen as he had other commitments and did not see the need for the evaluation. He offered little about the reason for his hospitalization other than to recount the fact that he was cold and wanted to be in a warmer climate.

He denied drug involvement, said that he did not wish to return to school, and hoped that he could start to build boats when he left the hospital. He was quite noncommittal about problems and did not think he belonged in the hospital.

He offered little information about specifics in relation to his college experience, about his relationship to his parents, or reference any other problems in his life. He begrudgingly acknowledged that he had used both LSD and cannabis in high school and also while at college, but said this was not a problem for him. He denied hallucinations, delusions, or suicidal ideation. His relatedness suggested an aloof, superficial, mildly irritated, and somewhat guarded manner. He rarely spoke or initiated conversation except to respond to test material or to inquire why the examiner was asking particular questions. He did not manifest appreciable signs of upset. There was no sign of attentional or concentration disruption or unevenness. His affect was constricted, rather bland and nondescript, whereas his mood reflected a continual somber and serious demeanor during the time he was seen for the evaluation.

Tyler's object representation material is presented in Table 6.9, followed by interpretive comments and therapeutic recommendations in relation to the MOA and SCORS information.

Impressions and Recommendations. The SCORS material initially suggests that Tyler's complexity of representations of self and others is characterized by percepts lacking differentiation and any type of emotional depth or substance. His relatedness portrays an avoidant, egocentric, and superficial quality. His thinking, although not bizarre or psychotic in nature, is somewhat odd and eccentric. Tyler's portrayal of another object relations dimension, affect–tone, reflects his sense that relationships and people's feelings and affects are minimally acknowledged. The TAT stories suggest relatedness defined by an empty, barren, and virtually nonexistent emotional landscape, although there is the possibility that he is warding off and attempting to contain upsetting material, suggested by the sparse and terse quality of his productions.

Turning to the object relations dimension of emotional investment in relationships, he largely views others as a means to obtain gratification and as helpful objects for self-soothing. Both of his TAT stories depict female figures as nurturant, concerned, and as helpers. There is again the sense of an egocentric and self-absorbed quality to his representations, with others being minimally embellished or defined except as they exist to meet one's needs and provide succorance.

His sense of social causality again reveals the self-absorbed and egocentric nature that largely defines his representational world on other SCORS scales. Both stories are significant for what they do not provide.

TABLE 6.9
MOA and SCORS Responses for Case 15

TAT object representation measures

Card 2:   "A girl just returning from school. She's eager to get fed before she helps in the fields. She's wondering whether to ask her mother if lunch has been prepared. She goes and eats food . . . don't know . . . helps in the fields I guess."

Scores

Complexity of representations of people—Level 2
Affect–tone—Level 2
Capacity for emotional investment and moral standards—Level 1
Understanding of social causality—Level 2

Card 4:   "A man is stressed. He's been missing a ball game on television. Wife or girlfriend is trying to relax him. Don't know how he feels. He ends up . . . they both go and sit in front of the television together."

Scores

Complexity of representations of people—Level 2
Affect–tone—Level 3
Capacity for emotional investment and moral standards—Level 2
Understanding of social causality—Level 2

Rorschach object representation measures

Card III.   "I can see little bits of mirrored images of two figures, possibly human, possibly birds. The head, the body . . . the nose looks human. Or could look like birds . . . the nose is protruding and could be a beak."

MOA score: 4

Card VII.   "Picture of two girls . . . a mirror image, possibly a feather in the hair.

MOA score: 4

"A wolf maybe . . . actually attached to the head of the girl. Head and body . . . the girl's head is coming off the wolf's head. It's attached. Shape of it all. Don't know, just hanging onto it. It might have some kind of single horn."

MOA score: 3

Card VIII.   "Part of the . . . red there is two rats or possibly a rat and a frog. Looks like they're just climbing. Rat on the left or a rat and frog combination . . . shape of them and they both look the same."

MOA score: 4

Card X.   "Crabs up there. Maybe fiddler crabs. Has a centralized body with legs on either side. Maybe could be spiders . . . moving along on the sand."

MOA score: 2

Highest MOA score: 2
Lowest MOA score: 4
Mean MOA score: 3.40
Mode MOA score: 4

They are lacking in appreciable depth and reveal unexplained transitions and actions. His stories are somewhat odd and illogical and again there is little sense that behavior is motivated by inner thoughts, feelings, or conflicts.

Turning to the MOA material, inspection of Table 6.9 reveals that he produced only five scorable responses. Of these, three were scale point 4 responses, and one was a scale point 3. His representational schema suggests that self and others are defined by a faltering and poorly articulated sense of cohesion and autonomy. One does not have the impression that Tyler's view of the world is tainted by percepts defined by malevolence and harm. More likely, he experiences a diffuse and poorly integrated sense of himself projecting a still obviously fragile and unstable relatedness that calls forth the need for mirroring and succorance in a manner reminiscent of what was seen in the SCORS material. His one scale point 2 response is also defined by a tentative, unsure, and confusing response in which he is unable to definitively decide on whether the percept is human or animal. More ominous is the second response to Card VII (the wolf attached to the head of a girl). This suggests clear cognitive slippage, idiosyncratic and illogical thought organization, and most likely represents the residuals of the more disorganized and obvious psychotic presentation that prompted his admission 3 weeks earlier.

Both the SCORS and MOA information provide a glimpse at an inner landscape defined by an overall representational quality indicative of a poorly articulated and fragile sense of self and others. Tyler's investment in the interpersonal domain appears fleeting, avoidant, and tentative, although he currently does not project that the world is a place where imminent harm or malevolence is an eventuality or an enduring component of relationships. His current behavior within the context of a structured milieu provides a strong parallel to both his MOA and SCORS responses, as well as to his previous behavior at home and in his final year of high school, based on the reports of his parents.

Extrapolating from the object representation findings to the treatment situation, it is important to emphasize that this young man appears to be showing incremental progress in recompensating from an acute psychotic episode and he has done so without any psychopharmacological assistance, as he has steadfastly refused medication. Continued inpatient treatment would still be indicated to ensure further stabilization and to firm up an aftercare program, which would likely see him returning home to live with his parents and initiating outpatient psychological treatment.

The question of how available this young man is for individual psychotherapy must still be held in abeyance, although the object representational material certainly raises possible scenarios. He will benefit from an approach that employs structure, feedback, and a reality-based focus designed to encourage a working connection and to foster his continued personality restoration (Kohut, 1977; Modell, 1976). This may not be the easiest of tasks given his avoidant and tentative object relatedness, which serves to protect him from perceived threats to his integrity and autonomy. To minimize the risk of Tyler taking flight and dropping out of treatment, the initial goal of building a therapeutic alliance should be explicitly stated and defined as the primary focus of the work (Horowitz, 1989). In fact, the emphasis on the continued maintenance of an enduring mutative relational experience should comprise a primary concern. With patients like Tyler, the results of the projective material indicate an introjective depressive organizational configuration. In instances like this, the psychotherapeutic experience will emphasize a forum wherein a premium on the establishment and support of relatedness is highlighted (Blatt, 1995; Blatt & Ford, 1994). Gradually it will be important to address conflictual material in relation to the developmental issues around separation and individuation. It will also be essential to eventually move toward helping Tyler realize and articulate a more differentiated and integrated perspective of himself and others. It will be important to evaluate the role that his parents should play in the treatment. Whether they should be actively involved in adjunctive family psychotherapy, or might be more appropriately involved in periodic consultations, are issues that should be addressed as part of the overall treatment plan.

7

Pathways of Trauma: The Impact of Chronic, Complex Abuse and Neglect Experiences on Object Representations and Relatedness

Clinicians who assess and treat adolescents are increasingly informed by a burgeoning literature that attests to the link between present psychopathology and either current or earlier experiences of abuse or trauma. As a result of research efforts, largely since the mid-1980s, it is now possible to observe the multiple effects and pathways of different types of trauma and abusive experiences on a child's or adolescent's short-term adaptation in emotional, behavioral, cognitive and interpersonal areas (Browne & Finkelhor, 1986; Conte & Schuerman, 1988; Eth & Pynoss, 1985; Friedrich, 1988; Friedrich, Urquiza, & Beilke, 1986; Gomes-Schwartz, Horowitz, & Sauzier, 1985; Krystal, 1978; Mannarino & Cohen, 1986; Monane, Leichter, Otnow Lewis, 1984; Terr, 1991).

It is also increasingly possible to witness how children and adolescents assimilate and integrate abuse and trauma experiences over time, and how these impact on long-term functioning and adaptation (Bagley & Ramsey, 1985; Briere & Runtz, 1988; Cicchetti & Beeghly, 1987; Herman, Perry & van der Kolk, 1989; Terr, 1991; Watkins & Bentovim, 1992; Westen, Ludolph, Block, et al., 1990). As van der Kolk and Fisler (1994) observed, the frequent sequelae of abusive and significantly neglectful experiences usually results in adaptational efforts reflecting a chronic inability to integrate and modulate emotional, cognitive, and behavioral responses. These subsequently give rise to an array of behaviors designed to regulate internal affective states and impulses. Self-destructive patterns of behavior, eating disorders, dissociative episodes, substance abuse, and increased aggression against others serve to define the clinical presentations in many adolescents seen for consultation.

The manner in which abuse alters object relations development and functioning depends on a multitude of factors, but many adolescents who were subjected to more chronic and severe abuse manifest consistent indication of altered, damaged, and distorted representations of self and others in an effort to maintain their psychological integrity. This may result in self representations tainted by a global sense of badness and contamination (Herman, 1992) that, over time, define the child's identity and assume an important adaptive function by preserving the primary attachment to the parents, albeit in a pathogenic manner.

Ironically, as Herman advised, "The profound sense of inner badness becomes the core around which the abused child's identity is formed, and it persists into adult life" (p. 105). Thus, the adolescent's self representations are defined by a rigid, exaggerated, and split quality. This inner schemata is frequently and vividly portrayed in the case of borderline adolescents, a psychiatric population who consistently reveal significant histories of abuse and trauma (Herman et al., 1989).

Abuse and trauma also result in related failures of integration and developmental arrest in the child's object representations involving others. Herman's observations indicate that the child's initial identifications and connectedness often result in exaggerated, yet brittle and highly idealized images of at least one adult or parental figure, often the abuser. But this inevitably leads to a situation where the child is increasingly aware of the disparity between the idealized representations and the omnipresent reality of abuse and trauma, with this pressure often precipitating the emergence of more overt psychopathology, or for the moment, the maintenance of a pathological state of equilibrium in which object representations are split and polarized. This perpetuates a psychological scenario in which the child or adolescent is incapable of developing an integrated inner representation of the object as a safe, nurturant, and consistent caregiver.

In a climate where abuse is ongoing, it is virtually impossible for the child to internalize a sense that others are trustworthy, emotionally available, and predictable. Object representations thus reflect a template which is fluid, incomplete, and meager—positive emotional experiences may be unpredictably replaced by episodes of terror—thus, a cycle is initiated wherein stable positive representations cannot coalesce or become prepotent because of the neverending possibility of the specter of yet another invasion and violation to the integrity of the self. Thus, as Herman (1992) concluded, the exposure to abuse and trauma has a dramatic and drastic impact on an adolescent's psychological functioning, reflected in aberrant ego functioning and, ultimately, in relatedness:

> Thus, under conditions of chronic child abuse, fragmentation becomes the central principle of personality organization. Fragmentation in conscious-

ness prevents the ordinary integration of knowledge, memory, emotional states, and bodily experiences. Fragmentation in the inner representations of the self prevents the integration of identity. Fragmentation in the inner representations of others prevents the development of a reliable sense of independence within connection. (p. 107)

Perhaps, then, the clearest and most comprehensible example of the child's experience is akin to a kind of emotional dichotic listening task in which neverending, competing, and contradictory information is repeatedly presented, with the dictum that he or she somehow has to organize the emotionally charged material into a message having coherence and integrity. This, of course, represents an impossible task for the infant or younger child because of underdeveloped cognitive information-processing capabilities. The sequelae is likely to reflect more involved, pervasive, enduring, and dire psychological consequences embodied in symptoms reflecting behavioral, somatic, and mood disturbances. The latency-age child who is subjected to trauma or chronic abusive experiences will also display symptomatology that reflects, in the extreme, the indication of posttraumatic stress disorder, or may again manifest an array of behavioral, somatic, emotional, cognitive, learning, or interpersonal problems—the predictable outgrowth of extreme environmental stressors. The adolescent, depending on his or her personality, will most often represent abuse and trauma experiences along a continuum of varied psychiatric problems and syndromes (e.g., depression, antisocial orientation, posttraumatic states, anorexia nervosa and bulimia, somatization disorder, substance abuse and dependence). More extreme psychological postscripts would include those adolescents presenting with dissociative and personality disorders as well as major depressive reactions and suicidality.

Since the mid-1980s, increasing evidence pointed to a strong connection between more severe adolescent developmental disorders (i.e., borderline states) and a multitude of antecedent conditions emphasizing varied environmental experiences of multiple, more severe and chronic abuse, neglect, and trauma, including early loss, multiple caretakers, exposure to violence, family chaos, and significant neglect (Ludolph et al., 1990; Zanarini, Gunderson, Marino, Schwartz, & Frankenburg, 1989).

These more severe instances of chronic, unremitting, and extreme invasive experiences were designated as *Type II trauma* by Terr (1991), and they differ from *Type I trauma* experiences that emanate from exposure to a single, catastrophic experience. Type I trauma usually results in posttraumatic disorders, following the criteria defined by *DSM–IV*. The aftermath does not reflect the massive denials, numbing, self-anesthesias or personality problems noted in the victims of type II.

The sequelae of Type II trauma is quite different according to Terr. Her thoughts emphasized the ongoing preservative efforts of the psyche and self in mobilizing coping and defensive strategies well-known to clinicians: repression, pervasive denial, dissociation, self-hypnosis, aggression against the self, and identification with the aggressor. Pathological personality problems and characterological changes may begin to emerge in latency and later in adolescence. There is increased consolidation and integration of abuse experiences that are, in the extreme, represented by personality states indicative of more primitive developmental levels of functioning and organization (e.g., borderline and narcissistic disorders).

Herman (1993) also raised concerns about the current *DSM–IV* typology, and advocated for the establishment of diagnostic criteria that acknowledges the difference between different types of trauma and abuse (i.e., acute vs. chronic), citing that more ongoing, severe, and recurrent experiences, labeled as disorders of extreme stress not otherwise specified (DESNOS) have a markedly different sequelae and ultimately more pervasive and deleterious impact on the individual's adjustment.

Several studies established a compelling link between borderline personality disorder in adolescence and histories of sexual abuse (Bryer, Nelson, Miller, & Krol, 1987; Herman et al., 1989; Ogata et al., 1990; Westen, Ludolph, Misle, Ruffins & Block, 1990; Westen, Ludolph, Block, et al., 1990). These efforts are important for several reasons: (a) they demonstrated a strong association between borderline personality disorder and antecedent histories of chronic, complex trauma including physical and sexual abuse, as well as ongoing exposure to domestic violence; (b) they tracked the sequelae of postoedipal sexual abuse and documented the ultimate deleterious impact on enduring object relations; and (c) they documented the impact of disrupted attachments and dysfunctional family experience (i.e., Type II trauma) on subsequent social functioning and adaptation.

In the 1990s, a number of investigators (Freedenfeld et al., 1995; Holaday, Armsworth, Swank, & Vincent, 1992; Holaday & Whittenberg, 1994; Leifer et al., 1991; Ornduff et al., 1994; Westen, Ludolph, Lerner, et al., 1990) began to utilize projective devices (e.g., TAT and Rorschach) as instruments in empirical investigations designed to examine the effects and sequelae of trauma and abuse with respect to children and adolescents. The implementation of projective devices to investigate postabuse experiences in children was prompted by several concerns involving the reliability and validity of introspective and retrospective measures (McNally, 1991), which primarily rely on anecdotal observations and behavioral measures such as self-report, behavioral checklists, and parental reports. Information and results generated from these devices are difficult to interpret because they are often subject to bias, reveal considerable variability, and lack conceptual clarity.

As a result of these concerns, McNally and others (Allen, 1994; Conte & Schuerman, 1988) observed the need for clinicians and researchers to utilize new methods for assessing the aftermath of abuse and trauma experiences as they pertain to children and adolescents. They offer procedures and devices emphasizing nonbehavioral psychological processes that are altered and possibly transformed by abuse and trauma experiences. These may serve as subsequent mediators between trauma and the ensuing posttraumatic problems victimized children and adolescents experience in their future adaptational efforts. With this concern in mind, several studies reviewed here attempted to illustrate how psychological processes, specifically object representations, are altered by abuse experiences, and how these measures may then be conceptualized as cogent mediating variables informing clinicians about the course and direction of future object relatedness.

Several efforts of Westen and colleagues (cf. Westen, Ludolph, Block, et al., 1990; Westen, Ludolph, Lerner, et al., 1990) suggest prototypical efforts in this regard. These efforts illustrate that empirical material (TAT results) can be utilized to identify a likely causal link between trauma experiences and current object relations in adolescent patients. Findings also point to the importance of distinguishing several interrelated but distinct dimensions of object relations functioning as assessed by the SCORS. The results also highlight the importance of viewing object representational material as important mediating structures that direct future social functioning and relatedness.

Finally, additional recent investigations (Freedenfeld et al., 1995; Ornduff, Freedenfeld, Kelsey, & Critelli, 1994) also directed their efforts toward examining how object relations functioning is influenced by experiences of physical abuse and by experiences of sexual abuse, respectively. These efforts utilized the SCORS to assess object representations, and results attested to the utility of employing empirical measures to define a strong link between abuse experiences and subsequent object relations functioning. Object representations of both physically and sexually abused children revealed representational schemata whereby others were portrayed as more primitive and malevolent and where interpersonal transactions were imbued with punitive and negative affective connotations.

Ornduff et al. (1994) offered that these results have important implications for diagnosis and treatment. TAT results using SCORS material revealed a relationship between documented sexual abuse and impaired object relations functioning, a finding that lends important empirical support to an earlier cited body of anecdotal clinical research. Moreover, these findings provide for clear and focused therapeutic work in that the goals of treatment for abused patients involves the restoration and integration of fragmented aspects of self and others. There is an attendant need to temper and modulate intense affects and to gradually modify malevolent perceptions of the environment. There is also the need to assist young patients in recognizing dysfunctional and destructive patterns of past relationships, and the attendant expectation of abuse and maltreatment, in order to preclude future involvement in a pattern of abusive relationships—a cycle familiar to clinicians.

In the sections to follow, three adolescent cases are presented. All reflect examples where the history documents clear, chronic, and multiple episodes of abuse and extreme environmental maltreatment, again most appropriately referred to as Type II trauma (Terr, 1991). The intent is to illustrate how trauma and abuse experiences are reflected in object representations measures (e.g., MOA, SCORS) and how this information may then be utilized to generate a composite of different dimensions of adolescents' object relations functioning. The cases also illustrate how these measures provide critical information in the development of hypotheses and prognostications regarding therapeutic options and likely response to treatment.

CASE 16: JOEY, A YOUNGSTER WITH A HISTORY OF PHYSICAL, SEXUAL, AND EMOTIONAL ABUSE

Overview

Joey is a 12-year, 9-month-old male who was seen at the request of his preadoptive social worker and therapist who were seeking updated psychological assessment in order to shed light on possible motivational factors that might account for the escalation of acting out behavior in his preadoptive placement. He had been in his current preadoptive placement for the past 3 years and his parents were now raising serious reservations about completing the adoption process given the difficulties he was having and the impact this was creating on the family. He was portrayed as increasingly oppositional, verbally abusive, and isolative at home. He was manifesting symptoms of encopresis and nocturnal enuresis, behaviors that had not been manifest since he had entered his current placement almost 3 years earlier. He was described as vulgar and obsessed with sexual issues, making frequent reference to his sexual prowess and contacts with various girls at school. His grades had slipped and he also displayed a more oppositional and disrespectful attitude toward his teachers. With his peers, he maintained superficial and measured involvement, bragging about his drug and alcohol use and his antisocial escapades, behavior that was probably not actually taking place according to reports of those who knew him best—his parents and teachers.

His developmental history is remarkable for severe, chronic, and multiple experiences of abuse and trauma during the first 5 years of life. Joey was physically abused by his father, according to court records, with this beginning in infancy. He was also sexually abused by his father, as were his two older sisters. This abuse commenced when he was approximately 4 and consisted of intermittent anal penetration, ending when Joey was placed in foster care at age 5. His father and mother were both alcoholic and his mother, while physically present, was not able to protect Joey or his siblings from their father's frequent explosive outbursts and sexual assaults. His father died in an automobile accident while driving under the influence of alcohol. Shortly thereafter, Joey and his two sisters were placed in three different foster homes when he was age 5 because of their mother's increased alcoholism and severe neglect. At age 6, Joey was placed in a preadoptive home where he remained for almost 3 years. This placement was terminated following the birth of the family's first child when Joey began to show subtly abusive behavior toward the infant.

Joey was seen for a multidisciplinary developmental assessment at a medical center. A psychological evaluation, including projective tests, was part of the process. The results of the Rorschach and TAT object representation measures are presented in Table 7.1, followed by interpretations and a commentary relating to diagnostic and disposition concerns.

Impressions

During the administration of projective devices, Joey presented as angry, irritated, anxious, and unhappy. He rarely spoke and generally refused to elaborate on his responses when asked to do so, frequently shrugging his shoulders and, on two occasions, flipping the cards across the table. He tended to blame others for his current plight and saw little connection between the problems and symptoms he was manifesting and inner or external stress. He expressed anger at his preadoptive parents and said he did not care if he lived there any longer. His relatedness suggested an angry, avoidant, wary, and superficial tie to the examiner and this did not appreciably alter over time.

Interpretation of Rorschach object representation material begins to raise serious concerns about this young adolescent's sense of self and others. At best, he appears capable of a superficial, fleeting connectedness; at worst, his world view is one of potential harm, attack, and loss of self-integrity. His response to Card IX, wherein he depicts aliens being engulfed by fire, raises questions of intrusive material around the death of his abusive father who died in a fiery car crash while intoxicated. His genre suggests the possibility that a more defined paranoid wariness will increasingly color his perceptions of the world. There are already clear indications that his wary, cautious, and angry–avoidant demeanor and connection to his environment may be the harbinger of a more schizoid

TABLE 7.1
MOA and SCORS Responses for Case 16

TAT object representation measures

Card 2:	"She's a schoolgirl ... walked across a tobacco field ... she fell in a pig pen. That's it ... don't know. Guess she feels sad ... don't know. No ... nothing else."
Scores	
	Complexity of representations of people—Level 1
	Affect–tone—Level 2
	Capacity for emotional investment and moral standards—Level 1
	Understanding of social causality—Level 1
Card 4:	"She's looking at grandfather. Don't know ... just visits with him ... don't know." [flips card across the table]
Scores	
	Complexity of representations of people—Level 2
	Affect–tone—Level 2
	Capacity for emotional investment and moral standards—Level 1
	Understanding of social causality—Level 2

Rorschach object representation measures

Card II.	"Two monsters fighting ... yeah. See ... red stuff is their blood cause they're beating each other up."
MOA score:	5
Card III.	"Two people picking up bags ... that's all I can see. Just picking them up, going away I guess."
MOA score:	2
Card VIII.	"Statue of two lions ... just there. Looks like two of them ... look the same. Tree there too."
MOA score:	4
Card IX.	Two aliens there ... arms ... eyes some kind of battle ... shooting fire. See the fire ... burning them. Don't know ... stupid." (flips card across the table)
MOA score:	5

Highest MOA score:	2
Lowest MOA score:	5
Mean MOA score:	4
Mode MOA score:	5

or paranoid stance as increased adolescent demands are superimposed on an already damaged and primitive personality structure.

The TAT object representation material converges to project an equally concerning portrait vis-à-vis his object relations functioning. The consistent tenor defining his representations suggests poor and underdeveloped differentiation between self and others. Even where others are acknowledged, they are depicted in a basic and incoherent manner. Relationships are barren, capricious, and in some instances, nonexistent. Relations are hardly portrayed with any positive affective valence. To the contrary, the predominant affective tenor is one of a low level and chronic apathy and emptiness with hints that he wards off more pervasive despair via his curt, terse, and irritated displeasure with the material. His ability to understand why he or others behave and feel the way they do reflects an inability to demonstrate a rudimentary sense of social causality. His interpersonal concerns suggest a profoundly eccentric, self-absorbed, and isolated quality, quite in line with previously noted impressions in which guardedness, isolation, and avoidance are prominent.

Commentary

The projective material converges with clinical material provided by Joey's therapist, preadoptive parents, and social worker to reveal a chronically troubled and increasingly disturbed young adolescent. It is likely he will leave his preadoptive placement and be referred for residential treatment in order to provide more intensive treatment and containment. The history of chronic, complex trauma and abuse that characterized much of his first 6 years left an indelible mark, one that made it difficult for him or his two sets of preadoptive parents to surmount.

It is difficult to say what went wrong in the past 6 years. He received ongoing and regular psychotherapy with several therapists at the child welfare agency, which oversaw his preadoptive placement. Still, therapists came and went as did the preadoptive parents, thus repeating a familiar scenario of settling in only to see people ultimately leave and abandon him. Joey now appears to stand on the edge of a precipitous cliff. Faced with the emerging and ever-increasing demands of adolescence, he is ill-equipped to come to grips with those new tasks and demands that are difficult for youngsters with much fewer troubles. More so than ever, he requires an environment that will provide a multiplicity of concerted therapeutic interventions if he is to realize a more adaptive and less pathological adjustment to his world.

A residential treatment setting is probably most appropriate at this point, as it would potentially allow the essential and critical opportunity for a corrective emotional experience. His behavior necessitates more containment and it is possible that placement in foster care will not provide him with the mutative milieu he urgently needs if he is to be salvaged. In residential care, it will be essential to continue with his individual psychotherapy and the utmost premium should be placed on finding a therapist who will be available for at least the next year or two, the anticipated length of Joey's placement. The primary focus of his psychotherapy should involve the development of a consistent, predictable, safe place wherein Joey can present his concerns in relation to being "placed," with this being a bridge to the introduction of his feelings and thoughts in relation to more chronic and enduring core themes involving abandonment, rejection, and lack of trust. His response to therapy will hardly be positive and his transference will reflect an array of avoidant, distancing, and aggressive maneuvers designed to protect him from anticipated harm and ultimate rejection. It would be entirely appropriate to proceed very slowly with this youngster, initially engaging him with a therapeutic approach encouraging participation in activities and games of his choosing in order to facilitate connectedness in which he does not feel pressured and in which he can assume some sense of control and security, allowing for additional diagnostic material provided by transferential behavior, as well as allowing him to feel a sense of measured relatedness. In the long run, it will be important to acknowledge that apparent gains and what may appear to be the inkling of a working alliance may give way to acting out and regressive shifts. These will be a barometric measure of diffuse, potent, and understandable underlying affects connected to the core conflicts previously described.

The next case to be presented also involves an adolescent male, somewhat older, but also with a history of early, chronic, complex trauma and abuse. Introductory case information follows, along with later presentation of TAT and Rorschach object representation material outlined in Table 7.2. Interpretations and summary comments are then outlined.

CASE 17: DANIEL, EARLY ABANDONMENT, PHYSICAL AND EMOTIONAL ABUSE

Overview

Danny is a 14-year, 7-month-old adolescent who was seen for psychological assessment shortly after he was admitted to a residential children's center. Prior to his admission, he had spent most of the past 18 months in three separate psychiatric hospitals and was also placed in an adolescent shelter for 1 month. All of the hospitalizations were prompted by severe out-of-control aggressive behavior in the home setting and at school. He also expressed suicidal and homicidal ideation and intent. Discharge diagnoses included conduct disorder and posttraumatic stress disorder with delayed onset.

The early developmental history is somewhat obscure, although Danny was born and lived in El Salvador for the first 4 years of his life. His parents either abandoned him or were murdered when he was 3 years of age and he was subsequently placed in an orphanage until he was adopted at age 4 years, 6 months. Previous hospital records strongly suggest that he was malnourished, probably physically abused by his biological parents, and

TABLE 7.2
MOA and SCORS Responses for Case 17

TAT object representation measures	
Card 2:	"Kind of like . . . don't know. Some town I guess. Plantation and tobacco fields. Don't know . . . people just working hard. Don't know . . . can't see anything else. Nope."
Scores	
	Complexity of representations of people—Level 2
	Affect–tone—Level 2
	Capacity for emotional investment and moral standards—Level 2
	Understanding of social causality—Level 2
Card 4:	"Could look kinda like a movie. Wife that doesn't want to see her husband leave her, but he decides to go and lady becomes a widow . . . cause she doesn't want anyone else and he never returns. Don't know . . . he just goes to the city."
Scores	
	Complexity of representations of people—Level 3
	Affect–tone—Level 3
	Capacity for emotional investment and moral standards—Level 2
	Understanding of social causality—Level 2
Rorschach object representation measures	
Card III.	"Two people and a little butterfly. Head, back legs . . . just there."
MOA score:	2
Card VI.	"A cat . . . a dead cat . . . a run over cat. Reminds me of something that I saw on the road yesterday."
MOA score:	5
Card VIII.	"Two wolves . . . there and there. Look the same. Just there. Don't know."
MOA score:	4
Card IX.	"An explosion . . . like it's all colors . . . like a forest fire . . . all one big cloud of smoke and color . . . trees all burned up there."
MOA score:	6
Card X.	"Two little seahorses . . . there and there. Just looks like them."
MOA score:	2
Highest MOA score:	2
Lowest MOA score:	6
Mean MOA score:	3.80
Mode MOA score:	2

was a likely witness to extreme violence and pathos as he lived in a war-torn country.

Danny began to manifest behavioral difficulties shortly after he was adopted. These mainly consisted of oppositional and aggressive behaviors when demands were made on him to comply or when he felt frustrated. He had a particularly difficult time with his adoptive mother but also focused his angry feelings on his 8-year-old sister, whereas he tended to get along better with his father and 14-year-old sister. He was difficult to discipline and seemed to have particular problems with impulse control. His difficulties escalated when he entered kindergarten and he continued to manifest serious behavior problems, for example, fighting, impulsive acting out, and oppositional behavior. He was liked by his peers but they found it difficult to deal with his unpredictable manner and frequently shunned him after his outbursts and tirades, a pattern that persisted throughout much of his early schooling. His parents attempted to rectify the situation by placing him in a series of private schools, including a military school, but he continued to manifest unremitting conduct and behavioral problems, that is, lying, stealing, fighting, and ignoring rules. At home, his parents were increasingly unable to control or contain him and he was first hospitalized when he threatened his mother with a knife.

Danny's initial adjustment to residential treatment reflected an erratic course with periods of pronounced acting out (e.g., group vandalism, fighting, running away), which became more tempered and was replaced by a more passive–aggressive stance in which he was oppositional, verbally truculent, defiant, and moody in both the school setting and in his cottage. The staff also documented the emergence of symptomatology possibly suggestive of a posttraumatic state as exemplified by sleeping problems, behavioral hyperactivity, flashbacks involving "fire and explosions," crying, and increased diffuse anxiety. This clinical presentation coincided with the outbreak of war in the Middle East. More recently, he has been showing a more positive side and his goals are to attend the local public high school next year, obtain a part-time job after school, and transfer from the residence to a group home facility on the campus. Therapeutic interventions included weekly individual psychotherapy along with biweekly family psychotherapy. Despite the strained situation with his parents that existed for the past several years, Dan reported feeling close to them, looked forward to their visits, and also maintained regular telephone contact.

The psychologist who initially evaluated Danny initially was struck by his somewhat apprehensive and curt presentation. He was polite and compliant, yet fairly taciturn and reticent, rarely offering spontaneous material about his situation. A somber, serious, and occasionally irritable manner comprised his mood and affective reactivity. He tended to minimize and downplay the severity of his recent problems and said that he was sure these were behind him and that he was trying to do better so that he could reach the goals he had set for himself. His relatedness suggested a somewhat wary, cautious, and superficial quality, although he was reasonably cooperative and pleasant in a measured sort of way.

Impressions

Rorschach object representation measures are variable and converge with actual accounts of his relatedness in the initial stages of residential care. Danny's MOA scores range from 2 to 6 with the modal score being 2, suggesting a fairly intact and reasonably good capacity for relating, although there is the sense of some reserve and distance resulting in the reported superficial connection referenced by staff and his therapist. On other occasions, his sense of the world may be more ominous and distinct threats to the integrity of the self are anticipated. Whether or not these are tied to preoedipal experiences is certainly worth considering and could be grist for his continued therapeutic work. MOA results are in close accord with actual accounts of his overall functioning. He was clearly manifesting some capacity to engage with staff and peers, albeit in a somewhat superficial, aloof manner. At other times, he demonstrated a more aggressive, oppositional, and labile side in his dealings with others, particularly adults. Results raise concerns about conflicts in relation to integrating disparate aspects of self and others, with the likelihood of regressive shifts and acting out a continued possibility.

Danny's TAT material is also noteworthy for somewhat variable object relations functioning. In one case (Card 2), his story is strikingly barren. People are not differentiated in any manner and there is the hint that his avoidance and passive retreat are being employed to ward off uncomfortable feelings and thoughts. Because this card is usually seen as a family, and because this adolescent has "lost" his two families, issues of loss, abandonment, and fear of being cast aside probably temper his relatedness. The theme of loss and abandonment quickly comes to the fore in his next response on Card 4, wherein the man leaves never to return and the woman never becomes involved in another intimate relationship. One sees a more developed and elaborate indication of Dan's representational world, but even here there is a somewhat self-absorbed, egocentric quality to his functioning. He clearly articulates a major source of concern that again reflects his underlying conflict about being close and intimate, and to what this may ultimately lead.

Commentary

Despite the serious problems and compromised adjustment that have depicted this adolescent's situation for the past several years, there is reason for encouragement given the results of the current projective findings. They suggest obvious object relations strengths and provide important information about underlying problems and enduring concerns involving closeness, trust, and intimacy. The preoedipal years were certainly noteworthy for multiple episodes of trauma, abuse, and probable neglect, but there is evidence that his latency years, although troubled and turbulent, must have provided him with some sense of containment and meaningful relatedness. He was able to demonstrate some growth and experience a more quiescent, less conflicted, predictable sense of the world, although he was still uprooted and placed in several boarding schools.

At this juncture, he needs to experience an environment that will continue to provide the type of containment and holding needed to stabilize him as a prerequisite toward assisting him to realize the goals he has set for himself and reunite him with his family. He is certainly an appropriate candidate for supportive–expressive psychotherapy. This was already initiated along with the previously mentioned family psychotherapy. His individual work is quite likely to reach an impasse when he begins to approach material related to closeness, loss, and eventual abandonment. He will likely be accommodating, cooperative, and careful in his initial dealings, possibly giving way to more passive and active measures designed to avoid looking at the aforementioned conflict areas. His therapist might expect that at some point Danny will perceive him or her as uncaring, harsh, and rejecting, and it will be important to monitor acting out both in and out of therapy as this will probably be associated with painful material centering around perceived assaults on the self involving external events that produce disappointment, loss, and imagined or anticipated rejection. It will be critical for his therapist to maintain frequent contact with school and cottage personnel to head off episodes of splitting, and it will be equally important to monitor the process of the family psychotherapy as this will provide indispensable material for his individual work.

The last case to be presented involves an older female adolescent, age 18 years and 2 months, who also has a history of severe preoedipal abuse, neglect, and trauma followed by a troubled latency period and problematic early adolescence. Her TAT and Rorschach object representation material is presented in Table 7.3 followed by exposition of case material, clinical impressions, and final commentary in relation to treatment options and direction.

CASE 18: AMELIA, A HISTORY OF CHRONIC, COMPLEX TRAUMA

Overview

At the time of referral, this 18-year-old adolescent was seen for evaluation as she was residing in a supervised apartment setting. She was in her final year of secondary school and was experiencing difficulty abiding by the rules and regulations required in her living arrangement. She would have friends visit after curfew, did not comply with mandates against having friends stay overnight, and was periodically verbally abusive to the house manager. She was under the voluntary custody of the department of child welfare, with her adoptive mother initiating this process when Amelia was 16 years and 7 months of age.

TABLE 7.3
MOA and SCORS Responses for Case 18

TAT object representation measures

Card 2: "A teenage girl. Was born and raised on the farm and is going off to college. Dad is working. The mother is pregnant. She looks really depressed but she's not. She's really worried about her family but everything will work out in the end. Somehow things will get better. She will make it through school and get a job."

Scores

Complexity of representations of people—Level 3
Affect–tone—Level 2
Capacity for emotional investment and moral standards—Level 3
Understanding of social causality—Level 3

Card 4: "Looks like a movie. She's trying to convince her husband not to go off to the mines. If he does, he might get hurt in an explosion. He's in a, 'I don't care' mood. She begs him not to go but he goes. She was right. He gets caught in an explosion and is permanently in a wheelchair. They stay together . . . she's sad but she'll make it. He's struggling but will make it."

Scores

Complexity of representations of people—Level 3
Affect–tone—Level 3
Capacity for emotional investment and moral standards—Level 3
Understanding of social causality—Level 3

Rorschach object representation measures

Card I. "Two people pulling something. Two things look like people pulling. They have the figure there. Going in opposite directions of each other.

MOA score: 2

Card II. "Two people praying . . . kneeling and holding hands. Don't know, just looks like that. Hands are touching together."

MOA score: 1

Card III. "Two women washing clothes. Bent over and doing something and two pots here so it looks like they are washing clothes."

MOA score: 2

Card VI. "A very messed up violin. Has been smashed into two pieces and the strings are all busted. And this is all spread out and looks like it's in rough shape."

MOA score: 6

Card VII. "Two girls dancing, looks like they're dancing a ritual of some kind . . . some kind of family tradition . . . just does. Just liking each other's dancing. Don't see feet . . . just their upper bodies there."

MOA score: 2

Card VIII. "Two bears climbing up the mountain. Two animals walking up the side of something . . . way they are standing."

MOA score: 2

Card IX. "Two guys playing saxophones . . . some kind of musical instruments. Stands not in it . . . saxophones held to their mouths."

MOA score: 2

Highest MOA score: 1
Lowest MOA score: 6
Mean MOA score: 2.40
Mode MOA score: 2

147

She had been in her current living arrangement for 16 months with this placement being initiated when mother felt that she could not positively parent her daughter if Amelia continued to remain at home. Since being placed, Amelia and her mother have seen each other on a regular basis, with her mother more often coming to see her as she lives some distance away. Amelia is not currently involved in psychological therapy, having told her social worker that she does not feel it would be helpful to her at this point in her life.

The developmental history was remarkable for multiple episodes of physical and sexual abuse commencing at approximately 20 months of age and ceasing when Amelia was permanently removed from her mother's care at age 6. Shortly after birth, Amelia's mother entered a drug rehabilitation program where she remained until Amelia was 20 months of age, and Amelia remained with her during this time. The history suggests that the mother of a staff member provided most of the care for Amelia during her mother's early recovery from drug addiction. From the time she was 6 up until she was 9, Amelia was placed in five different foster placements with most of them being terminated because of her aggressive and self-destructive behavior. At age 9, she was placed in residential treatment where she remained for the next 3 years. Her initial adjustment was stormy and she remained aggressive, oppositional, and difficult to engage. Case material indicated that she gradually formed a positive alliance with her female therapist, who remained Amelia's therapist for her 3 years in care. Over time, she gradually settled down and was eventually placed in a preadoptive home when she was 12, subsequently being adopted by a single professional woman when she was 13. For the next 42 months, she remained in her adoptive home but continued to experience problems. She defied her mother's authority by breaking rules, sometimes became verbally and physically assaultive, and on one occasion ran away for 2 weeks. She experimented with drugs and alcohol, associated with troubled peers and frequently distanced herself from her mother. She was involved in ongoing psychotherapy, with her mother also taking part in intermittent mother–daughter sessions and consultations.

Impressions

When seen for psychological evaluation, Amelia impressed the examiner as lethargic and passively defiant when faced with test material, but more cooperative and involved when she was engaged in discussion about her life. She complained about having to take the tests again, saying she had done them since her early years in foster care. She did, however, agree to talk about her current life circumstances and her past, mentioning she had some memories of her life with her biological mother but had forgotten most of her early past. She related that she frequently "zones out," mostly at school but sometimes at home, and that people think she is having "spells" of some type. The examiner felt these would certainly constitute examples of self-induced hypnotic or dissociative episodes and indicated, at least in some instances, a preferred protective measure designed to ward off noxious affective material or intrusive memories. Previous medical and neurological consultations had ruled out any organic basis for her transient states of altered consciousness.

Her Rorschach object representation measures suggest the potential for fairly positive and consistent dealings with others as the majority of her MOA scores are 2s with one score of 1. She is likely to engage with others in a manner that suggests interest and involvement, although with some reserve and aloofness. The presence of an MOA response of 6 is not entirely ominous even though it does raise some concerns vis-à-vis underlying material that represent relations as imbued with malevolent and destructive elements. This response may be more linked to self representations, as there is more than ample material to raise the possibility of Amelia viewing herself as damaged and less than intact. The history suggested that although she has of late achieved a more harmonious and reasonably mature stance in her dealings with others, she can still be provocative, instigative, and capable of launching into infrequent verbal tirades usually directed toward her adoptive mother. Still, the overall picture based on the MOA material bodes positively, suggesting that she has the capacity to establish and maintain meaningful connections to others.

Similarly, TAT object representation measures generally suggest that Amelia's dealings in the interpersonal arena can be reasonably productive and adaptive, although the stories do convey a distinctly dour and dysphoric quality as noted by the Affect–Tone scores. There is some suggestion that she tends to ward off upsetting or depressing material by creating relatively positive but unelaborated scenarios when faced with adversity. This would be consistent with her self-report as well as accounts provided by her social worker. By her account, she zones out at times and she also spends considerable amounts of time in bed, sometimes missing school or appointments. In both of her stories, she seems to possess the basic capacity to view herself and others as somewhat complex, but usually in a more stereotypical manner, and there is the strong suggestion that representations are colored by underlying depressive affect. This renders her perceptions of relationships as imbued with struggle, pain, and sadness. Her representations also convey themes that hint at conflictual dependence and associated pressing concerns centering around separation–individuation issues particularly apparent in her Card 2 response.

Commentary

This adolescent presents a concerning history with the preoedipal years marred by significant episodes of chronic, complex trauma and abuse. Amelia's latency period was also unsettled with multiple foster home placements and finally a 3-year stint in residential care. Her adolescence has had its ups and downs. Although adopted, she increasingly battled with her adoptive mother and was finally placed in a semi-independent living situation at age 17. At present, she continues to have problems, but these are more benign than in the past, although she can still be obstreperous, combative, and cavalier about rules and regulations. Of equal concern is behavior that raises the likelihood that Amelia is depressed, although she tends to minimize this and denies the need to resume psychotherapy at this time in her life.

The psychological findings provided Amelia, her social worker, and mother with important diagnostic material and also information that could be readily translated into therapeutic programming.

In this case, there would be considerable reason to be encouraged by the results of the object representation material, as it indicates she has the resources to get along with others in a fairly positive manner and that somewhere along the way, she benefited from mutative experiences that allowed her to surmount her very problematic preoedipal and latency years. She may experience problems in her dealings with others, as she still maintains some measured distance in her dealings. The key to understanding why this is the case relates to findings gleaned from the SCORS material, in particular the Affect–tone dimension. Her interpersonal representations are tainted by a distinct dysphoric quality and she appears to have the expectation that close relationships are a struggle. Her behavior mirrors these findings as she actively and passively retreats and avoids the world when she finds it too demanding or taxing. Results raise the strong impression of a mild and ingrained depressive personality configuration that ultimately renders her adaptation problematic.

It would be entirely appropriate to push for resumption of psychotherapy as well as for a concomitant psychiatric consultation in order to evaluate her for a trial of antidepressant medication. Her reluctance to become involved in psychotherapy could probably be addressed by emphasizing that it would be more intended to address her current cycle of lethargy, inertia, and retreat in order to help her move on with her life rather than designed to uncover or focus on her past. Amelia, despite her assertions that she currently does not need someone's help, would probably be engaged over the course of time and it would be helpful to frame the referral as constituting a trial arrangement designed to address whether or not something positive would result. In lieu of individual treatment, another option could be referral to group psychotherapy as she might find this less intrusive and more palatable. It would provide her with opportunities for connection with other adolescents and would also allow for the opportunity to address issues in relation to separation–individuation, relationship concerns, and strategies around coming to grips with later adolescent demands. Finally, the option would also exist for family psychotherapy wherein she and her mother could be seen together, with this being appropriate because Amelia may find her way back into her mother's home at some point. This intervention would be less desirable than either individual or group treatment, although it would provide an opportunity for mother and daughter to strengthen their bond and create an arena where Amelia could, with her mother's support, examine issues in relation to separation and individuation.

SUMMARY

This chapter focused on three adolescents of different ages and presenting somewhat different clinical pictures, with the common denominator linking their situations the exposure to noxious environmental events involving multiple episodes of chronic, complex trauma (Terr, 1991) and prolonged abuse and neglect experiences during the preoedipal years. In two of the cases, the additional stress of multiple moves and rejections during the latency period constituted an additional stressor or potentially traumatic event. Despite their starts in life, it was possible to see, in at least two of the cases, reason for some optimism given the results of psychological test material, clearly complementing observations from those most familiar with these young patients, and offering reasons for cautious yet positive prognostications regarding the immediate future. The clinical material raises questions about how children cope with and assimilate sordid environmental experiences that transpire in the critical preoedipal years. Although it would hardly be appropriate to comment that Amelia and Danny are "out of the woods," it would be warranted to acknowledge their resilience and strength, and highlight that they both display obvious emotional resources that bode well as they continue along their adolescent passage.

The results suggest that corrective, mutative emotional experiences appeared to be a critical factor. This was observable in the cases of Amelia and Danny and not so clear in the case of Joey. The development of an enduring positive relationship may be sufficient to, at least in part, ameliorate the sequelae of abusive and neglectful experiences transpiring in the preoedipal developmental period. The current clinical material reflects a more optimistic tone as it suggests that adolescents who endured and been exposed to significant trauma and abuse in their earliest years were somehow able to demonstrate resiliency and a capacity allowing them to view their worlds in a manner that provides options for relatively healthy and appropriate relatedness and connection, provided they continue to receive external support and appropriate professional direction.

8

From Assessment to Treatment Planning: The Development of the Psychodynamic Formulation

The primary function of the dynamic formulation is to provide a succinct and comprehensive conceptualization of a given case, and thus provide a blueprint that directs and informs the ensuing treatment (Perry, Cooper, & Michels, 1987). The formulation provides the critical conceptual link between diagnosis and subsequent therapeutic interventions. With regard to children and adolescents, Shapiro (1989) advocated that the importance of the dynamic formulation remains even more critical in this rapidly changing, atheoretical climate. It still reflects an inexact fit between diagnosis, according to existing criteria (*DSM–IV*), specific child or adolescent's treatment needs, and the most appropriate course of therapeutic action. Thus, the role of the initial formulation is important and critically informative, especially in a workplace where time constraints provide a major test regarding the diagnostic mettle of the clinician.

The development of the dynamic formulation requires the clinician to adhere to four basic tenets outlined by Shapiro and Esman (1985): that (a) there is unconscious mental functioning; (b) manifest symptoms or problems are motivated, at least in part, by internalized conflicts, attitudes, beliefs, and assumptions involving self and others; (c) symptoms have meaning and significance to the child or adolescent, and these affect adaptation to the world by how they are construed in the larger social system; and (d) there is a critical role for displacing internalized conflicts and maladaptive relationships onto the therapist as transferential behaviors as an attempt to modify or negate the repetitive maladaptive behavior and symptoms. As Shapiro (1989) observed, transference behaviors most often occur in frequent, ongoing, and fairly regular intense relationships—

an obvious example being psychotherapy, but also in other arenas of the child or adolescent's life (e.g., tutoring, foster care, residential treatment). Shapiro's focus emphasized clear linkage to ego psychology, as primarily embodied in the theoretical positions advanced by Freud (1963), Mahler et al. (1975), and Pine (1988). However, he also acknowledged the role object relations theory and factors play in the diagnostic formulations in his offerings, stressing, "issues of self esteem regulation and the child's history of human relations that stamp his/her object relations are central to his/her reaction patterns and represent a vital subsystem to be considered" (p. 676).

Shapiro's thoughts rely on a database drawing on a variety of sources emphasizing the organization and integration of information into a conceptual schemata linking historical, current, conscious, and unconscious material. The present paradigm introduces psychological test data as the pivotal ingredient providing the grist for thoughts and prognostications in relation to structural developmental personality attributes and dimensions, as well as those regarding the major directions, levels, and ultimate course of the treatment. Or, as Blatt and Lerner (1983b) observed:

> A systematic assessment of the human responses on the Rorschach will allow the diagnostic clinician to draw inferences about the representational configurations of an individual's inner world. This assessment should have important implications for understanding the nature of the psychopathology, as well as various aspects of the therapeutic relationship, including expected progressive and regressive shifts, that are likely to emerge, potential avenues of recovery and/or change, and information pertinent to specific types of treatment interventions which may be mutative. (p. 10)

The psychodynamic formulation provides a relatively brief yet comprehensive, integrative, dynamic working model of the adolescent's central relationship issues and conflicts with regard to his or her internal and external transactions with self and others.

As Perry, Cooper, and Michels (1987) advised, the formulation has four components:

1. A brief summary of the case that defines the adolescent's current problems and symptoms, placing them in the context of the adolescent's current life situation and developmental history, with this including major precipitants and the primary diagnosis.

2. Reference to nondynamic factors that may have contributed to the psychiatric disorder, with these often including information noted on Axis III and IV of the *DSM–IV* (e.g., juvenile diabetes, asthma, epilepsy, chronic neglect, various types of abuse, other noxious physical or external factors relating to the primary diagnosis).

3. A psychodynamic explanation of the central conflicts, describing their role and function vis-à-vis the current clinical presentation and their genetic origins in the developmental history.

4. Prognostications with regard to how the defined conflicts are likely to manifest and play out in the treatment situation.

More elaborated description of the specific parts of the dynamic formulation follows, with attention to referencing where psychological test data is introduced.

PART I: THE SUMMARIZING STATEMENT

The initial paragraph should introduce why this particular adolescent presents with a given *DSM–IV* diagnosis and attendant symptoms at this point in time. It should succinctly identify the patient, the most salient precipitating events, the extent and quality of object relations, the most relevant aspects of the history (particularly as they relate to the current situation), and those prominent behaviors and symptoms addressed by the formulation. This section should provide an abstract of the clinical situation, not a detailed psychosocial exposition of the adolescent. It should address who the patient is, how he or she arrived at the problematic place, and what are the concerns needing to be addressed.

PART II: DESCRIPTION OF NONDYNAMIC FACTORS

This second paragraph, according to Perry et al., should identify the essential nondynamic variables that could have contributed to the primary psychiatric disturbance, that is, the *DSM–IV*, Axis I diagnosis. These relate mostly to information recorded on Axis III and IV and could involve, for example, substance abuse; family problems or parental discord; sexual, physical, or emotional abuse and neglect; or any one of a variety of physical disorders or conditions (e.g., Crohn's disease, Tourette's syndrome, epilepsy, diabetes, leukemia, orthopedic problems, cerebral palsy). Clinicians working with adolescents who manifest major organic conditions, or who were subjected to chronic, complex trauma experiences, still have the major task of deciphering to what degree the manifest primary psychiatric disorder is a function of the aforementioned factors or situational precipitants. More importantly, they must ascertain to what extent, and in what way these adverse events and circumstances coalesce, impact, and influence object relations functioning.

PART III: PSYCHODYNAMIC EXPLANATION
OF CENTRAL CONFLICTS

This third part of the formulation is akin to the interpretation, wherein integrative inferences are developed based on material provided by MOA and SCORS object representation material. Unlike the psychotherapeutic interpretation, this information is primarily for the clinician's benefit as it provides for the development of a dynamic working model of the adolescent's inner landscape. As Perry et al. observed, the explication of central conflicts involves several steps highlighting an ongoing, sequential, inductive–deductive conceptualization process on the part of the clinician.

The initial step concerns the identification of a small and finite number of pervasive issues or themes that characterize the adolescent's current problems and presenting symptomatology, and can be connected to historical material. Related to this is the task of defining how the patient's attempts were both maladaptive, producing acute symptoms, or in other instances, more defined characterological involvement—and also adaptive as reflected in pockets of ego strength, adaptive object relatedness, and areas of productive functioning. A critical integrative and organizing principle is that central conflicts always portray opposing wishes, motives, and intentions, and can be both conscious and unconscious. Also, they suggest a repetitive pattern and link to genetic origins. For example, an older adolescent may consciously wish to be less aggressive and explosive in his relationships and honestly professes to have little insight into the development of these current behaviors. Unconsciously, his identification with an abusive, unpredictable father, whom he both feared and loved but repeatedly let him down resulted in a template that defines close relationships as oscillating between abuse and rejection. Unfortunately, his attempts to resolve the central conflict indicate prominent and repetitive displaced aggressive and abusive behavior toward his mother and siblings.

Following the delineation of central conflicts and major themes, the psychodynamic formulation is developed with the theoretical emphasis primarily on an object relations model, although it is also possible to construct the formulation employing other psychodynamic perspectives (e.g., ego psycholology or self psychology) that emphasize the importance of adolescents' inner life as instrumental in the understanding of their transactions and dealings in the worlds they traverse.

In adopting the object relations model, primary emphasis is placed on interpersonal issues, on the nature of the self and object representations, and on the prominent and central conflicts between them. As noted in earlier sections, representations are yoked to affective and motivational factors, with maturation and development reflecting more integrated and less contradictory or polarized representations regarding aspects of the self and others. It is important to address the evidence of developmental failure, arrest, and derailment that results in partial or incomplete integration of self and other. It is equally important to identify, where possible, additional indication of defensive misattributions (projections, displacements) in relation to aspects of self or others.

This section relies entirely on information gleaned from MOA and SCORS material, providing salient information about the various dimensions of the adolescent's object representations. Here, we witness how data generated from psychological test material can provide reliable and valid information that comprehensively articulates the dimensions and nuances of the adolescent's interpersonal domain as defined by object representation measures, how central conflicts are presented via this material, and offer perspective on how the adolescent attempts to resolve or cope with these conflicts via implementation of adaptive or maladaptive measures.

PART IV: PREDICTING RESPONSES TO THERAPEUTIC INTERVENTIONS

Prognostic hypotheses are generated in the final section of the formulation process. This refers to the meaning and assumptions the adolescent is likely to bring to bear when he or she engages in treatment or other relationships that, because of their frequency, duration, or intensity, will elicit strong affective material tied to earlier relationships. This section also addresses the issue of how positively or negatively the adolescent will react to, and subsequently utilize, therapeutic encounters, including specific psychological treatment, psychotherapy, or ancillary environmental interventions stressing interpersonal contacts emphasizing close, regular, and potentially intimate involvements (e.g., special education, court supervision, foster care, residential treatment, psychiatric hospitalization). From an object relations perspective, prognostications will emphasize which representations of self and others are most prepotent, likely to present themselves, and be impressively displayed within the context of the therapeutic encounter.

THREE ILLUSTRATIVE PSYCHODYNAMIC FORMULATIONS

Three adolescent patients are presented in order to describe the steps involved in the development of the formulation. Clinical material is designed to specifically introduce the young adolescent, the somewhat older adolescent and, finally, a patient in late adolescence in order to highlight distinct developmental differences in object relations functioning and to highlight commonality with respect to pathology as reflected by dimensions of object relations derailment and impairment.

Before proceeding to exposition of the dynamic formulation, the MOA and SCORS responses of the first adolescent, Bill, are detailed in Table 8.1.

TABLE 8.1
MOA and SCORS Responses for Case 19

TAT object representation measures	
Card 2:	"Guy plowing the field. He's slave of the two girls. She (girl with books) wants to marry him . . . thinks he's awesome. Mom says ok. They get married and live in farmhouse. Live with her, the mother . . . have horses. She likes him because he's a worker and has good biceps."
Scores	
	Complexity of representations of people—Level 2
	Affect–tone—Level 4
	Capacity for emotional investment and moral standards—Level 2
	Understanding of social causality—Level 2
Card 4:	"This looks like a soap opera. She cheated on her old boyfriend with this guy. Old boyfriend comes back to beat up the new boyfriend. She's holding back the new boyfriend from beating up the old boyfriend. The old boyfriend punches the new boyfriend in the head and knocks the girlfriend to the floor. The new boyfriend punched the old boyfriend three times in the head and kicks him in the nose. Old boyfriend falls to the ground. New boyfriend thinks he beaten up enough and calls ambulance. Ambulance comes and takes them away. Woman continues to cheat and ends up alone. Has nobody now because boyfriend goes to jail. She has heart attack and dies. New and old boyfriends get in another fight over whose fault it was that the woman died. Old boyfriend goes to the hospital again and new boyfriend goes to jail for life. Old boyfriend gets a new life."
Scores	
	Complexity of representations of people—Level 1
	Affect–tone—Level 1
	Capacity for emotional investment and moral standards—Level 1
	Understanding of social causality—Level 2
Rorschach object representation measures	
Card II.	"Looks like somebody just got shot in the head. This is their nose . . . here's where got shot and blood. Looks like got shot because there's a big hole in the head and this is their nose. This is the blood because it's red and went black."
MOA score:	6
Card III.	"A picture of a tarantula spider . . . just bit somebody. There's the tarantula and the people. Bit off their legs and they went snap and this is a pool of blood. This is another skeleton he bit up."
MOA score:	6

(Continued)

TABLE 8.1
(Continued)

Card IV.	"Don't know what this looks like. A guy leaning on a tree. Arms, legs, back of head . . . tree."
MOA score:	3
Card VI.	"Looks like an animal snake trying to get out of the old skin. This is him climbing out and leaving the old skin back here . . . because the old skin is already off. Head peeling a little."
MOA score:	3
Card VII.	"Looks like a circle of people . . . people waiting in a circle for someone to come in. There's the people all joined together. Maybe those are people . . . because they are in a circle. Because of this . . . where someone is going to come in [bottom] and go through in there."
MOA score:	3
Card VIII.	"Two animals going up over a mountain. Legs, body. This is the mountain they are going up. Their front feet are going out onto another rock."
MOA score:	2
Card VIII.	"A skeleton of another . . . that the wolves have been chewing on. This is the other animal. Looks like a bear . . . looks like all meat, all thick and chewed. Because it has holes in it and stuff."
MOA score:	6
Card IX.	"Looks like a messed up tree . . . three trees growing into each other. These are the limbs. The two other trees are covered up by the branches. All the leaves are together."
MOA score:	3
Card X.	"Whole bunch of animals in the woods having a meeting. Spiders, snakes, little fish. Because they're all in the same spot. That's where animals are . . . in the woods."
MOA score:	2

Highest MOA score:	2
Lowest MOA score:	6
Mean MOA score:	4.30
Mode MOA score:	6

Case 19: Bill, A 13-Year-Old With Depression

Part I: Summary Statement. This is a 13-year-old seventh grader who is having considerable difficulty in school. He is described by his teachers as inattentive and distracted and has difficulty completing assignments. Concerns are raised as to whether or not he exhibits attention deficit disorder with hyperactivity or some other diagnosis that would account for his attentional problems and apparent inability to focus at school. Previous psychological assessments by school personnel ruled out a learning disorder but repeatedly pinpointed attentional problems, with psychiatric consultation being recommended in order to assess the appropriateness of a

trial of stimulant medication. He is characterized as a pleasant and respectful student by his teachers and does not have difficulty getting along with
his peers, although his involvements tend to be superficial. His teachers feel
he has poor self-esteem and note that he frequently makes self-disparaging
comments in relation to his performance. At home, he has a somewhat
strained and tense relationship with his mother and her new live-in male
partner. Bill can be moody, insolent, difficult, and oppositional, preferring
to isolate himself in his room. At times he expresses a desire to live with his
father and stepmother, but this does not appear possible given the fact that
a recent shift in physical custody did not run smoothly, and Bill is now back
with his mother.

Part II: Nondynamic Factors. Intrafamilial discord and tensions were
always part of this youngster's life. His parents were divorced when he
was 6 years old. Subsequently, his mother was involved in several
relationships that did not work out, and Bill was involved with three
male figures who were characterized as oscillating between being "strict
and punitive" and somewhat inconsistent in their involvements. Other
male figures had no role in parenting or disciplining Bill while residing
in the home. Bill was also a witness to incidents of domestic violence
involving his mother and one of her partners; on several occasions police
were called by neighbors. When visiting his biological father's home, Bill
frequently finds himself fighting with his stepmother's children, two boys
younger than himself, with his father somewhat removed from discipli-
nary involvement, acceding to his wife's decisions regarding punishment
or consequences. As a result, Bill often feels singled out, slighted, and not
supported by either his father or stepmother. Additional developmental
factors are unremarkable.

Part III: Dynamic Formulation. Dynamically, Bill's manifest behavior
serves to belie significant and concerning inner turmoil, in part reflected
by his attentional problems, tied to anxiety and stress regarding central
conflicts: his inability to integrate the good and bad representations of
himself and others, and his difficulty moving on and asserting more
independent, self-assured aspects of himself without feeling comfortable
or secure with these strivings, given his rather fragile status vis-à-vis
attainment of an initial and secure sense of dependency. What looks to
be fairly good object relatedness outside of the home (e.g., his ability to
connect with teachers and peers) suggests a superficial and fragile quality
that crumbles when demands for more intimate and close relationships
are presented, as is the case with relationships within the family.

His sense of self and others reflects a predominant assumption that
close involvements are ultimately punitive, nonnurturant, and destruc-

tive; more specifically, he views the world in a manner suggesting that closeness or dependency is equated with dire consequences. To be loving, connected, and intimate connotes the possibility of serious trouble, eventually resulting in the loss of one's basic security and protection. This youngster's difficulties reflect preoedipal origins with the suggestion that initial needs for connection and dependence were at best met with inconsistent responses from caretakers and resulted in self representations imbued with a sense of badness and inadequacy. Subsequent revisions and modifications of object representations indicate arrest, as mutative experiences were lacking during latency—he now increasingly sees the world of others as unavailable, moody, angry, and destructive, with this building on an object representation foundation that already suggested skewed and negatively imbued percepts of self and others.

At this juncture, one must be concerned about continued difficulties at home, and in the near future about the nature of his relationships with peers. With his mother, he is likely to continue to repetitively enact a scenario stressing a moody, strident, omnipotent, and combative stance. This does not signify phase-specific strivings toward more individuated functioning, but instead reflects "stuckness" in relation to not having earlier dependency needs satisfied. With his father, one may see a less intense variation of this with probable displacement of conflict onto his stepmother. In the peer arena, the projective results suggest two possible types of relatedness may eventuate: one in which he becomes intensely and immediately involved with little sense of what relationships are about, but that they somehow all have a happy ending (e.g., TAT Card 2 story); or in a more concerning scenario, he may play out the representation of relationships that are heavily charged with themes of rejection, rebuff, infidelity, and retaliation—in effect, repeating the installments of the chapters embodied in his mother's relationships during much of the latency years.

Part IV: Predicting Responses to the Therapeutic Situation. It is likely that one would observe at least two major responses to treatment depending on the therapeutic modality. Supposing that individual treatment is undertaken, Bill will probably present as superficially involved, pleasant, compliant, and docile, with this giving way to a more resistant posture as demands are placed on him for involvement and participation around exploration of problems, as the situation dictates closeness and more connectedness. At this point, he may become more anxious, avoidant, and increasingly aggressive in his transactions as he experiences the gradual emergence of his central conflicts in relation to dependency–closeness and rebuff–destruction. This will require containment, active involvement, and therapeutic interventions that will ultimately enable him to juxtapose and introduce modified expectations and perceptions against ingrained and strongly embedded object relations information, which has resulted in his current clinical problems.

In another scenario, where a family psychotherapy approach involving Bill and his mother is advocated, he may again present as initially deferential, subservient, and noncommittal as to his role in the treatment, with this shifting to a more aggressive, intense, and attacking posture toward his mother, or possibly the therapist, as he again reenacts his ingrained sense of male–female transactions or his hostile–dependent connection to his mother. Again, it is likely that object representation material will be an informing source with respect to the transference manifestations and behavior likely to emerge in a more family-oriented treatment. It will be important to implement adjunctive approaches that emphasize psychoeducational work with his mother, father, and stepmother in order to inform them of the reasons why Bill conducts himself the way he does, pointing out links between his behavior and his central conflicts. Advice, direction, and guidelines as to effective ways of relating and parenting the young adolescent should be underscored.

The second adolescent to be presented is a 15-year-old female who was seen by a multidisciplinary child assessment team in an outpatient setting. Preliminary MOA and SCORS material is outlined in Table 8.2, followed by presentation of the clinical formulation.

**Case 20: Amber, a 15-Year-Old With
Separation–Individuation Difficulties**

Part I: Summary Statement. Amber, a 15-year-old female, presented a history of longstanding learning problems for which she continues to receive special educational assistance. Currently in the ninth grade, she also manifests problems with self-esteem, according to reports from teachers and parents. She has marginal involvement with peers with this appearing to reflect her choosing, as she is not shunned or ostracized. Her attendance at school reflects a serious problem as she missed many school days over the course of the past few years, complaining of diffuse aches and pains, and on occasion, migraines for which she was treated. They are now under control.

School avoidance and earlier separation problems are noted when she entered school and persisted up until the present. Even before this, she presented as a cranky, difficult toddler who was clingy, preferred to play alone or to stay close to her mother who worked within the home. More recently, her parents expressed concerns about her psychological adjustment citing her negative self-image, school avoidance, and tendency to isolate herself while at home. Her 20-year-old sister is also described by

TABLE 8.2
MOA and SCORS Responses for Case 20

TAT object representation measures	
Card 2:	"I don't know. The girl is on her way to school. Walking by the farm. She still walks to school. She wants to go back home and go to bed . . . she's tired. She doesn't do it . . . goes to school. Has to. Starts the morning. They're just working on the farm."
Scores	
	Complexity of representations of people—Level 2
	Affect–tone—Level 3
	Capacity for emotional investment and moral standards—Level 2
	Understanding of social causality—Level 2
Card 4:	"Woman is trying to hug that guy. I don't know what happens. He just walks away . . . gonna' be late for work. I don't know. He feels like he's gonna' be late for work . . . mad. She feels like she wants a hug."
Scores	
	Complexity of representations of people—Level 2
	Affect–tone—Level 3
	Capacity for emotional investment and moral standards—Level 2
	Understanding of social causality—Level 2
Rorschach object representation measures	
Card I.	"Bat with holes in it . . . got hurt . . . got shot I guess."
MOA score:	6
Card III.	"I don't know. Two waiters pulling on a tray and food is flying all over the place . . . the red stuff. I thought of it."
MOA score:	2
Card VII.	"Two girls with their butts stuck together . . . joined there. I don't know."
MOA score:	3
Card IX.	"I don't know. Guess it could be two witches. Leaning on a giant crystal ball . . . something like that I guess. Yeah."
MOA score:	3

Highest MOA score:	2
Lowest MOA score:	6
Mean MOA score:	3.50
Mode MOA score:	3

her parents as having problems suggestive of depression, but she avoids seeking help.

Part II: Nondynamic Factors. Her father has a history of heavy alcohol involvement and verbally abusive behavior when drinking. Her mother has always had a somewhat depressive quality to her personality by her report; and her older sister is also reportedly depressed. Amber has a 2-year history of migraines, resulting in a pediatric neurological consultation. She responded to medication and the migraines have all but disappeared. However, these did result in significant school absences during the past 2 years. Temperamentally, she is portrayed as an adolescent who was always shy, avoidant, and on the periphery of her peer group. Interactions within the family emphasize that she can be demanding, clingy, sometimes lethargic, labile, and overly sensitive. Although her parents attempted to broach the possibility of Amber being seen for psychological consultation, she steadfastly balked, maintaining that she can solve her own problems. Her parents subsequently backed off and began to explore family psychotherapy as an intervention.

Part III: Dynamic Formulation. Amber's current behavior and adaptation at home and in the school setting has clear parallels and antecedents to her earlier functioning, both in latency and during the preoedipal period, where she presented in a similar manner as to the present. A basic constitutional predisposition represented by her shy, anxious, and avoidant nature is a contributory factor in setting the stage for subsequent object relations problems first referenced in early childhood. Projective material delineates conflicts between wishes for closeness and excessive immature dependency, approaching a symbiotic quality, with this being juxtaposed against representations that connote that such yearnings are potentially fraught with disappointment, rebuff and, in the extreme, possible disaster (i.e., rejection and possibly abandonment).

Amber's sense of self and others reflects clear lines of demarcation. She has not yet come close to displaying a rudimentary sense of how different aspects of herself and others are part of a greater, integrated whole. This splitting represents a prominent defensive strategy, albeit an increasingly ineffectual one, in which she wards off yet assimilates, in a primitive manner, unconscious aggressive wishes and impulses in relation to self and others. Faced with increasing developmental and environmental demands to move on, she finds herself with a dilemma—to proceed may be equated with the possible loss of emotional support and nurturance but to continue to stay where she is may eventuate in being confronted with disappointment, loss, and continued conflict with respect to her interpersonal involvements. The ever-increasing innate and more encompassing stresses of middle adolescence are now superimposed and impacting on a rather unstable organizational structure, wherein the current behavior and emotional presentation converge and coalesce to represent a concerning clinical situation warranting consideration of immediate therapeutic attention.

Part IV: Predicting Responses to the Therapeutic Situation. The decision of the parents to proceed with a therapeutic course involving family psychotherapy seems appropriate and indicated for several reasons. Most importantly, Amber's loud protests and adamant refusal to engage in individual treatment should be respected. Given her responses to projective material, she would not have an easy time connecting or establishing a therapeutic alliance, although there is some indication this could take place given enough time. She could be expected to provide resistance, avoidance, and a distancing stance in her transferential behavior—with this being the manifest presentation of her representational schemata, directing her to maintain her distance, lest she be rebuffed or discarded if she becomes too close or engaged. Although this interpersonal presentation would provide a potentially critical vista to help her better understand herself and others, this would likely entail a fair amount of time and effort, and would perhaps not be the most appropriate or efficacious therapeutic trek on which to embark.

It would be more indicated to recommend a course of family psychotherapy, as all members of the family are struggling with developmental problems and conflicts that have resulted in clear symptomatology in the mother, father, older sister, and certainly with Amber. Within the context of a family approach, it would be possible to work directly with the parents around the need to create a holding environment for Amber that would gradually allow her some sense of more mature dependency and allow her, as well as other family members, to become more unique and individuated in their relatedness. Misperceptions and misattributions vis-à-vis self and others should gradually be altered and redefined.

At some point, it would be important to revisit the possibility of considering individual psychotherapy for Amber, with this being an outgrowth of family work or in conjunction with ongoing family psychotherapy. This would foster increased opportunity for examining age-appropriate separation–individuation issues, providing her with a forum where she can begin to move a bit beyond the confines of the family and consider the greater world of self and others. At this juncture, individual work would provide an opportunity to tease apart the social contingencies of her emotions, impulses, and feelings as she embarks on a journey involving the initiation of new attachments with peers and others outside the realm of her family.

The third adolescent to be discussed is a 19-year-old female who was referred for psychological evaluation by her therapist who had seen her for three sessions and was looking for additional diagnostic information and closure. Initial MOA and SCORS information is outlined in Table 8.3, with this being followed by the presentation of the dynamic formulation.

Case 21: Emily—A 19-Year-Old With a Severe Adjustment Disorder and Depression

Part I: Summary Statement. Emily recently began psychotherapy for her eating disorder, anorexia nervosa, which had its onset 2 years ago in her senior year of high school. She is now a sophomore at a nearby community

TABLE 8.3
MOA and SCORS Responses for Case 21

TAT object representation measures

Card 2:   "She's a farm girl . . . leaving her folks to go to school and her family
                   stays to work. Feels kind of bad that they have to work so hard.
                   She eventually leaves the farm and gets an education."

Scores

                   Complexity of representations of people—Level 3
                   Affect–tone—Level 3
                   Capacity for emotional investment and moral standards—Level 3
                   Understanding of social causality—2

Card 4:   "Looks like he's very angry at someone. He wants to go off and talk
                   or yell. Maybe this is his mother . . . trying to reason or stop him.
                   She's concerned about him. Talks to him for a while and he calms
                   down."

Scores

                   Complexity of representations of people—Level 3
                   Affect–tone—Level 3
                   Capacity for emotional investment and moral standards—Level 3
                   Understanding of social causality—Level 3

Card 6GF: "She looks surprised by something he said. Looks like he's watching
                   over her . . . doesn't look like he approves at all. She feels badly I
                   guess. He just tells her what she's doing wrong and what he thinks
                   she should be doing. She just . . . says nothing . . . listens to him."

Scores

                   Complexity of representations of people—Level 3
                   Affect–tone—Level 3
                   Capacity for emotional investment and moral standards—Level 3
                   Understanding of social causality—Level 3

Rorschach object representation measures

Card II.   "Two human figures with their hands together . . . humans I guess."
MOA score: 1
Card III.   "Two people . . . that's all. Two people."
MOA score: 2
Card VI.   "Two women . . . heads are facing each other. Don't see anything
                   else."
MOA score: 2
Card VIII.   "I don't really . . . this looks like an animal and this looks like another
                   animal . . . just walking along."
MOA score: 2

Highest MOA score: 1
Lowest MOA score: 2
Mean MOA score: 1.75
Mode MOA score: 2

---

college, continues to reside with her parents, and expresses plans to transfer to a 4-year school next year. She was recommended for psychological therapy by her primary care physician who now feels that psychotherapy is indicated; she also initiated a trial of Imipramine following last week's office visit. Emily's developmental history is rather unremarkable according to her therapist, who advises that it was difficult to obtain much more than cursory information in relation to Emily's upbringing and earlier functioning. Her therapist depicts her initial therapeutic involvement as fairly controlling in a passive–avoidant manner; she is insistent that her parents not be involved in her treatment even though her therapist has expressed the need to consult with them in order to obtain additional background information.

There is no history of psychological or psychiatric treatment. She was, and continues to be, a competent student. Her father is described as rather obsessive and controlling and somewhat distant emotionally, whereas her mother is represented as sometimes infantilizing; but on the whole, Emily does not reference major parent–child conflict now or in earlier developmental periods. The oldest of three, she also gets along reasonably well with her 17-year-old sister and 14-year-old brother, reporting typical tiffs here and there. Although Emily denies being depressed, both her primary care physician and therapist raised this as a referral concern. The question of a depressive disorder secondary to her anorexia nervosa is one consideration here, although the treating professionals also raise questions of a predisposition toward a depressive disorder separate from the eating disorder.

Part II: Nondynamic Factors. By her report, Emily was always reserved, shy, and somewhat self-effacing. She mentions having a small, select group of friends with whom she socializes, although not on a regular basis; she dates occasionally, but does not have a regular boyfriend. She is conscious about her weight and related that she lost approximately 20 pounds over the course of the past 2 years, with this being accomplished by restricting food and maintaining regular adherence to a rigid exercise regimen. Her family history is unremarkable for eating disorders and there is no suggestion of major psychological problems in either her parents or siblings. Depressive disorders are not noted in the family constellation. Emily's greater medical history is unremarkable.

Part III: Dynamic Formulation. Emily's current difficulties appear embedded in conflicts that highlight developmental derailment with respect to separation–individuation issues and demands. She appears to equate assertiveness and strivings for greater autonomy with the distinct possibility that she will not measure up or be good enough in her endeavors.

TAT material raises the possibility that identifications with a strong-willed, controlling, and perhaps critical father, coupled with an identification with a mother who seemed more compassionate but could be infantilizing resulted in self representations imbued with doubt, hesitation, and a need to be more in control as witnessed by her eating disorder. Her therapeutic presentation to this point emphasized a slow moving chess game with her therapist. Moving on in her life also appears to be equated with disappointing or letting others down, possibly her mother, but this is a speculative hypothesis and requires more information, as reasons for this premise are not yet entirely clear. It appears likely that she also experienced difficulty in integrating disparate self and object representations, with the indication that she wards off and splits unacceptable parts of the self and others to avoid feeling out of control and vulnerable to feelings of failure or criticism.

She is conflicted around issues of closeness and intimacy, displaying on the one hand an apparent capacity to initiate and sustain close ties, but on the other hand, she holds back and maintains reserve, preferring to keep her distance and perhaps avoid exposure to disappointment or criticism. There is also the suggestion that her basic temperament and disposition, from what little information is available, always reflected a somewhat taciturn, reserved, and tentative–avoidant type of relatedness. She has reached a critical juncture as the demands for branching out are now interpreted as imminent and are taking their toll, being reflected in her current symptomatology (e.g., exacerbation of her eating disorder), certainly an apt metaphor for her issues in relation to identity consolidation, which would encompass the need to address object relations modifications and alterations in relation to self and others.

Part IV: Predicting Responses to the Therapeutic Situation. The decision by Emily's physician to initiate a trial of a tricyclic antidepressant is a critical initial intervention and one that should hopefully result in stabilization of her eating disorder as well as possibly clarifying the degree and nature of the depressive symptomatology (e.g., whether it is a secondary affective component of the eating disorder, or reflects a more primary concern in its own right). In treatment, Emily will probably continue to present as she did in the initial sessions. That is, she will be cautious, reserved, and subtly controlling, presenting material she feels comfortable with and hopes will meet with her therapist's acceptance and approval. Looming in the background will be her fears that she will not meet the therapist's expectations and this may result in the situation where her therapist needs to be more focused and confrontative in an attempt to bring conflicts regarding being ineffectual and incompetent to the fore.

Emily would seem to be an appropriate candidate for a psychotherapeutic approach emphasizing a supportive–expressive treatment and inviting her participation in teasing out the factors that led to the development of her eating disorder. But on a cautionary note, and relying on information gleaned from object representation material, the therapeutic approach should be respectful of her disposition, emphasizing a need to enable her to participate in a manner allowing her to feel some control and comfort lest she be left exposed and vulnerable. This is a situation where severe and extreme transference reactions will probably not emerge, but the more likely scenario will involve a gradual slowing down, passive–avoidant, and immobilizing repertoire of reactions designed to, consciously and unconsciously, communicate the emergence of the affectively charged material Emily is having difficulty acknowledging and integrating.

SUMMARY

The aforementioned clinical presentations provided examples of how the dynamic formulation is generated from projective material. Specifically, MOA and SCORS data were used to illustrate and define the central psychodynamic conflicts in three adolescent patients. The primary emphasis was on utilizing object relations tenets as the theoretical reference point in clarifying the exact nature of the respective adolescent's psychological difficulties. The chapter emphasized how object representation measures provide a key to understanding how current symptomatology reflects varying degrees of object relations derailment, and how object representation material offers the clinician a comprehensive, psychological blueprint to refer to in the planning and development of treatment options and direction.

9

Object Representation and Changes in Clinical Functioning: Positive and Negative Therapeutic Sequelae in Adolescence

Information obtained from initial patient assessment, specifically projective techniques, provides the therapist with important and meaningful sources of data with which to facilitate and direct the treatment process (Alpher, Perfetto, Henry, & Strupp, 1990). The clinical vignettes presented in chapter 6 offer the opportunity to witness different types of distortions and variations in the content and structure of adolescents' representational worlds as a function of their unique inner pyschopathology. These *inner maps* (Horowitz, 1977) or *representational schemata* comprise invaluable sources of material that can inform, direct, and guide subsequent therapeutic endeavors. Moreover, information gleaned from SCORS and MOA material provide guidelines regarding the specific changes that need to transpire in the adolescent's representational world if he or she is to progress toward higher, more adaptive, differentiated levels of object relatedness.

With this diagnostic information, therapists are guided by assumptions and principles derived from object relations theory, for example, that the therapeutic relationship and nontherapeutic mutative experiences (Blatt & Ford, 1994) provide an enduring arena where distortions and deficiencies in object representations can be reworked and modified. Provided that psychological or other interventions had some positive impact, the end result should reflect representations of self and others that are more articulated, bounded, and suggest increased empathic relatedness (Blatt & Wild, 1976).

There has been a gradual increase in psychotherapy outcome studies with children and adolescents since the mid-1980s (Lutz, 1992; Pfeiffer &

Strzelecki, 1990). This was prompted by concerns of accountability. Outcome studies encouraged the development of behavioral and psychological measures to demonstrate the efficacy of psychological treatment. Change criteria in children and adolescents may take any of several manifest forms: improvement in interpersonal functioning, positive change in academic grades, decrease in referral symptoms, improvement in parents' or teachers' observations in relation to behavior, self-report changes. But as Abraham, Lepisto, Lewis, Schultz, and Finkelberg (1994) observed, there were few attempts to document changes in deeper structural psychological variables that may be related to and accompany treatment.

This does appear to be changing, as several recent studies used projective material as outcome or change criteria—for example, utilizing the Rorschach in an inferential test–retest manner (Exner & Andronikof-Sanglade, 1992; Weiner & Exner, 1991). Several investigators recently began to utilize projective tests, employing a nomothetic paradigm, to assess psychological change in children and adolescents who were involved in long-term residential treatment (Abraham et al., 1994; Gerstle, Geary, Himelstein, & Reller-Geary, 1988; LaBarbera & Cornsweet, 1985). The findings of Abraham and colleagues (Abraham et al., 1994) are most relevant as they directly relate to adolescents with more severe psychological disturbance. Their findings attest to the importance of the Rorschach in documenting personality change. After 2 two years of residential treatment, these adolescents demonstrated improved self-perception and more realistic self-appraisal, along with more interest in others. Increased interpersonal comfort with less detachment and avoidance was also suggested.

Other investigators also used projective material in a more idiographic fashion in order to document changes in structural–developmental personality attributes as they relate to psychotherapeutic experiences. Blatt and Ford (1994) reported significant object representation changes in older adolescents and young adults who were involved in intensive, long-term, psychoanalytically oriented treatment. The MOA scale predicted therapeutic gain in the capacity to establish meaningful interpersonal relations and to change symptomatically. Gruen and Blatt (1990) found that two seriously disturbed patients manifested significant changes in their representational structures following long-term, dynamic treatment. Here, growth in representational structures followed a developmental continuum and revealed that integration and consolidation of conflicting self representations was dependent on the resolution of core psychological conflicts reflected in parental representational material enacted in the transference relationship.

Blatt and colleagues (Blatt, Wiseman, Prince-Gibson, & Gatt, 1991) used an object representation measure, the Object Relations Inventory (ORI), to investigate the relationship between changes in object representations and changes in clinical functioning as measured by the Global Assessment Scale (GAS), a structured behavior rating device. Findings suggested that hospitalized older adolescents and young adults had, at the time of discharge, significantly modified their representations of others (parental figures) and that this was associated with corresponding changes in overt behavior. The results led the investigators to conclude that the quality of object representation is a useful and important psychological measure for evaluating the degree of therapeutic progress.

Two clinical examples are presented in order to illustrate several points. First, in one case an idiographic perspective provides a cogent vantage point to document subtle, important object representational change that is a function of therapeutic experiences, and is supported by accompanying changes in clinical functioning and object relatedness. In another instance, object representation data affords a more articulate and multi-dimensional perspective on a young adolescent's troubled world, more so than is realizable if one attempts to decipher his manifest faltering clinical presentation. In this latter case, the material is most informative in capturing nuances of representational and relatedness derailment, serving notice to his therapist and others about the need to seriously reconsider initial treatment options and proposed levels of treatment.

CASE 22: TIM, AN ADOLESCENT SEXUAL OFFENDER

Tim was a 13-year, 3-month-old young adolescent when he was first seen for psychological assessment some 2 months after being admitted to a residential children's center. Prior to this, he was hospitalized on a child psychiatric unit for a 3-month period. This was prompted by several considerations: escalation of behavior problems (stealing, fighting), the discovery that he had been sexually abusing his young female cousins and sister for at least 1 year, and suicidal ideation and threats accompanied by mood swings.

His developmental history suggested an early history of considerable chaos, upheaval, neglect, and abuse—physical and sexual, as well as emotional. Tim was the oldest of two; he has a sister who is 3 years younger. His parents divorced when he was 3 years of age, and reports from social service personnel suggest that his father was alcoholic and physically abusive to Tim's mother, but not to the children. Following his parent's divorce, Tim's mother had involvements with many different male partners and moved frequently, up until Tim was approximately 7. At this time, she became involved with Tim's stepfather, who physically, sexually, and emotionally abused Tim and his sister until they were removed from his mother's care when he was 10 years of age. Tim and his sister were subsequently placed with a paternal aunt—a single parent with two young female children.

Tim's initial adjustment to residential treatment indicated some relatively benign initial problems—for example, sarcastic and derisive verbal taunts directed toward staff and peers, mistrust and wariness, obstinate and oppositional behavior—with this gradually giving way to more appropriate relatedness and connection to staff and peers. Clinical sequelae of abuse suggested nightmares, difficulty sleeping, intrusive memories and flashbacks, and transient dissociative episodes. Psychiatric consultation raised the question of possible auditory hallucinations and probable depressive symptoms suggested by suicidal thoughts.

Tim's initial psychological treatment program called for a variety of therapeutic interventions: weekly individual psychotherapy with a male therapist, weekly group psychotherapy in the adolescent sexual offenders program, psychopharmacological treatment with a tricyclic antidepressant (i.e., Imipramine, 25 mgs., t.i.d.), and special educational tutoring to remedy problems with mathematics.

When seen for his initial psychological evaluation, Tim presented as a tall, appropriately attired young adolescent who looked his stated age. He was cooperative and pleasant, but related in a reticent and subdued manner. Tim exhibited a narrow and constricted affective presentation; he did not appear to be anxious, upset, or troubled by the nature of the various tasks. His mood suggested a somewhat sad, somber, and serious quality, although he denied being depressed when queried by the examiner. His attentional functioning was even and sustained with no suggestion of unevenness or disruption. Odd, unusual, or inappropriate ideation was not elicited. His relatedness suggested a superficial quality—although not unpleasant, he presented as somewhat distant, passive, and removed, maintaining this posture over the course of the assessment.

Tim's object representation measures reflecting his responses to the SCORS and the MOA are presented in Table 9.1, followed by interpretations and recommendations in relation to treatment considerations.

Impressions and Recommendations

The initial SCORS material reveals a depleted, barren, nondescript, undifferentiated representational sense of others and what they are all about. There is not the sense that Tim views the world as particularly malevolent or hostile. His interactions seem empty and superficial, and people seem alone and mired in their own troubles or unhappiness. His rendition of the girl being "depressed" on Card 2 of the TAT parallels his own current situation. His capacity to initiate and sustain ties with

TABLE 9.1

MOA and SCORS Responses for Case 22

TAT object representation measures

Card 2:	"A girl coming back from school. Walking, just looks over and sees people . . . a family. Lady next to a tree. Don't know. She just keeps walking . . . she goes home. Depressed I guess . . . because she's got homework."

Scores

Complexity of representations of people—Level 2
Affect–tone—Level 3
Capacity for emotional investment and moral standards—Level 1
Understanding of social causality—Level 2

Card 4:	"I don't know, looks like they could have got married and they're out to a movie. The girl is all happy. That's really it. No . . . can't see anything else here."

Scores

Complexity of representations of people—Level 2
Affect–tone—Level 4
Capacity for emotional investment and moral standards—Level 1
Understanding of social causality—Level 1

Rorschach object representation measures

Card IV.	"Like you know . . . could be Big Foot . . . just kind of leaning up against a tree."
MOA score:	3
Card VII.	"Looks like two girls looking at each other. Yeah. That's all I can see here."
MOA score:	2
Card X.	"I don't know . . . kind of looks like bugs here up at the top . . . don't know . . . kind of leaning against a tree or something."
MOA score:	3

Highest MOA score:	2
Lowest MOA score:	3
Mean MOA score:	2.66
Mode MOA score:	3

others, peers or adults, is particularly compromised. It is difficult to ascertain if he has any interest in others—his representations reflect an isolated, detached, and lonely type of existence. Although there is a hint that he is troubled by his inner feelings and emotions, suggested by the fact that he retreats from elaboration regarding internal states, this raises the question of an avoidant style of dealing with the world. Again, one questions how much this is tied to a pervasive and chronic unhappiness that globally colors his sense of the world.

On another measure of object representation, the MOA, Tim produced only three scorable responses. Two are scored scale point 3 and the other is a scale point 2 response. Although the latter response connotes some capacity and interest for relatedness, it does convey reserve and superficial involvement. The former responses reveal a sense of self imbued with feelings of vulnerability, poorly defined autonomy, and a quality of neediness. More primitive and disorganized representations of self and others are not manifest in the protocol, a sign of encouragement given the history that raised the possibility this adolescent's internal world might reflect more malevolent and undifferentiated representational schemata in relation to self and others.

As noted, the treatment plan emphasized a multimodal approach within the context of a residential child center providing a total therapeutic milieu. Following this evaluation, Tim's individual therapist, teacher, and cottage director met with the psychologist who conducted the evaluation to discuss his likely response to various proposed interventions that were an outgrowth of the psychological assessment. His therapist was advised that Tim would likely view individual treatment as an arena where his fragile and vulnerable self representations would eventually emerge, but only after he felt some sense of competency and mastery allowing for risks and self-examination. Likewise, his teacher was advised that Tim would probably find it difficult to feel comfortable with success and failure given his shaky and limited ability to realistically appraise his status as a learner. Cottage staff were advised to be encouraging, firm, and responsive in an effort to draw him out and to actively pursue activity and responsibilities in that setting, gradually encouraging risk-taking and some sense of competence.

Two examples of psychotherapy vignettes serve to illustrate how MOA and SCORS material parallels and converges with Tim's clinical functioning, providing his therapist with a vivid window allowing for the exploration of Tim's misperceptions about self and others.

Scenario 1. After approximately 9 months in individual treatment, Tim disclosed a recurrent dream in which he and a friend were climbing a steep incline. He would start to lose his footing and begin to slide down a steep incline, attempting to grasp onto branches and bushes as he fell. He was never really able to halt his fall, but the dream would end before he was able to or he crashed onto a rocky ledge.

His therapist explored with him the apparent issues relating to conflicts about failing, about being vulnerable and not in control, along with the possible conflicts around being disappointed or let down by others when one really needed them—how difficult it was to lean on others when one could not be sure if they would be available to help out. Tim was somewhat apprehensive about his therapist's observations but gradually began to introduce material in his sessions that spoke to his difficulties in relying on others lest he be set adrift or dismissed. This set the therapeutic stage for more active discussion and examination of reality-based concerns (e.g., relationships, goals, feelings, and thoughts about his parents).

He began to evidence indication of a more articulated and defined sense of who he was, and was also showing increasing ability to see others as more complex and unique. After about 16 months of treatment, another vignette took place, again illustrating how initial MOA and SCORS data define nuances of an individual's object representations and the likely dimensions relating to critical aspects of the therapeutic relationship.

Scenario 2. During a game of chess, the therapist commented on Tim's apparent indifference and lack of attention to his move with Tim abruptly stating that he no longer wished to play. The therapist suggested an alternative move, attempting to be supportive and encouraging. But Tim refused any assistance. Exploration revealed that he had interpreted the comments as sarcastic, derisive, and patronizing, meaning that he was incompetent and stupid.

The therapist attempted to connect this with his recent behavior at school wherein he had become more obstreperous and sarcastic when offered assistance with his learning difficulties in mathematics. Tim admitted to feeling "stupid" because he was having difficulty in one area even though he was doing well in his other subjects. Further exploration led to material indicating that he equated asking for help with being incompetent and having to rely on others who might judge him harshly or write him off. He found it difficult for the first time in his life to depend on others and to ask for assistance, because his assumptions revealed concerns that others had never been helpful and that to look for support was to be potentially disappointed or weak.

Like many youngsters who manifest global and poorly articulated percepts about aspects of their self representations, Tim still displayed a cognitive style that reflected an "all or nothing" manner of looking at himself and precluded his realizing a more differentiated perspective on his resources and limitations (Harter, 1977). This did not allow for him to entertain the possibility that he might be less than competent in one area, or that he would need to "lean on" or depend on others for help, as this ultimately became translated into the assumption that he was someone who had limitations and glaring weaknesses.

Over the course of his first 2 years of residential treatment, Tim gradually demonstrated a more adaptive and less problematic adjustment. His relatedness with peers and staff improved, although he was still viewed as somewhat aloof and moody. Despite this, he was liked and respected by his peers and the adults with whom he had daily involvement. He made progress in the sexual offenders program and assumed responsibility for his transgressions with his young cousins and sister. He had reinitiated contact with his mother and she visited him intermittently. The tentative disposition called for Tim to be placed in a group home for adolescents in the community in which his aunt resided.

Follow-up psychological assessment was conducted approximately 2 years after Tim entered residential care, designed to provide updated impressions on his current psychological functioning. His object representational material is outlined in Table 9.2, followed by clinical impressions and updated treatment recommendations.

Impressions and Recommendations

The SCORS material reveals signs of an important positive shift in one representational area, the capacity for emotional investment, with this being seen in the increase in scores and by his narratives, which now portray enduring relationships in a relatively positive light. There is, however, still a basic and unelaborated quality regarding how he constructs his sense of how and why people relate in the way they do. His views of self and others do not convey isolation and detachment previously so prominent in his TAT stories 2 years earlier. Overall, he is guided by a representational template that enables him to depict, in an emotionally positive manner, themes of affiliation, connectedness, and relative closeness. This inner material parallels and is supported by the observations of those who deal with Tim on a regular basis: his teacher, cottage personnel, and his therapist.

Additional evidence of inner change is found in the updated MOA data. Although he continues to produce a limited number of scorable responses, four in all, they are now predominantly scale point 2 responses. He also produces one scale point 1 response, suggesting a more defined and clear sense of the capacity for mutual relatedness. His three scale point 2 responses still suggest that the majority of his connections with others will continue to emphasize an interest and ability to engage with some measure of reserve and distance being the case in most situations. Of importance, as well, is the fact that his self representations are more defined and autonomous, reflecting a perceptible shift when compared to previous material suggesting self representations imbued with vulnerability, a lack of cohesion, and neediness.

In Tim's case, significant changes in object representations transpired over the course of a 2-year period in residential treatment, and these measures are useful criteria for assessing the degree of therapeutic progress. His manifest clinical functioning, including object relatedness, showed incremental progress, as well, and this information was paralleled by both the SCORS and MOA measures of his object representations. Tim derived considerable benefit from his residential stay and in the process demon-

TABLE 9.2
MOA and SCORS Responses for Case 22

TAT object representation measures	
Card 2:	"Looks like this girl just came home from school. Her mom is pregnant. Father is in the field working. That's about all I can see here. They feel pretty good . . . go in and eat supper. Mother goes to rest and father has to go back to work again."
Scores	
	Complexity of representations of people—Level 2
	Affect–tone—Level 5
	Capacity for emotional investment and moral standards—Level 3
	Understanding of social causality—Level 2
Card 4:	"Like two people in love and the girl is trying to talk with him. I don't know. He drives away somewhere. They end up coming back and marrying one another."
Scores	
	Complexity of representations of people—Level 2
	Affect–tone—Level 3
	Capacity for emotional investment and moral standards—Level 3
	Understanding of social causality—Level 2
Rorschach object representation measures	
Card II.	"Two people . . . don't know . . . kind of look like guys with beards . . . looking at each other."
MOA score:	2
Card III.	"Two kids on a teeter–totter . . . going up and down."
MOA score:	2
Card VII.	"Looks like two women with ponytails . . . looks like they could be talking to each other."
MOA score:	1
Card X.	"I can see a horse here . . . and another one. Looks like they're running or something. That's all."
MOA score:	2
Highest MOA score:	1
Lowest MOA score:	2
Mean MOA score:	1.75
Mode MOA score:	2

strated important incremental signs of behavioral and emotional growth and maturation.

The second case to be discussed involves that of a 14-year, 2-month-old adolescent male seen for follow-up evaluation after 2 years of family psychotherapy interspersed with occasional individual sessions. In this instance, there were three therapists involved with this youngster and his mother. Two had left the agency, and one felt she was not able to connect with the family and transferred the case to a colleague who requested the psychological assessment, given this adolescent's highly troubled adjustment.

CASE 23: MICHAEL, AN ADOLESCENT
WITH DEPRESSION, CONDUCT PROBLEMS,
AND FALTERING PERSONALITY DEVELOPMENT

This 12-year, 7-month-old adolescent was seen at the request of his pediatrician, who referenced growing concern regarding Michael's escalating regressive and maladaptive behavior at home and in school. He lived
with his mother and 16-year-old half-sister. His father abandoned the
family when Mike was 4 years of age and had no subsequent contact
with the family. At home, Michael's adjustment varied considerably. He
alternated between periods of making excessive demands on his mother
for her undivided time and attention, voicing that his sister was favored.
He was physically and verbally abusive to his mother and sister, and
periodically destroyed furniture and objects in the home. At other times,
he was tearful, unhappy, and made reference to taking his life, although
he did not articulate a clear plan of action. He tended to be isolative, had
no real friends, and occupied himself with reading science fiction and
playing video games.

His adjustment to school reflected a similar erratic and uneven picture.
Despite average intellectual ability and no indication of a learning disorder, he generally performed poorly: he failed to complete assignments,
was defiant and oppositional, and fought and bickered with his classmates. He was involved in a weekly socialization group conducted by
the school adjustment counselor. He was described by his teacher as
difficult, unhappy, and unable to maintain relationships with peers unless
he was getting his way.

His early developmental history was remarkable for temper tantrums,
separation anxiety, and difficulties in getting along with his sister. Much
of his preschool care was provided by his maternal grandfather, who was
disabled and short-tempered, and who had minimal involvement with
Mike. This man died shortly after Mike entered the first grade. Mike's
early school history was marked by significant school refusal and difficulty leaving his mother. She frequently accompanied him to school
during his first 2 years and remained in the school setting until he settled
down. Mike's mother remarried when he was 8 years of age and his
stepfather also had minimal interest in assuming a major role in parenting.
He was distant, uninvolved, and entrusted major parenting duties to
Mike's mother, who found it increasingly difficult to cope with Mike's
tirades and outbursts.

Involvement in any type of psychological treatment did not materialize
until Mike was 12 years of age, and this involved a brief psychiatric
hospitalization following an argument at home in which he threatened
his mother and half-sister with a kitchen knife. He subsequently made

suicidal threats and the hospitalization transpired. In the child psychiatric unit, he was subdued, docile, compliant, and superficially involved with the other children in the program. He was discharged after a 15-day stay, with diagnostic impressions suggesting conduct problems and family dysfunction. Outpatient family psychotherapy was the primary aftercare recommendation.

Michael was first seen for psychological evaluation following this hospitalization. It had been difficult to enlist his participation when assessment was attempted while he was an inpatient. He proved to be a difficult youngster to engage and assess. Accompanied to the session by his mother, he initially demanded that she not leave the clinic. He was a youngster with sandy brown hair that partially covered his eyes. He was unsure why he was being assessed and offered little comment about his recent hospitalization, except to say that the staff was "stupid," and the other children, "jerks." Over time, his cooperation became more compromised and consisted of increasingly obstreperous and infantile outbursts. He became more anxious, provocative, and oppositional with the introduction of projective devices, proclaiming that he had done this before and did not need to do it again. He scaled the cards across the table, muttered obscenities, and demanded to see if his mother was still in the waiting room. His behavior became more compliant when the examiner firmly insisted on his cooperation and reassured him that his mother would remain nearby until the evaluation was completed. His relatedness remained detached and avoidant at best and he did not deviate appreciably as the evaluation continued. His affect suggested an unhappy, petulant, and moody quality with little sign of contentment or a lighter side being manifest.

Michael's initial SCORS and MOA object representation material is presented in Table 9.3, followed by clinical impressions and treatment recommendations.

Impressions and Recommendations

Initial SCORS material emphasizes that representations of others are undifferentiated, minimally elaborated, and lacking any emotional qualities. His sense of the world tends to be highly egocentric and self-absorbed with little suggestion that he has any appreciable interest or desire in connecting with others. His TAT stories are odd, somewhat illogical, and his own issues and inner conflicts intrude and serve to distort and blur his sense of separateness from others. Michael has little sense of what motivates himself or others. There is virtually no appreciation that behavior is guided by thought, feelings, and emotions; his stories are fairly noncausal with the likelihood that he lacks the critical capacity to make much sense out of his or others' functioning. Although his descriptions

TABLE 9.3
MOA and SCORS Responses for Case 23

TAT object representation measures	
Card 2:	"These are stupid. I don't know. Just farming and getting ready for winter. And they ... I don't know. That girl is going to school ... won't go. Guess she feels sick. Don't know. Unhappy I guess ... because she's sick."
Scores	
	Complexity of representations of people—Level 2
	Affect–tone—Level 2
	Capacity for emotional investment and moral standards—Level 1
	Understanding of social causality—Level 2
Card 4:	"I don't know ... can't see what ... could be a boyfriend and a girlfriend. Looks like my sister and her boyfriend. Go out on a date, come home ... and ... don't know. Could have sex I guess. Don't know. How many more of these do we have to do?"
Scores	
	Complexity of representations of people—Level 2
	Affect–tone—Level 3
	Capacity for emotional investment and moral standards—Level 1
	Understanding of social causality—Level 1
Rorschach object representation measures	
Card II.	"Don't know ... nothing much. Could be a bird that's been shot ... can see the blood here and here."
MOA score:	6
	"The whole thing looks like a rocket of some type has blown up something ... maybe could ... be building or something. That's all ... just smoke and fire all around there."
MOA score:	6
Card III.	"Different ... could be two people, here and here. Looks like they're kissing or ... yeah, just kissing."
MOA score:	1
Card IV.	"Don't know about this one. Could be, looks like a large monster standing there ... eating something ... looks like that. Could be eating a person or something."
MOA score:	6
Card IX.	"An explosion ... all the colors look like fire there. Don't know ... could be like these two, here and here ... are just all on flames. Can't see anything else."
MOA score:	6
Highest MOA score:	1
Lowest MOA score:	6
Mean MOA score:	5
Mode MOA score:	6

181

of relationships are superficial at best, and more often than not, portrayed by an empty, nonexistent, and barren quality, this is not particularly troubling to him, as significant affective material does not accompany his representations.

Supplemental object representational material (MOA responses) provide additional reason for concern. Of his five scorable responses, four are at scale point 6; his remaining one is a scale point 1. This latter response indicates some potential intact capacity for relatedness juxtaposed against more ominous percepts that illustrate considerable focus on body damaging, attacking, and malevolent interactions. Equally apparent is the portrayal of the victim–victimizer dichotomy wherein the mutilated, disfigured, and destroyed percepts alternate with equally malevolent and aggressive interactions in which a monster devours others. Overall, these responses raise serious concerns about this young adolescent's ability to get along in the world given his inner representational template of expectations of harm, malevolence, and loss of integrity.

As noted, this young adolescent and his mother were subsequently involved in a rather uneven course of family psychotherapy for a 2-year period. During this time, Michael's behavior at school stabilized somewhat with this probably attributable to the fact that he was assigned a male aide who helped to direct and contain his behavior. In this setting, he remained involved in a boys' socialization group; but as the school adjustment counselor noted, he still was very much on the periphery of the group. His demeanor paralleled MOA material. He provoked, taunted, and occasionally fought with group members; at other times, he apparently set himself up to be ostracized, rebuffed, and excluded, even though a few members of the group made attempts to reach out to him.

At home, his behavior oscillated between periods of being highly disagreeable (still prone to be verbally provocative and attacking), and periodically out of control (i.e., destroying furniture and punching holes in walls). At other times, he was isolative and distanced himself from his mother, stepfather, and sister. He complained he would rather live elsewhere and that the rules were unreasonable.

As he entered the seventh grade, Michael's academic performance slipped considerably owing to the fact that he was now in a new school. He made a fairly unremarkable initial social adjustment, as he had acquired a few friends and had not been involved in major altercations. The reports of his new teachers were more of a concern, as all of them saw an isolated, withdrawn, and potentially troubled youngster who could on occasion show poor impulse control and poorly modulated anger, expressed by storming out of class or being verbally assaultive and attacking.

The second psychological assessment took place shortly after he turned 14 and was initiated by the newest therapist who had only recently become involved with Michael and his mother. Two incidents prompted the referral. In one instance Michael had become embroiled in a heated exchange with his stepfather and threatened him with a baseball bat, with this prompting a call for police assistance. Following this, Michael began to balk at attending school and spoke to his school guidance counselor about suicidal ideation. This information was passed to the family's therapist, who advised the mother that in view of Michael's deterioration in functioning, he was initiating psychological and psychiatric consultations in order to provide updated diagnostic impressions.

The follow-up SCORS and MOA material is outlined in Table 9.4, followed by clinical impressions and therapeutic recommendations.

Impressions and Recommendations

Relative to the first assessment, the current SCORS material reveals subtle positive shifts in his object representations, although there is still the sense that he sees others in a predominately unidimensional, simplistic manner with minimal awareness of their internal states. The strikingly egocentric perceptions that comprised the previous material have given way to a more conventional, albeit still somewhat self-absorbed map that directs perceptions of how others feel, think, and relate. It is difficult for Michael to experience much satisfaction from his interpersonal relationships. Others exist, move about, and relate in a removed and detached manner (TAT Card 2), and where there is some type of involvement, it is precarious and potentially short-lived (TAT Card 4). Again, one has the sense of an estranged, detached, and isolated adolescent whose representations of others, although not particularly imbued with malevolent or negative attributions, suggest that his relatedness will be compromised and characterized by an avoidant and tentative stance toward others.

The follow-up MOA material is of equal concern when current results are compared to his earlier protocol. All of his present eight MOA scores are scale point 6 responses, whereas 2 years earlier he produced four scale point 6 responses, but he also produced one scale point 1 response. Presently, Michael's self representations reflect faltering self–object differentiation and clear boundary disturbance. His representations of self are poorly defined, tainted by themes suggesting concerns with eroding and highly compromised integrity, expectations of harm and malevolence, and the sense that relationships are generally destructive. The victim–victimizer scenario is reflected in responses suggesting fears of abject harm and destruction juxtaposed against another response representing a powerful, attacking, and destructive object. Of concern is the fact that there is no indication that relatedness can involve anything more than relationships emphasizing dire possibilities.

TABLE 9.4
MOA and SCORS Responses for Case 23

TAT object representation measures

Card 2:
"A guy digging up crops. Pregnant lady leaning against a tree, hoping he'll get through it alive. Bunch of houses and rocky land. Go in the house and start eating. The young girl looks worried . . . don't know why. The guy . . . no telling . . . can't see his face. Pregnant lady looks happy . . . maybe because she's pregnant."

Scores

Complexity of representations of people—Level 2
Affect–tone—Level 3
Capacity for emotional investment and moral standards—Level 2
Understanding of social causality—Level 2

Card 4:
"A guy and a wife I guess. Don't know . . . she's hugging him. Has to do a job she doesn't want him to do. Well he has a positive look on his face . . . she sort of looks worried. He comes back safely. Or she gets word that he's been killed and she's sad."

Scores

Complexity of representations of people—Level 3
Affect–tone—Level 2
Capacity for emotional investment and moral standards—Level 2
Understanding of social causality—Level 2

Rorschach object representation measures

Card I.
"A bat. Looks like that bat was shot in two places . . . or someone painted it to look that way. Can see the holes."

MOA score: 6

"Might be a fly that was splattered . . . all over the place . . . hit with a fly swatter."

MOA score: 6

Card II.
"Looks like a guy with rest of head missing. Well it disappeared . . . could have got shot or in some type of explosion . . . blood there."

MOA score: 6

Card III.
"A massive fly with no wings. Someone could have ripped them off. Or could have been born that way."

MOA score: 6

"Look at this way and could be an ant with no back end. Someone cut off the back end of the ant . . . legs were torn off."

MOA score: 6

Card IV.
"Looks like a squished rat. Looks like someone ran a truck over it. All splattered."

MOA score: 6

Card VI.
"Looks like . . . could be a cat that was dissected . . . can see the parts kind of hanging there."

MOA score: 6

Card X.
"Could be a hippopotamus . . . has mouth wide open and could be eating those animals there and there."

MOA score: 6

Highest MOA score: 6
Lowest MOA score: 6
Mean MOA score: 6
Mode MOA score: 6

184

In the follow-up disposition conference with the mother, school personnel, and newest therapist, the psychologist shared impressions and concerns relating to the need to reconsider and alter the treatment direction based on Michael's faltering behavioral adjustment at home and his marginal adaptation at school. Referral for a residential placement was the primary recommendation. This was based in part on psychological test material highlighting prominent and consistent impairment, distortions, and highly compromised object representations mirrored by his erratic, unpredictable, and increasingly troubled behavioral adjustment, especially in the home setting. The SCORS and MOA material suggested a more aggressive and integrated therapeutic course was indicated. His mother, despite her good intentions, appeared increasingly unable to provide containment, structure, and an adequate environment to parent her son. Michael required a setting that would enable him to quell his acting out and begin to experience and internalize stability, predictability, and consistency. Of paramount concern was the fact that he had demonstrated recent serious loss of impulse control (e.g., threatening his stepfather with a baseball bat) and also voiced intrapunitive ideation (i.e., suicidal and self-destructive thoughts).

SUMMARY

This chapter was designed to illustrate two points relating to assessment and treatment. First, with respect to both of these adolescents, the initial assessment of object representations informs and advises clinicians as to how differences in the content and structure of object representations dictate the most appropriate type and subsequent level of therapeutic intervention. Second, object representation measures provide the clinician with a sense of how effective therapeutic interventions have been. This is reflected by examining measures demonstrating the modification of how adolescents view themselves and others—that is, how their object representations were altered and modified.

In the first case, that involving Tim, the nature of the therapeutic treatment was largely predetermined by the fact that he was in a setting emphasizing a multimodal treatment paradigm. Initial measures of object representation served to define potential treatment pitfalls as well as critical therapeutic interventions that would expedite and promote improved and more differentiated inner modifications with respect to his sense of self and others. Follow-up impressions attested to the utility of SCORS and MOA data in providing information that perceptible inner changes and alterations of this adolescent's inner object representational template had occurred following 2 years of residential treatment. These

changes were corroborated by documented improvement in clinical functioning.

In another instance, the case of Michael, there was less indication of
internal or behavioral change and the follow-up assessment is noteworthy
for highlighting ongoing concerns about this adolescent's derailed and
faltering developmental course. This provided critical information about
the urgency to reconsider the previous treatment interventions and to
alter the course of future therapeutic directions, given the results of MOA
and SCORS material, paralleled by observations and accounts of manifest
behavior. Both referenced major concerns about this young adolescent's
adjustment and the sense that aggressive and more intensive intervention
was indicated in order to address his increasingly compromised adaptation to early adolescence. Still, given obvious and warranted concerns,
object representational measures serve an important clinical function.
Directing the need to consider change in the therapeutic course, and
pointing to the need to advocate for more intensive and concerted treatment, they attest to the utility of these measures in choreographing therapeutic direction.

Object representation material also provides an important and illumi-
nating source of inner information that may hint at changes in object
relatedness. In these instances, object representation material provided
critical diagnostic and therapeutic information, cautioning the clinicians
about the need to reconsider previous treatment options and goals.

10

Concluding Observations and Remarks

In undertaking this project, I had several distinct and rather clear objectives in mind. These served to provide a sense of cohesiveness and integration that, I hope, will result in an appreciation of how the final effort reflects a tapestry, weaving aspects of theory, clinical observation, and concerns relating to object representation assessment and subsequent treatment considerations with adolescent patients.

Before proceeding with a discussion of specific objectives, a comment on the overriding goal providing the major impetus for undertaking this project seems warranted. I was greatly influenced and excited by the possibilities of introducing the tenets of object relations theory into my own immediate clinical work emphasizing psychological assessment, but I was frustrated by the paucity of research directly relating to children and adolescents. The work of Tuber (1992) and Westen (1991b) provided an introduction to empirical measures designed to capture and articulate the breadth and depth of children's and adolescents' object representations, the inner "hard drive" or template that informed and directed manifestations of object relatedness.

This led me to the attempt to utilize object representation measures, the MOA, first developed by Urist (1977), and the SCORS, which originated from the efforts of Westen and colleagues (Westen et al., 1985) in the evaluation of object relations functioning in younger children (Kelly, 1996). I was encouraged by the response of colleagues who found that these measures, employed in an idiographic approach to the consideration of TAT and Rorschach material, could offer clinical and heuristic possibilities in relation to assessment as treatment.

Wishing to expand my own knowledge and to broaden the clinical possibilities and application of both the MOA and SCORS, I embarked on the undertaking of this volume—the phenomenological assessment of object representation in normal and troubled adolescents—in the hopes of building on a clinical literature that still afforded a scant perspective on how adolescents of different ages and with varying degrees of psychological disturbance portrayed their sense of self and others on standardized projective devices. I was particularly interested in illustrating how object representation information could be transformed and translated into specific and relevant dynamic information to inform, guide, and alert clinicians regarding the treatment process (i.e., transference manifestations, level of treatment, types of therapeutic interventions, potential pitfalls).

Thus, general considerations relating to extending and applying the object representations assessment with adolescents was an overriding goal. But, as mentioned previously, this work was also directed by more specific and circumscribed objectives.

First, I made an attempt to demonstrate that object representations material (e.g., information derived from MOA and SCORS data) would provide the clinician with cogent and relevant sources of diagnostic information not readily obtainable if the primary emphasis was placed on the reliance of manifest behavior, or on material obtained from actuarial scales. The clinical material here attests to the fact that a major current taxonomy like the *DSM–IV* cannot provide more than a screening or classificatory function. In contrast, employment of object representation material opens the door for consideration that adolescents with ostensibly the same disorder may present vastly different structural–developmental panoramas vis-a-vis their sense of self and others—a personality dimension that is of concern when one considers treatment options and directions.

Second, I wanted to illustrate the differences between normal and maladjusted adolescents in order to provide the reader with a sense of how object representation is manifest in clinical versus nonclinical adolescent clients, given the dearth of studies. Object relations continue to develop and to reflect subtle linear increases through the adolescent developmental period, an exception being the SCORS dimension. It involves affect-tone and does not reflect linear change (Westen et al., 1991).

Case material provided ample testimony to the effect that younger and older adolescents who were demonstrating significant clinical dysfunction and well-documented problems with relatedness could be readily identified as having inner representational templates that mirrored their manifest dealings with their interpersonal worlds. Scrutiny of protocols revealed a close correspondence between MOA and SCORS data; these two object representational measures provided convergent indices that complemented one another and provided a cogent, reliable, and valid composite of an adolescent's representational schema of self and others.

A third objective involved taking a more in-depth look at an array of disturbed adolescents with varying clinical presentations in order to ascertain whether those with more severe developmental derailments and significantly compromised adaptation (e.g., borderline presentations, psychotic disorders) would manifest more global and primitive object representation functioning, or if their functioning would reflect unevenness, variability, and shifts tied to specific activating and arousing situations (Westen, 1991b).

A fourth objective involved the consideration of how actual events in childhood have a causal impact on the formation of psychological structures, in this case, object representations. I attempted to look more closely at three adolescent situations remarkable for multiple and chronic noxious incidents emphasizing extreme environmental stress and abuse, that is, chronic complex trauma (Terr, 1991). Manifestations of object representation and clinical functioning were evaluated in order to portray the varied and different sequelae and developmental passages related to trauma experiences in both the preoedipal and latency years.

A fifth objective involved illustrating how object representational material could be translated and transformed into relevant and informative caveats that would inform, direct, and guide clinicians in their initial treatment formulations and subsequent therapeutic endeavors. Object representation information provided the clinician with the type of representational changes that needed to eventuate if the adolescent was to progress to higher developmental levels of functioning (Blatt & Lerner, 1983b).

Material from both the MOA and the SCORS was shown to be vital in alerting clinicians to the expected and likely parameters of relatedness that would transpire in the therapeutic arena—for example, nuances of transference phenomena, the nature of the relatedness, and the appropriate level and mode of therapy given self and object representational differentiation. This information was also seen as critical in prognostications about the ability of an adolescent to tolerate different types of therapeutic experiences. In several instances, certain adolescents were available for a psychotherapeutic venture emphasizing an introspective, insight-oriented approach. In other cases, a treatment experience that placed a premium on the development of corrective and reparative relatedness comprised the initial, enduring, and essential task of the therapeutic work.

Object representation material was also shown to be a sensitive and valid indicator related to therapeutic changes in the cases of two adolescents. In one instance, more adaptive and mature patterns of intra- and intersubjective relatedness was the outgrowth of concerted multimodal therapeutic interventions, with this being amply endorsed by testimony as to substantive improvement in clinical functioning. In another instance, the sequelae was not as positive, as the adolescent continued to manifest continued signs of faltering adjustment. Here, object representation material still served a vital function—alerting and advising for more immediate and aggressive treatment interventions in order to stem the tide of an escalating clinical course.

The completion of a book marks an ending of sorts, but it heralds a beginning, as well. Serving to provide and convey the author's message, observations, and thoughts in relation to a particular topic or concern, it also provides a springboard or catalyst for others. I find myself musing about a myriad of possible clinical and research paths that could follow in relation to the assessment and therapeutic arenas, and my hope is that this work will be the impetus for stimulating curiosity in my colleagues.

Some specific closing thoughts and future directions worth considering come to mind. With respect to the assessment of representations and relatedness, it will be important to continue with investigations of how adolescents with diverse forms of psychopathology arrive at developmental positions that portray derailed and uneven representations and parallel problems with relatedness. Do preoedipal, adverse environmental situations impact and influence representations to the same degree as do later incidents of trauma and environmental stress occurring in the postoedipal years? Westen's (1990) research suggests this is probably the case, but there is certainly the need for future investigators to accord continued attention to such issues in order to evaluate how specific environmental events and situations impact on representations and subsequent relatedness.

Intriguing possibilities are suggested by considering the concomitant evaluation of the parents of adolescents who manifest various patterns of impaired and disordered self and object representations. Would the parents of an adolescent with more pronounced personality derailment (e.g., borderline state) show similar indication of uneven, disorganized, and impaired object representation? In another instance offering possible preventive implications, it would be worth considering how an adolescent mother's self and other representations provide cogent information that might potentially inform clinicians about the likelihood of attachment problems, as well as presaging the possibilty that parent–child relatedness could be compromised at a later developmental point. Some work (Levine & Tuber, 1993) was conducted in this area involving object representational assessment measures other than the MOA or SCORS and opportunities for future work are manifold.

In the treatment domain, it would be interesting and informative to continue with efforts to document enduring object representational changes as a function of psychological interventions, that parallel significant alterations in clinical functioning. Is it possible to witness significant representational change as a function of short-term, individual psychotherapy? Would different types of psychological modalities (i.e., group psychotherapy or differing family therapy treatments) impact representations? Would other interventions impact and produce shifts in representational and relational functioning—psychopharmacological, environmental changes, such as residential placement?

The reader might think of many other questions and lingering concerns, suggesting that new paths and directions need to be traversed. I hope this effort attested to the validity and clinical utility of assessment approaches incorporating an idiographic object relations perspective to the evaluation and consideration of projective data involving adolescents.

References

Abraham, P. P., Lepisto, B. L., Lewis, M. G., Schultz, L., & Finkelberg, S. (1994). An outcome study: Changes in Rorschach variables of adolescents in residential treatment. *Journal of Personality Assessment, 62,* 505–514.

Achenbach, T. M., & Edelbrock, C. S. (1983). *Manual for the Child Behavior Checklist and Revised Child Behavior Profile.* Burlington: University of Vermont, Department of Psychiatry.

Acklin, M. W. (1995). Integrative Rorschach interpretation. *Journal of Personality Assessment, 64,* 235–238.

Allen, S. N. (1994). Psychological assessment of posttraumatic stress disorder. *Psychiatric Clinics of North America, 17,* 327–349.

Alpher, V., Perfetto, G., Henry, W., & Strupp, H. (1990). The relationship between the Rorschach and assessment of the capacity to engage in short-term dynamic psychotherapy. *Psychotherapy, 27,* 224–229.

American Psychiatric Association. (1994). *Diagnostic and statistical manual of mental disorders* (4th ed.). Washington, DC: Author.

Ames, L. B., Metraux, R. W., & Walker, R. N. (1971). *Adolescent Rorschach responses: Developmental trends from ten to sixteen.* New York: Brunner/Mazel.

Appelbaum, S. A. (1990). The relationship between assessment and psychotherapy. *Journal of Personality Assessment, 54,* 791–801.

Aronow, E., Reznikoff, M., & Moreland, K. L. (1995). The Rorschach: Projective technique or psychometric test? *Journal of Personality Assessment, 64,* 213–228.

Bagley, C., & Ramsey, R. (1985). Disrupted childhood and vulnerability to sexual abuse: Long term sequels with implications for counseling. *Journal of Social Work and Human Sexuality, 4,* 33–47.

Baron-Cohen, S. (1993). Children's theories of mind: Where would we be without the intentional stance? In M. L. Rutter & D. F. Hay (Eds.), *Development through life: A handbook for clinicians* (pp. 59–82). Oxford, England: Blackwell.

Beardslee, W. R., Schultz, L. H., & Selman, R. L. (1987). Level of social–cognitive development, adaptive functioning, and *DSM–III* diagnoses in adolescent offspring of parents with affective disorders: Implications of the development of capacity for mutuality. *Developmental Psychology, 23,* 807–815.

Bellak, L. (1993). *The T.A.T., C.A.T., and S.A.T. in clinical use* (5th ed.). Boston: Allyn & Bacon.

Bentivegna, S. W., Ward, L. B., & Bentivegna, N. P. (1985). Study of a diagnostic profile of the borderline syndrome in childhood and trends on treatment outcome. *Child Psychiatry and Human Development, 15*, 198–205.

Beres, D., & Joseph, E. (1970). The concept of mental representation in psychoanalysis. *International Journal of Psycho-Analysis, 51*, 1–9.

Berg, M. (1982). Psychological testing of the borderline patient: A guide for therapeutic action. *American Journal of Psychotherapy, 36*, 536–546.

Berg, M. (1986). Diagnostic use of the Rorschach with adolescents. In A. I. Rabin (Ed.), *Projective techniques for adolescents and children* (pp. 111–141). New York: Springer.

Blatt, S. J. (1990). Interpersonal relatedness and self-definition: Two personality configurations and their implications for psychopathology and psychotherapy. In J. L. Singer (Ed.), *Repression and dissociation: Implication for personality theory, psychotherapy & health* (pp. 299–335). Chicago: University of Chicago Press.

Blatt, S. J. (1991). A cognitive morphology of psychopathology. *Journal of Nervous and Mental Disease, 179*, 449–458.

Blatt, S. J. (1995). The destructiveness of perfectionism: Implications for the treatment of depression. *American Psychologist, 50*, 1003–1020.

Blatt, S. J., Brenneis, B., Schimek, J. G., & Glick, M. (1976). Normal development and psychopathological impairment of the concept of the object on the Rorschach. *Journal of Abnormal Psychology, 85*, 364–373.

Blatt, S. J., Chevron, E. S., Quinlan, D. M., & Wein, S. (1975). *The assessment of qualitative and structural dimensions of object representation in spontaneous description of significant figures.* Unpublished manuscript, Yale University.

Blatt, S. J., & Felsen, I. (1993). "Different kinds of folks may need different kinds of strokes": The effect of patients' characteristics on therapeutic process and outcome. *Psychotherapy Research, 3*, 245–259.

Blatt, S. J., & Ford, R. Q. (1994). *Therapeutic change: An object relations perspective.* New York: Plenum.

Blatt, S. J., Ford, R. Q., Berman, W., Cook, B., & Meyer, R. (1988). The assessment of therapeutic change in schizophrenic and borderline young adults. *Psychoanalytic Psychology, 5*, 127–158.

Blatt, S. J., & Lerner, H. D. (1983a). Investigations in the psychoanalytic theory of object relations and object representation. In J. Masling (Ed.), *Empirical studies of psychoanalytic theories* (pp. 189–249). Hillsdale, NJ: The Analytic Press.

Blatt, S. J., & Lerner, H. D. (1983b). The psychological assessment of object representation. *Journal of Personality Assessment, 47*, 7–28.

Blatt, S. J., & Ritzler, B. A. (1974). Thought disorder and boundary disturbance in psychosis. *Journal of Consulting and Clinical Psychology, 42*, 370–381.

Blatt, S. J., & Shichman, S. (1983). Two primary configurations of psychopathology. *Psychoanalysis and Contemporary Thought, 6*, 187–254.

Blatt, S. J., Tuber, S., & Auerbach, J. (1990). Representation of interpersonal interactions on the Rorschach and level of psychopathology. *Journal of Personality Assessment, 54*, 711–728.

Blatt, S. J., & Wild, C. M. (1976). *Schizophrenia: A developmental analysis.* New York: Academic Press.

Blatt, S. J., Wiseman, H., Prince-Gibson, E., & Gatt, G. (1991). Object representations and change in clinical functioning. *Psychotherapy, 28*, 273–283.

Bleiberg, E. (1984). Narcissistic disorders in children. *Bulletin of the Menninger Clinic, 48*, 501–517.

Bleiberg, E. (1991). Mood disorders in children and adolescents. *Bulletin of the Menninger Clinic, 55*, 182–204.

Blos, P. (1967). The second individuation process of adolescence. *The Psychoanalytic Study of the Child, 22,* 162–186.

Bowlby, J. (1969). *Attachment and loss* (Vol. 1: Attachment). New York: Basic Books.

Briere, J., & Runtz, M. (1988). Symptomatology associated with childhood sexual victimization in a nonclinical adult sample. *Child Abuse and Neglect, 12,* 51–59.

Browne, A., & Finkelhor, D. (1986). Impact of child sexual abuse: A review of the research. *Psychological Bulletin, 99,* 66–77.

Bruchkowsky, M. (1989). *Affect and cognition in the development of empathy in middle childhood.* Unpublished manuscript. Toronto, Ontario, University of Toronto.

Bryer, J. B., Nelson, B. A., Miller, J. B., & Krol, P. A. (1987). Childhood sexual and physical abuse as factors in adult psychiatric illness. *American Journal of Psychiatry, 144,* 1426–1430.

Bryt, A. (1979). Developmental tasks in adolescence. *Adolescent Psychiatry, 7,* 136–146.

Campbell, M., & Cueva, J. E. (1995). Psychopharmacology in child and adolescent psychiatry: A review of the past seven years. Part II. *Journal of the American Academy of Child and Adolescent Psychiatry, 34,* 1262–1272.

Carlson, G. (1979). Lithium carbonate use in adolescents: Clinical indications and management. *Adolescent Psychiatry, 7,* 410–418.

Case, R. (1988). The whole child: Toward an integrated view of young children's cognitive, social, and emotional development. In A. D. Pellegrini (Ed.), *Psychological basis for early education* (pp. 155–184). New York: Wiley.

Chess, S., & Thomas, A. (1984). *Origins and evolutions of behavior disorders: From infancy to early adulthood.* New York: Brunner/Mazel.

Chethik, M. (1986). Levels of borderline functioning in children: Etiological and treatment considerations. *American Journal of Orthopsychiatry, 56,* 110–119.

Cicchetti, D., & Beeghly, M. (1987). Symbolic development in maltreated youngsters: An organizational perspective. In D. Cicchetti & M. Beeghly (Eds.), *Atypical symbolic development* (pp. 47–67). San Francisco: Jossey-Bass.

Coates, S., & Tuber, S. (1988). The representation of object relations in the Rorschachs of extremely feminine boys. In H. Lerner & P. Lerner (Eds.), *Primitive mental states on the Rorschach* (pp. 647–654). New York: International Universities Press.

Cohen, H., & Weil, G. R. (1972). *Tasks of emotional development.* Lexington, MA: Lexington Books.

Colby, A., & Kohlberg, L. (1987). *The measurement of moral judgement* (Vol. 1: Theoretical foundations and research validation). Cambridge, England: Cambridge University Press.

Conners, C. K. (1982). Parent and teacher rating forms for the assessment of hyperkinesis in children. In P. A. Keller & L. G. Ritt (Eds.), *Innovations in clinical practice: A source book* (Vol. 1, pp. 302–312). Sarasota, FL: Professional Research Exchange, Inc.

Conte, J. R., & Schuerman, J. R. (1988). The effects of sexual abuse on children: A multidimensional view. In G. Wyatt & G. Powell (Eds.), *Lasting effects of child sexual abuse* (pp. 157–169). Beverly Hills, CA: Sage.

Curry, J. F., & Thompson, R. J. (1979). The utility of behavior checklist ratings in differentiating developmentally disabled from psychiatrically referred children. *Journal of Pediatric Psychology, 4,* 345–352.

Damon, W. (1975). Early conceptions of positive justice as related to the development of logical operations. *Child Development, 46,* 301–312.

Damon, W. (1981). Exploring children's social cognition on two fronts. In J. Flavell & L. Ross (Eds.), *Social cognitive development: Frontiers and possible futures* (pp. 13–29). New York: Cambridge University Press.

Downey, G., & Walker, E. (1989). Social cognition and adjustment in children at risk for psychopathology. *Developmental Psychology, 25,* 835–845.

Dunn, J. (1987). Understanding feelings: The early stages. In J. Bruner & H. Haste (Eds.), *Making sense: The child's construction of the world* (pp. 26–40). London: Methuen.

Dunn, J., & Munn, P. (1987). The development of justification in disputes with mother and sibling. *Developmental Psychology, 23,* 791–798.

Eagan, J., & Kernberg, P. (1984). Pathologic narcissism in childhood. *Journal of the American Psychoanalytic Association, 32,* 39–62.

Elkind, D. (1985). Cognitive development and adolescent disabilities. *Journal of Adolescent Health Care, 6,* 84–89.

Erikson, E. H. (1959). Identity and the life cycle. *Psychological Issues, 1,* 50–100.

Eth, S., & Pynoss, R. S. (Eds.). (1985). *Post-traumatic stress disorder in children.* Washington, DC: American Psychiatric Press, Inc.

Exner, J. E. (1978). *The Rorschach: A comprehensive system* (Vol. 2: Current research and advanced interpretation). New York: Wiley.

Exner, J. E., & Andronikov-Sanglade, A. (1992). Rorschach changes following brief and short-term therapy. *Journal of Personality Assessment, 59,* 59–71.

Exner, J. E., & Weiner, I. B. (1992). *The Rorschach: A comprehensive system* (Vol. 3: Assessment of children and adolescents). New York: Wiley.

Exner, J. E., & Weiner, I. B. (1995). *The Rorschach: A comprehensive system* (Vol. 3: Assessment of children and adolescents; 2nd ed.). New York: Wiley.

Federn, P. (1952). *Ego psychology and the psychoses.* New York: Basic Books.

Freedenfeld, R. N., Ornduff, S. R., & Kelsey, R. M. (1995). Object relations and physical abuse: A TAT analysis. *Journal of Personality Assessment, 64,* 552–568.

Freud, A. (1963). The concept of developmental lines. *Psychoanalytic Study of the Child, 18,* 245–265.

Freud, A. (1965). *Normality and pathology in childhood.* New York: International Universities Press, Inc.

Friedrich, W. N. (1988). Behavior problems in sexually abused children: An adaptational perspective. In G. E. Wyatt & G. J. Powell (Eds.), *Lasting effects of child sexual abuse* (pp. 171–192). Beverly Hills: Sage.

Friedrich, W. N., Urquisa, A. J., & Beilke, R. (1986). Behavior problems in sexually abused young children. *Journal of Pediatric Psychology, 11,* 47–57.

Gacano, C., & Meloy, J. R. (1994). *The Rorschach assessment of aggressive and psychopathic personalities.* Hillsdale, NJ: Lawrence Erlbaum Associates.

Gardner, G. (1960). Adjustment difficulties during adolescence. In M. Stuart & S. P. Prugh (Eds.), *The healthy child: His physical, psychological and social development* (pp. 165–194). Cambridge, MA: Harvard University Press.

Gerstle, R. M., Geary, D. C., Himelstein, P., & Reller-Geary, L. (1988). Rorschach predictors of therapeutic outcome for inpatient treatment of children: A proactive study. *Journal of Clinical Psychology 44,* 277–280.

Gilligan, C. (1982). *In a different voice: Psychological theory and women's development.* Cambridge, MA: Harvard University Press.

Goddard, R., & Tuber, S. (1989). Boyhood separation anxiety disorder. *Journal of Personality Assessment, 53,* 239–252.

Goldberg, E. H. (1989). Severity of depression and developmental levels of functioning in eight sixteen-year-old girls. *American Journal of Orthopsychiatry, 59,* 167–178.

Gomes-Schwartz, B., Horowitz, J. M., & Sauzier, M. (1985). Severity of emotional distress among sexually abused pre-school, school-age, and adolescent children. *Hospital and Community Psychiatry, 36,* 503–508.

Greco, C. M., & Cornell, D. G. (1992). Rorschach object relations of adolescents who committed homocide. *Journal of Personality Assessment, 59,* 574–583.

Greenberg, J., & Mitchell, S. (1983). *Object relations in psychoanalytical theory.* Cambridge, MA: Harvard University Press.

Gruen, R. J., & Blatt, S. J. (1990). Changes in self and object representation during long-term dynamically oriented treatment. *Psychoanalytic Psychology, 1,* 399–422.

Harder, D., Greenwald, D., Wechsler, S., & Ritzler, B. (1984). The Urist Rorschach Mutuality of Autonomy scale as an indicator of psychopathology. *Journal of Clinical Psychology, 40,* 1078–1083.

Hart, B., & Hilton, S. (1988). Dimensions of personality organization as predictors of teenage pregnancy risk. *Journal of Personality Assessment, 52,* 116–132.

Harter, S. (1977). A cognitive–developmental approach to children's expression of conflicting feelings and a technique to facilitate such expression in play therapy. *Journal of Consulting and Clinical Psychology, 45,* 417–432.

Hartmann, H. (1958). *Ego psychology and the problem of adaptation.* New York: International Universities Press, Inc.

Hauser, S. T., Borman, E. H., Powers, S. I., Jacobson, A. H., & Noam, G. G. (1990). Paths of adolescent ego development: Links with family life and individual adjustment. *Psychiatric Clinics of North America, 13,* 489–509.

Hay, D. F. (1994). Prosocial development. *Journal of Child Psychology and Psychiatry, 35,* 29–71.

Hayes, S. N. (1993). Treatment implications of psychological assessment. *Psychological Assessment, 5,* 251–253.

Herjanic, B., & Reich, W. (1982). Development of a structured psychiatric interview for children: Agreement between child and parent on individual symptoms. *Journal of Abnormal Child Psychology 10,* 307–324.

Herman, J. L. (1992). *Trauma and recovery.* New York: Basic Books.

Herman, J. L. (1993). Sequelae of prolonged and repeated trauma: Evidence for a complex posttraumatic syndrome (DESNOS). In J. R. T. Davidson & E. B. Foa (Eds.), *Posttraumatic stress disorder: DSM–IV and beyond* (pp. 213–228). Washington, DC: American Psychiatric Press, Inc.

Herman, J. L., Perry, J. C., & van der Kolk, B. A. (1989). Childhood trauma in borderline personality disorder. *American Journal of Psychiatry, 146,* 490–495.

Hodges, K., McKnew, D., Cytryn, L., Stern, L., & Kline, J. (1982). The Child Assessment Schedule (CAS) diagnostic interview: A report on reliability and validity. *Journal of the American Academy of Child and Adolescent Psychiatry, 21,* 468–473.

Hoffman, M. E. (1984). Interaction of affect and cognition in empathy. In C. Izard, J. Kagan, & R. Zajonic (Eds.), *Emotions, cognition and behavior* (pp. 103–131). Cambridge, England: Cambridge University Press.

Holaday, M., Armsworth, M., Swank, P., & Vincent, K. (1992). Rorschach responding in traumatized children and adolescents. *Journal of Traumatic Stress, 5,* 119–129.

Holaday, M., & Whittenberg, T. (1994). Rorschach responding in children and adolescents who have been severely burned. *Journal of Personality Assessment, 62,* 269–279.

Holt, R. (1975). The past and future of ego psychology. *Psychoanalytic Quarterly, 44,* 500–576.

Horner, A. (1979). *Object relations and the developing ego in therapy.* New York: Aronson.

Horowitz, M. (1977). Structure of processes of change. In M. Horowitz (Ed.), *Hysterical personality.* New York: Aronson.

Horowitz, M. J. (1989). *Nuances of technique in dynamic psychotherapy* (pp. 332–399). Northvale, NJ: Aronson.

Ipp, H. (1986). *Object relations of feminine boys: A Rorschach assessment.* Unpublished doctoral dissertation, York University, Toronto, Canada. DAI-B 47/08, P. 3525, Feb., 1987.

Jacobson, E. (1964). *The self and the object world.* New York: International Universities Press.

Kavanaugh, G. (1985). Changes in patients object representations during psychoanalysis and psychoanalytic therapy. *Bulletin of the Menninger Clinic, 49,* 546–564.

Kelly, F. D. (1986). Assessment of the borderline adolescent: Psychological measures of defensive structure and object representation. *Journal of Child and Adolescent Psychotherapy, 3,* 199–206.

Kelly, F. D. (1995). *The psychological sequelae of chronic, complex trauma in latency age children: Rorschach indices.* Unpublished manuscript.

Kelly, F. D. (1996). *Object relations assessment in younger children: Rorschach and TAT measures*. Springfield, IL: Thomas.

Kernberg, O. (1966). Structural derivatives of object relationships. *International Journal of Psychoanalysis, 47*, 236–253.

Kernberg, O. (1967). Borderline personality organization. *Journal of the American Psychoanalytic Association, 15*, 641–685.

Kernberg, O. (1975). *Borderline conditions and pathological narcissism*. New York: Aronson.

Kernberg, P. (1989). Narcissistic personality disorder in childhood. *Psychiatric Clinics of North America, 12*, 671–695.

Kissen, M. (1986). *Assessing object relations phenomena*. Madison, CT: International Universities Press.

Kleiger, J. H. (1992). A conceptual critique of the EA:es comparison in the Comprehensive Rorschach System. *Psychological Assessment, 4*, 288–296.

Klein, M. (1948). *Contributions to psychoanalysis, 1921–1945*. London: Hogarth.

Klein, M. (1952). The mutual influences in the development of ego and id. *The Psychoanalytic Study of the Child, 7*, 51–53.

Klein, G. (1976). *Psychoanalytic theory*. New York: International Universities Press, Inc.

Kocan, M. (1991). Changes in self and object representation as revealed by reflection response. *Journal of Personality Assessment, 56*, 35–44.

Kohut, H. (1966). Forms and transformations of narcissism. *Journal of the American Psychiatric Association, 14*, 243–272.

Kohut, H. (1968). The psychoanalytic treatment of narcissistic personality disorders: Outline of a systematic approach. *The Psychoanalytic Study of the Child, 23*, 86–113.

Kohut, H. (1971). *The analysis of the self*. New York: International Universities Press, Inc.

Kohut, H. (1977). *The restoration of the self*. New York: International Universities Press, Inc.

Kohut, H. (1984). The role of empathy in psychoanalytic cure. In A. Goldberg & P. Stepansky (Eds.), *How does analysis cure?* (pp. 172–191). Chicago: University of Chicago Press.

Korenblum, M. (1993). Diagnostic difficulties in adolescent psychiatry: Where have we been and where are we going? *Adolescent Psychiatry, 19*, 58–76.

Krohn, A. (1972). *Levels of object representation in manifest dreams and projective tests*. Unpublished doctoral dissertation, University of Michigan.

Krohn, A., & Mayman, M. (1974). Object representation in dreams and projective tests: A construct validation study. *Bulletin of the Menninger Clinic, 38*, 445–466. DAI-B 33/11, P. 5520, May, 1973.

Krystal, H. (1978). Trauma and affects. *Psychoanalytic Study of the Child, 33*, 81–116.

Kwawer, J. S., Lerner, H. D., Lerner, P. M., & Sugarman, A. (1980). *Borderline phenomena and the Rorschach test*. New York: International Universities Press.

LaBarbera, J. D., & Cornsweet, C. (1985). Rorschach predictors of therapeutic outcome in a child psychiatric inpatient service. *Journal of Personality Assessment, 49*, 120–124.

Lamia, M. C. (1982). The revision of object representations in adolescent males. In S. C. Feinstein (Ed.), *Adolescent Psychiatry, 10*, 199–207.

Leifer, M., Shapiro, J., Martone, M., & Kassem, L. (1991). Rorschach assessment of psychological functioning in sexually abused girls. *Journal of Personality Assessment, 56*, 14–28.

Lerner, H. D. (1986). Object representation and the Rorschach. In M. Kissen (Ed.), *Assessing object relations phenomena* (pp. 127–142). Madison, CT: International Universities Press, Inc.

Lerner, P. (1992). Toward an experiential psychoanalytic approach to the Rorschach. *Bulletin of the Menninger Clinic, 56*, 451–464.

Lerner, H. D., & Lerner, P. M. (1988). *Primitive mental states and the Rorschach*. Madison, CT: International Universities Press, Inc.

Lerner, H. D., & St. Peter, S. (1984). Patterns of object relations in neurotic, borderline and schizophrenic patients. *Psychiatry, 47*, 77–92.

Levine, L. V., & Tuber, S. B. (1993). Measures of mental representation: Clinical and theoretical considerations. *Bulletin of the Menninger Clinic, 57*, 69–87.

Lofgren, D. P., Bemporad, J., King, J., Lindem, K., & O'Driscoll, G. (1991). A prospective follow-up study of so-called borderline children. *American Journal of Psychiatry, 148*, 1541–1547.

Ludolph, P., Westen, D., Misle, B., Jackson, A., Wixom, J., & Wiss, F. C. (1990). The borderline diagnosis in adolescence: Symptoms and developmental history. *American Journal of Psychiatry, 147*, 470–476.

Lustman, J. (1977). On splitting. *The Psychoanalytic Study of the Child, 32*, 119–154.

Lutz, S. (1992). In search of outcomes. *Modern Healthcare*, 24–29.

Mahler, M. (1963). Thoughts about development and individuation. *The Psychoanalytic Study of the Child, 18*, 307–314.

Mahler, M. (1974). Symbiosis and individuation. *The Psychoanalytic Study of the Child, 29*, 89–106.

Mahler, M., Pine, F., & Bergman, A. (1975). *The psychological birth of the human infant: Symbiosis and individuation*. New York: Basic Books.

Mannarino, A., & Cohen, J. (1986). A clinical–demographic study of sexually abused children. *Child Abuse and Neglect, 10*, 17–23.

Masterson, J. F. (1976). *Psychotherapy of the borderline adult: A developmental approach*. New York: Brunner/Mazel.

Masterson, J. F., Baiardi, J., Fischer, R., & Orcutt, C. (1992). Psychotherapy of borderline and narcissistic disorders in the adolescent: Establishing a therapeutic alliance. *Adolescent Psychiatry, 18*, 3–25.

Mayman, M. (1963). Psychoanalytic study of self-organization with psychological tests. In B. T. Wigdor (Ed.), *Recent advances in the study of behavior change: Proceedings of the academic assembly on clinical psychology* (pp. 97–111). Montreal: McGill University Press.

Mayman, M. (1967). Object representation and object relationships in Rorschach responses. *Journal of Projective Techniques and Personality Assessment, 31*, 17–24.

Mayman, M. (1968). Early memories and character structure. *Journal of Projective Techniques and Personality Assessment, 32*, 303–316.

Mayman, M. (1976). Psychoanalytic theory in retrospect and prospect. *Bulletin of the Menninger Clinic, 40*, 199–210.

Mayman, M. (1977). A multi-dimensional view of the Rorschach movement response. In M. Rickers-Ovsiankina (Ed.), *Rorschach psychology* (pp. 229–250). New York: Robert E. Krieger.

Mayman, M., & Krohn, A. (1975). Developments in the use of projective tests in psychotherapy outcome research. In I. Waskow & M. Parloff (Eds.), *Psychotherapy change measures* (pp. 151–169). Washington, DC: National Institute of Mental Health.

Mayman, M., & Ryan, E. (1972). *Level and quality of object relationships: A scale applicable to overt behavior and to projective test data*. Unpublished manuscript, Psychology Department, University of Michigan.

McNally, R. (1991). Assessment of post-traumatic stress disorder in children. *Psychological Assessment, 48*, 531–537.

Meloy, J. R., & Singer, J. (1991). A psychoanalytic view of the Rorschach Comprehensive System "Special Scores." *Journal Personality Assessment, 56*, 202–217.

Meyer, J., & Tuber, S. (1989). Intrapsychic and behavioral correlates of the phenomena of imaginary companions in young children. *Psychoanalytic Psychology, 6*, 151–168.

Modell, A. H. (1976). The holding environment and the therapeutic action of psychoanalysis. *Journal of the Psychoanalytic Association, 24*, 285–308.

Monane, M., Leichter, D., & Otnow Lewis, D. (1984). Physical abuse in psychiatrically hospitalized children and adolescents. *Journal of the American Academy of Child Psychiatry, 23*, 653–659.

Noam, G. G., & Houlihan, J. (1990). Developmental dimensions of DSM–III diagnoses in adolescent psychiatric patients. *American Journal of Orthopsychiatry, 60*, 371–377.

Ogata, S. N., Silk, K. R., Goodrich, S., Lohr, N. E., Westen, D., & Hill, E. (1990). Childhood abuse and clinical symptoms in borderline patients. *American Journal of Psychiatry, 147*, 1008–1013.

Ornduff, S. R., Freedenfeld, R. N., Kelsey, R., & Critelli, J. (1994). Object relations of sexually abused female subjects: A TAT analysis. *Journal of Personality Assessment, 63*, 223–238.

Ornstein, A. (1981). Self-pathology in childhood: Developmental and clinical considerations. *Psychiatric Clinics of North America, 4*, 435–454.

Palombo, J. (1990). The cohesive self, the nuclear self, and development in late adolescence. *Adolescent Psychiatry, 17*, 338–359.

Parmer, J. C. (1991). Bulimia and object relations: MMPI and Rorschach variables. *Journal of Personality Assessment, 56*, 266–276.

Perry, S., Cooper, A., & Michels, R. (1987). The psychodynamic formulation: Its purpose, structure and clinical application. *American Journal of Psychiatry, 144*, 543–550.

Petti, T. A., & Vela, R. M. (1990). Borderline disorders of childhood: An overview. *Journal of the American Academy of Child and Adolescent Psychiatry, 29*, 327–337.

Pfeiffer, S. I., & Strzelecki, S. C. (1990). Inpatient psychiatric treatment of children and adolescents: A review of outcome studies. *Journal of the American Academy of Child and Adolescent Psychiatry, 29*, 847–853.

Piaget, J. (1954). *The construction of reality in the child*. New York: Basic Books.

Piaget, J., & Inhelder, B. (1969). *The psychology of the child*. London: Routledge.

Pine, F. (1974). On the concept "borderline" in children. *The Psychoanalytic Study of the Child, 29*, 341–368.

Pine, F. (1988). The four psychologies of psychoanalysis and their place in clinical work. *Journal of the American Psychoanalytic Association, 36*, 315–340.

Pine, F. (1990). *Drive, ego, object and self: A synthesis for clinical work*. New York: Basic Books.

Pistole, D., & Ornduff, S. R. (1994). TAT assessment of sexually abused girls: An analysis of manifest content. *Journal of Personality Assessment, 63*, 211–222.

Puig-Antich, J., & Tabrizi, M. A. (1983). The clinical assessment of current depressive episodes in children and adolescents: Interviews with parents and children. In D. P. Cantwell & G. A. Carlson (Eds.), *Affective disorders in childhood and adolescence: An update* (pp. 157–180). New York: Spectrum.

Rapaport, D., Gill, M., & Schafer, R. (1968). *Diagnostic psychological testing*. New York: International Universities Press, Inc.

Rinsley, D. B. (1968). Economic aspects of object relations. *International Journal of Psycho-Analysis, 49*, 38–48.

Rinsley, D. B. (1980). Diagnosis and treatment of borderline and narcissistic children and adolescents. *Bulletin of the Menninger Clinic, 44*, 147–170.

Rogeness, G. A., Hernandez, J. M., Macedo, C. A., Amrung, S. A., & Hoppe, S. K. (1986). Near-zero plasma dopamine–B–hydroxylase and conduct disorder in emotionally disturbed boys. *Journal of the American Academy of Child and Adolescent Psychiatry, 25*, 521–527.

Rubenstein, A. H. (1980). The adolescent with borderline personality organization: Developmental issues, diagnostic considerations, and treatment. In J. S. Kwawer, H. Lerner, P. Lerner, & A. Sugarman (Eds.), *Borderline phenomena and the Rorschach test* (pp. 441–447). New York: International Universities Press.

Rutter, M. (1989). Pathways from childhood to adult life. *Journal of Child Psychology and Psychiatry, 30*, 23–53.

Ryan, E. R. (1973). *The capacity of the patient to enter an elementary therapeutic relationship in the initial psychotherapeutic interview.* Unpublished doctoral dissertation, University of Michigan. DAI-B 35/01, P.522, July, 1974.

Ryan, R. M., Avery, R. R., & Grolnick, W. S. (1985). A Rorschach assessment of children's mutuality of autonomy. *Journal of Personality Assessment, 49,* 6–12.

Ryan, N. D., Meyer, V., Dachille, S., Mazzie, D., & Puig-Antich, J. (1988). Lithium antidepressant augmentation in TCA-refractory depression in adolescents. *Journal of the American Academy of Child and Adolescent Psychiatry, 27,* 371–376.

Sandler, J. (1992). Comments on the self and its objects. *Adolescent Psychiatry, 18,* 395–406.

Sandler, J., & Rosenblatt, B. (1962). The concept of the representational world. *The Psychoanalytic Study of the Child, 17,* 128–145.

Schafer, R. (1954). *Psychoanalytic interpretation in Rorschach testing.* New York: Grune & Stratton.

Schafer, R. (1968). *Aspects of internalization.* New York: International Universities Press, Inc.

Schwab-Stone, M., Towbin, K. E., & Tarnoff, G. M. (1991). Systems of classification: *ICD–10, DSM–III–R,* and *DSM–IV.* In M. Lewis (Ed.), *Child and adolescent psychiatry: A comprehensive textbook* (pp. 422–434). Baltimore: Williams & Wilkins.

Selman, R. L. (1980). *The growth of interpersonal understanding: Developmental and clinical analysis.* New York: Academic Press.

Shapiro, E. R. (1982). The holding environment and family therapy with acting-out adolescents. *International Journal of Psychoanalytic Psychotherapy, 9,* 209–231.

Shapiro, T. (1989). The psychodynamic formulation in child and adolescent psychiatry. *Journal of the American Academy of Child and Adolescent Psychiatry, 28,* 675–680.

Shapiro, T., & Esman, A. (1985). Psychotherapy with children and adolescents: Still relevant in the 1980's. *Psychiatric Clinics of North America, 8,* 909–921.

Spear, W. E., & Sugarman, A. (1984). Dimensions of internalized object relations in borderline and schizophrenic patients. *Psychoanalytic Psychology, 1,* 113–129.

Stricker, G., & Healey, B. (1990). Projective assessment of object relations: A review of the empirical literature. *Journal of Consulting and Clinical Psychology, 2,* 219–230.

Sugarman, A. (1986). Self-experience and reality testing: Synthesis of an object relations and ego psychological model on the Rorschach. In M. Kissen (Ed.), *Assessing object relations phenomena* (pp. 51–75). Madison, CT: International Universities Press, Inc.

Sugarman, A., Bloom-Feshbach, S., & Bloom-Feshbach, J. (1980). The psychological dimensions of borderline adolescents. In J. S. Kwawer, H. D. Lerner, P. M. Lerner, & A. Sugarman (Eds.), *Borderline phenomena and the Rorschach test* (pp. 469–494). New York: International Universities Press, Inc.

Sutherland, J. (1963). Object relations theory and the conceptual model of psychoanalysis. *British Journal of Medical Psychology, 36,* 109–124.

Sutherland, J. D. (1980). The British object relations theorists: Balint, Winnicott, Fairbairn, Guntrip. *Journal of the American Psychoanalytic Association, 28,* 829–860.

Sutherland, J. D. (1983). The self and object relations. *Bulletin of the Menninger Clinic, 47,* 524–541.

Terr, L. (1991). Childhood traumas: An outline and overview. *American Journal of Psychiatry, 148,* 10–20.

Thomas, T. (1987, February). *A Rorschach investigation of borderline and attention deficit disorder children.* Paper presented at the mid-winter meeting of the Society for Personality Assessment, San Francisco.

Tuber, S. (1983). Children's Rorschach scores as predictors of later adjustment. *Journal of Consulting and Clinical Psychology, 51,* 379–385.

Tuber, S. (1989a). Assessment of children's object representations with the Rorschach. *Bulletin of the Menninger Clinic, 53,* 432–441.

Tuber, S. (1989b). Children's object representations: Findings for a non-clinical sample. *Psychological Assessment, 1,* 146–149.

Tuber, S. (1992). Empirical and clinical assessments of children's object relations and object representations. *Journal of Personality Assessment, 58,* 179–197.

Tuber, S., & Coates, S. (1989). Indices of psychopathology in the Rorschachs of boys with severe gender identity disorder: A comparison with control subjects. *Journal of Personality Assessment, 53,* 100–112.

Tuber, S., Frank, M., & Santostefano, S. (1989). Children's anticipation of impending surgery. *Bulletin of the Menninger Clinic, 53,* 501–511.

Urist, J. (1977). The Rorschach test and the assessment of object relations. *Journal of Personality Assessment, 41,* 3–9.

Urist, J. (1980). Object relations. In R. H. Woody (Ed.), *Encyclopedia of clinical assessment* (Vol. 1; pp. 821–833). San Francisco: Jossey-Bass.

Urist, J., & Shill, M. (1982). Validity of the Rorschach Mutuality of Autonomy Scale: A replication using excerpted responses. *Journal of Personality Assessment, 46,* 450–454.

Vaillant, G. E. (1987). A developmental view of old and new perspectives of personality disorders. *Journal of Personality Disorders, 1,* 146–156.

van der Kolk, B., & Fisler, R. E. (1994). Childhood abuse and neglect and loss of self-regulation. *Bulletin of the Menninger Clinic, 58,* 145–168.

Watkins, B., & Bentovim, A. (1992). The sexual abuse of male children and adolescents: A review of current research. *Journal of Child Psychology and Psychiatry, 33,* 197–248.

Weiner, I. B. (1994). The Rorschach inkblot method (RIM) is not a test: Implications for theory and practice. *Journal of Personality Assessment, 62,* 498–504.

Weiner, I. B., & Exner, J. E. (1991). Rorschach changes in long-term and short-term psychotherapy. *Journal of Personality Assessment, 56,* 453–465.

Werner, H. (1948). *Comparative psychology of mental development.* New York: International Universities Press, Inc.

Werner, H., & Kaplan, B. (1963). *Symbol formation: An organismic–developmental approach to language and the expression of thought.* New York: Wiley.

Westen, D. (1990). Towards a revised theory of borderline object relations: Contributions of empirical research. *International Journal of Psychoanalysis, 71,* 661–693.

Westen, D. (1991a). Clinical assessment of object relations using the TAT. *Journal of Personality Assessment, 56,* 56–74.

Westen, D. (1991b). Social cognition and object relations. *Psychological Bulletin, 109,* 429–455.

Westen, D. (1993). *Social Cognition and Object Relations Scale: Q-sort for TAT data.* Unpublished manuscript.

Westen, D., Barends, A., Leigh, J., Mendel, M., & Silbert, D. (1988). *Social Cognition and Object Relations Scales (SCORS): Manual for coding interview data.* Unpublished manuscript, University of Michigan at Ann Arbor.

Westen, D., Klepser, J., Ruffins, S. A., Silverman, M., Lifton, N., & Boekamp, J. (1991). Object relations in childhood and adolescence: The development of working relationships. *Journal of Consulting and Clinical Psychology, 59,* 400–409.

Westen, D., Lohr, N., Silk, K., Gold, L., & Kerber, K. (1990). Object relations and social cognition in borderline personality disorder and depression: A TAT analysis. *Psychological Assessment, 2,* 355–364.

Westen, D., Lohr, N., Silk, K., Kerber, K., & Goodrich, S. (1985). *Social Cognition and Object Relations Scale (SCORS): Manual for coding TAT data.* Department of Psychology, University of Michigan at Ann Arbor.

Westen, D. Ludolph, P., Block, J., Wixom, J., & Wiss, F. C. (1990). Developmental history and object relations in psychiatrically disturbed adolescent girls. *American Journal of Psychiatry, 147,* 1061–1068.

Westen, D., Ludolph, P., Lerner, H., Ruffins, S., & Wiss, F. C. (1990). Object relations in borderline adolescents. *Journal of the American Academy of Child and Adolescent Psychiatry, 29*, 338–348.

Westen, D., Ludolph, P., Misle, B., Ruffins, S., & Block, J. (1990). Physical and sexual abuse in adolescents with borderline personality disorder. *American Journal of Orthopsychiatry, 60*, 55–66.

Westen, D., Ludolph, P., Silk, K., Kellam, A., Gold, L., & Lohr, N. (1990). Object relations in borderline adolescents and adults: Developmental differences. *Adolescent Psychiatry: Developmental and Clinical Studies, 17*, 360–384.

Winnicott, D. W. (1960). The theory of the parent–infant relationship. *International Journal of Psychoanalysis, 41*, 585–595.

Zanarini, M. C., Gunderson, J. G., Marino, M. F., Schwartz, E. D., & Frankenburg, F. R. (1989). Childhood experiences of borderline patients. *Comprehensive Psychiatry, 30*, 18–25.

Zinner, J., & Shapiro, R. (1972). Projective identification as a mode of perception and behavior in families of adolescents. *International Journal of Psychoanalysis, 53*, 523–530.

Ziskin, J., & Faust, D. (1988). *Coping with psychiatric and psychological testimony* (4th ed.). Marina del Rey, CA: Law and Psychology Press.

Author Index

Subject Index